Thomas Childe Barker

Aryan civilization

Its religious origin and its progress with an account of the religion, laws, and institutions of Greece and Rome

Thomas Childe Barker

Aryan civilization
Its religious origin and its progress with an account of the religion, laws, and institutions of Greece and Rome

ISBN/EAN: 9783337131449

Printed in Europe, USA, Canada, Australia, Japan

Cover: Foto ©ninafisch / pixelio.de

More available books at **www.hansebooks.com**

Aryan Civilization:

ITS RELIGIOUS ORIGIN AND ITS PROGRESS,

WITH AN ACCOUNT OF THE

Religion, Laws, and Institutions,

OF GREECE AND ROME,

Based on the Work of

DE COULANGES.

BY THE REV. T. CHILDE BARKER,
Vicar of Spelsbury, Oxfordshire,
AND LATE STUDENT OF CH. CH.

PARKER, 337, STRAND, LONDON;
G. B. SMITH, CHIPPING NORTON;
Or may be had of the Author.
1871.

PREFACE.

THE first edition of La Cité Antique, by Monsieur FUSTEL DE COULANGES, Historical Professor at Strasbourg, appeared in 1864, and has since been crowned by the French Academy. Perhaps no other treatise could be found more useful for educational purposes or affording a clearer insight into the spirit of antiquity. The distinctive features of it are the use of Sanscrit for further purposes than those of philology, and a comparison of the laws and institutions of the Greeks and Romans with those of the ancient Hindoos. Greek and Roman civilization is shewn to have been based upon the worship of men's dead ancestors; from which worship, and not so much from the right of labour, were derived the idea of property and the old laws of succession. Among the points proved is the identity of the ancient *gens* with the primitive family, and the revival of the patriarchal theory for at least a portion of the Aryan race. The extent to which religion pervades all Greek and Roman institutions, customs, offices, is impressed on the mind by a detailed examination, and the author shews in a very interesting manner how kings were but priests from whom political power might be taken without destroying their royalty; how the census was once but a ceremony of purification; and the triumph nothing but the performance of a vow. The latter part of the work points out how much analogy there is between the histories of all ancient cities, and that they all really passed through the same series of revolutions, and consequently may be studied together. The chapters in which it is explained how all were eventually conquered by one particular city, especially merit perusal.

It may seem presumptuous, after this, to say that the present is not an exact translation of DE COULANGES' work; but it was thought wiser to deviate from it in some respects. For one thing, the attempt has been made to compress that writer's matter into about three-fifths of the original space; not by the omission, it is hoped, of anything valuable, but by suppressing repetitions, recapitulations, expansions, and summaries that might fairly be dispensed with. The liberty, too, of exercising an independent judgment has been taken occasionally; additions have been made for clearness; and it is trusted that the work will be more agreeable to English readers for having passed freely through a kindred mind, than if it had been literally translated.

ROME, 1869.

SYNOPSIS.

			PAGE
CHAPTER	I.	Fire-Worship, and	1
CHAP.	II.	The Worship of DEAD ANCESTORS,	6
CHAP.	III.	Confused into one Domestic Worship,	11
CHAP.	IV.	constituted, by initiation,	13
CHAP.	V.	THE FAMILY, with its slaves,	17
CHAP.	VI.	With the strict necessity for its being continued,	19
CHAP.	VII.	With its pure marriage, only for procreation of children,	21
CHAP.	VIII.	With its power of adoption and emancipation,	24
CHAP.	IX.	With its relationship by the males only,	26
CHAP.	X.	With its peculiar right of property,	28
CHAP.	XI.	Primogeniture, and right of males to succeed,	36
CHAP.	XII.	With its exaggerated paternal authority,	45
CHAP.	XIII.	And (for heathens) superior morality.	50
CHAP.	XIV.	The Family became the Gens, with its clients	54
CHAP.	XV.	Several Gentes { uniting in a new worship } made a CURIA, or φρατρια	65
CHAP.	XVI.	Several Curiæ, as religious ideas extended, made a TRIBE	68
CHAP.	XVII.	As a new religion sprung up,	69
CHAP.	XVIII.	Several Tribes made a STATE or CITY, civitas	74
CHAP.	XIX.	Then the CITY (URBS) was built	79
CHAP.	XX.	In the CITY the founder was worshipped,	87
CHAP.	XXI.	And other gods;	90
CHAP.	XXII.	With whom the citizens had communion in public repasts	97

			PAGE
CHAP.	XXIII.	A list of the public feasts constituted the Calendar	100
CHAP.	XXIV.	Religion is discernible in the Census, ...	102
CHAP.	XXV.	In the Assembly and Army, ...	104
CHAP.	XXVI.	In the Rituals, ...	108
CHAP.	XXVII.	And Annals, ...	110
CHAP.	XXVIII.	In the office of King, ...	113
CHAP.	XXIX.	As well as that of the Magistrate ..	119
CHAP.	XXX.	Religion was the foundation of the Law, and ..	124
CHAP.	XXXI.	Made the distinction between Citizen and Stranger	130
CHAP.	XXXII.	It gave strength to Patriotism, and made the Exile wretched	134
CHAP.	XXXIII.	It caused the profound separation between ancient states	137
CHAP.	XXXIV.	And rendered more hostile the relations in war ..	141
CHAP.	XXXV.	It stamped the characters of both Roman and Athenian, and	145
CHAP.	XXXVI.	Caused the want of Individual Liberty ..	154
CHAP.	XXXVII.	Revolutions arose from (1) decay of old beliefs,	157
CHAP.	XXXVIII.	(2) from position of the clients, ...	158
CHAP.	XXXIX.	And that of the plebeians	162

FIRST REVOLUTION.

CHAP.	XL.	Kings are deprived of political power, and ..	166
CHAP.	XLI.	Aristocracies govern	176

SECOND REVOLUTION.

CHAP.	XLII.	Primogeniture disappears; and the Gens, or Family, is dismembered	179
CHAP.	XLIII.	Clients get freed, and disappear in the plebs ..	182

THIRD REVOLUTION.

CHAP.	XLIV.	Plebeians are admitted into the city, ..	193
CHAP.	XLV.	Old laws are modified, and	214
CHAP.	XLVI.	A new principle of government beginning to prevail over the old one, men vote ..	222

FOURTH REVOLUTION.

			PAGE
CHAP. XLVII.	An aristocracy of wealth failing to establish itself,		226
CHAP. XLVIII.	Democracy prevails, ..	.. .. ..	231
CHAP. XLIX.	The rich are in continual strife with the poor for their property. Tyrants are common		234
CHAP. L.	The revolutions of Sparta were similar	..	244
CHAP. LI.	Philosophy and new beliefs join in preparing for	..	251
CHAP. LII.	The Roman Conquest, and	.. ..	258
CHAP. LIII.	The Advent of Christianity ..	.. ..	281

INTRODUCTION.

It is acknowledged on all hands that religion lies widely and deeply at the bottom of politics. Struggles between the spiritual and secular power, wars of rival creeds, and risings for liberty of conscience attest its great importance. Even where religion has shrunk from direct political action, it has still, indirectly, shewn itself the most powerful agent of civilization by moulding the character of nations, by settling their habits, and slowly transforming their institutions. And when we would investigate the causes why one people differs from another in condition and happiness, religion must have a place for consideration perhaps before race, climate, geographical position. The history of the ancient Jews, the history of Europe in the Middle Ages, and the history of modern times have all been carefully studied with an eye to religion.

Historians of Greece and Rome have only regarded mythology and the fables of the Olympian gods, a religion which sprung up when the character, laws, and institutions of those peoples had been already formed, and which tended as much to dissolve society as to constitute it. The immorality of the Olympian Mythology well deserves the condemnation which Plato passed upon it; and, though it had the merit of being less narrow than the worship of the Lares, and presented gods accessible to more people, yet for the main influences which moulded Spartan, and Roman, and Athenian into what they were in their best days, we must look to a purer form of worship, a religion taken not from outward physical nature, but from the soul and conscience, and which, being connected with thoughts of man's hereafter, was therefore more solemn and awe-inspiring than any of the fables propagated by wandering bards.

Doubtless, as God has revealed himself not only in the conscience but also in outward nature, the mind requires both manifestations to be reconciled in its belief. On this account, all old religions say something on Cosmogony. And now-a-days the reconciliation of revelation and science is the most interesting, as well as the most prominent, of problems. Believers in Christianity find both requirements satisfied, when they see presented to their adoration the Incarnate Deity at once the greatest of moralists and the Lord of nature. But the Græco-Latin race seems to have taken its objects of belief unequally, and even alternately, from either source. It oscillated between the two at different periods of its history, as a river, that has once received a bias, no longer flows in a direct line through the plain, but swings from side to side in wide and wider curves. The last and best-known of the Greek and Roman religions was that of the Olympian deities, who were personifications of different objects in nature. It will not be necessary here to recite all the traditions that prove the newness of this worship. Greece and Italy always preserved a recollection of the day when society existed, but Jupiter was unknown. The next older but also contemporary worship was that of the dead, under the names of Lares, Penates, ἥρωες, δαίμονες. This form of religion came from reflection on the soul of man and its state in the next world. But even this was accompanied by yet another sort of belief, which aimed, perhaps, at explaining the phænomena of the outward world, and which was, in fact, a half-forgotten and wholly misunderstood worship of fire, a form of worship mixed up and lost in the worship of the household gods.

Greek and Roman institutions were for the most part developed from this confused mixture of religions. It will be our object in this treatise to shew that to this worship they owed (besides its moral effects),

1st, The institution of the FAMILY, with its exaggerated paternal authority, its absolute right of property, and its peculiar rules of inheritance.

2ndly, How this same religion enlarged and extended the family through the gens, and the curia, till it formed a CITY, where it ruled with despotic sway, being the source of all rules, customs, and offices.

3rdly, We shall see that the isolation and exclusiveness of the primitive family was entirely inconsistent with the principle of association in cities; and that, new opinions on religion springing up at the same time, a series of REVOLUTIONS was the result, by which society was transformed.

We shall be attempting to investigate the form of society in times before Homer sung or Rome was founded, and must therefore have recourse to the earliest sources of information. The hymns of the Vedas express the first religious thoughts of the Eastern Aryas, and in the Laws of Manou certain passages may be found of an extremely remote date. But the sacred books and earliest hymns of the old Hellenes, like those of the Italians, have all perished, and one might be at a loss how to recall the record of generations which have left no written text, if the past was ever really dead. For the truth is, however long man may have forgotten his own history, he still bears about in himself some traces of the past. At each period he is the summary and product of preceding ages, and on examination may distinguish what those ages were by what remains in his belief, language, and customs. There are customs still subsisting in Hindoostan identical with those of the earliest periods, and which explain Greek and Roman history. There are legends, which, however false, prove modes of thought that subsisted in the period from which they were derived. The etymology of a word may reveal an old opinion or custom; and we find men in classical times continuing to practice at marriages, at funerals, and on feast-days, certain ceremonies which no longer answer to their belief. All these customs, stories, words, and rites, if closely examined, may end by giving us with some truth an idea of what the Aryas believed from fifteen to twenty centuries before Christ.

THE ARYAS.

ARYAS is the name (probably meaning noble) which was given to themselves by the ancestors of the leading nations of Europe and India, when as yet they were a small people of Central Asia feeding their flocks near the sources of the Oxus. The brief account here appended will help to the better understanding of the following pages. It is more probable that they left their ancient seats gradually and slowly, than that they emigrated in large bodies at one time. The western branch has been termed Iranian, and may be divided into (1) Greek-Latin, (2) Celts, (3) Slavo-Germanic. An examination of different languages enables us to form some conclusions as to what was their condition before their separation. The following is the principle upon which such conclusions are formed. If a word is found to be the same in the languages of both branches of the race, the thing indicated by that word was known by the race before the separation. But if we find different words for the same thing, most likely the knowledge of the thing indicated was acquired afterwards. From the similarity of names we conclude the undivided people knew barley, rye, corn, which they ground, and of which they made flour. But they were not sufficiently advanced in agriculture to know the use of the plough: because the Sanscrit word for plough is not anything like *aratrum*, but *karsh*, and the root *ar* only means to tear. They had evidently long been a pastoral people; so, many objects and ideas are expressed in Sanscrit (their earliest remaining tongue), with reference to cattle; as, for instance, the hours of the day, wealth, poverty, violence, deceit. They seemed to see cattle even in the clouds and stars. We find they had wine, pears, cherries, and nuts, but the plum-tree was still a sloe. On the height they knew the pine, the fir, and the cedar; and on the plain the poplar, the ash, the elm, the willow, and the alder. They had houses or cabins with doors to defend them against the snow and cold which made their climate rigorous. When they moved from place to place, they travelled in chariots with axles, drawn by yoked oxen. War was waged under kings by warriors armed with pike, lance, and javelin. Many metals were known, of which the commonest was bronze, but the use of iron was most likely acquired after the separation. Finally, we find mention of a sea, probably the Caspian whilst still one with Lake Aral.

ARYAN CIVILIZATION.

CHAPTER I.

FIRE-WORSHIP.

IN the house of every Greek or Roman was an altar, and upon the altar, fire always burning. Every evening it was covered up with ashes, that the wood might not be entirely consumed, and every morning the householder's first care was to renew the flame. His legitimate wife, after due initiation, had the honoured duty of keeping up the fire, in the absence of the master. The fire did not cease to burn until the family had altogether perished, and an extinguished hearth in early days meant the same thing as an extinguished family.[1]

It is evident from the strictness with which this custom was kept up that it was no insignificant practice, but that it certainly expressed some ancient belief. Not every sort of wood would do to feed the fire; certain trees only could be used,[2] and those of a kind too sacred for common use. It was a religious precept that the fire should always be kept pure,[3] which meant, literally, that no filthy object ought to be cast into it, and figuratively, that no blame-worthy action should be performed in its presence. There was one day in the year (it was the first of March with the Romans) when every family was bound to put out its fire and light another again immediately. But in order to renew the flame, certain.

---

[1] Homer, Hymns, xxix. Orphic Hymns, lxxxiv. Hesiod., *Opera*, 732. Æsch., *Agam.*, 1056. Eurip., *Herc. Fur.*, 523, 599. Thuc., i., 136. Aristoph., *Plut.*, 795. Cato, *De re Rust.*, 143. Cicero, *Pro domo*, 40. Tibullus, i., 1, 4. Horace, *Epod.*, 43. Ovid, *A. A.*, i. Virgil, ii., 512.

[2] Virgil, *Æn.*, vii., 71. Festus, v. *Felicis*. Plutarch, *Numa*, 9.

[3] Eurip., *Herc Fur.*, 715. Cato, *De re Rust.*, 143. Ovid., *Fast.*, iii., 698.

rites must be scrupulously observed. Flint and steel were forbidden to be used for this purpose.[1] Two processes only were allowed, the concentration of the solar rays into a focus, and the rubbing together of two pieces of a given sort of wood. Doubtless, originally the fire was looked upon as the earthly representative of the Sun in heaven, whom men adored as the great centre of movement and heat.[2] But it is questionable whether anything of this was known or remembered in later times. Still men continued offering to the fire, as to a god, flowers, fruit, incense, wine, and victims. Its protection was implored; it was entreated to bestow health, riches, manhood. A prayer to the fire has been preserved in the Orphic hymns,[3] and runs as follows:—" Render us always flourishing, always happy, O fire: thou who art eternal, beautiful, ever young; thou who nourishest, thou who art rich, receive favourably these our offerings, and in return give us happiness and sweet health." Thus could they see in the fire a god benevolent enough to maintain man's life, rich enough to feed him with gifts, and strong enough to protect the house and family.

A man did not leave his house without a prayer to the fire; and on his return, before embracing wife and children, he was bound to adore and invoke the fire. So Æschylus has represented Agamemnon, on his return from Troy, not as thanking Jupiter, nor carrying his joy and gratitude to the temple, but as offering his thanksgiving before the fire in his house. The dying Alcestis,[4] as she is giving up her life for her husband, thus addresses the fire of her house:—
" Mistress, I go beneath the earth, and for the last time fall before thee and address thee. Protect my infant children; give to my boy a tender wife, and to my girl a noble husband. Let them not die, like their mother, before the time, but may they lead a long and happy life in their father-land."

The sacred fire was a sort of providence in the family. Sacrifices were offered to it, and not merely was the flame

---

[1] Ovid., *Fast.*, iii., 143. Macrob, *Sat.*, i., 12. Julian., *Speech on the Sun.*
[2] E. Burnouf., *Revue des deux Mondes.* August, 1868.
[3] Hymns, Orphic, 84. Plant., *Captiv.*, ii., 2. Tibull., i., 9, 74. Ovid., *A. A.*, I, 637. Plin., *Hist. Nat.*, xviii., 8.
[4] Eurip., *Alc.*, 162—8. Cato, *De re Rust.*, 2. Eurip., *Herc. Fur.*, 523.

supplied with wood, but upon the altar were poured wine, oil, incense, and the fat of victims. The god graciously received these offerings and devoured them. Radiant with satisfaction, he rose above the altar, and lit up the worshipper with his brightness. Then was the moment for the suppliant humbly to invoke him and give heart-felt utterance to his prayer.

Especially were the meals[1] of the family religious acts. To the god was due a prayer at the beginning and end of the repast. He must have first-fruits of the food before any one could eat, and a libation of the wine before any one could drink. No doubt was entertained of his presence, or that he really ate and drank, for did not the mounting flame prove it? So god and man held communion.[2]

Such was their belief; and though it is true that these notions faded away and were forgotten as a creed, yet resulting customs and forms of words remained, whence the veriest unbeliever could not free himself; and we find even Horace and Ovid[3] still supping before the hearth whilst they offered prayers and made libations in its honour.

The laws of Manou in their present shape reveal to us the religion of Brahma as completely established, and even tending to its decline; but they have retained the vestiges of this more ancient worship of the sacred fire, reduced indeed to a secondary position, but not entirely destroyed. The Brahmin has his fire to keep up night and day, and to feed with peculiar sorts of wood. And as from the Greeks and Romans the fire-god received wine, so from the Hindoo he has the fermented drink called *soma*. The family meal also is religious, being conducted according to specified formulas. Prayers are addressed to the fire, as in Greece, and it is presented with first-fruits of rice, of butter, and of honey. We read that "the Brahmin should not eat of the rice of this year's harvest, before he has offered the first-fruits to the hearth-fire. For the sacred fire is greedy of grain, and when it is not honoured it will devour the existence of the negligent Brahmin."

---

[1] Æsch., *Agam.*, 1015. Ovid., *Fast.*, vi., 315.
[2] Plutarch, *Quest. Rom.*, 64; *Comment on Hesiod.*, 44. Homer, *Hymns*, 29.
[3] Horace, *Sat.*, ii., 6, 66. Ovid., *Fast.* ii., 631. Petron, 60.

The Rig-Veda has many hymns addressed to the fire-god Agni. In one it is said:—"O Agni, thou art the life, thou art the patron of man. In return for our prayers, bestow glory and riches on the father of a family who now addresses thee. Agni, thou art a wise protector and a father; to thee we owe life; we are of thy household." So the hearth-god was, as in Greece, a tutelary deity. Men asked of him abundance, and that the earth might be productive. He was prayed to for health, and that a man might long enjoy the light and arrive at old age like the sun at his setting. Even wisdom is demanded, and pardon for sin. For as in Greece the fire-god was essentially pure, so not only was the Brahmin forbidden to throw anything filthy into his fire, but he might not even warm his feet at it. The guilty man, also, as in Greece, might not approach his own hearth before he was purified from the stain he had contracted.

Assuredly the Greeks did not borrow this religion from the Hindoos, nor the Hindoos from the Greeks; but Greeks, Italians, and Hindoos belonged to one and the same race, and their ancestors at a very early period had lived together in central Asia. There they had learnt this creed, and established their rites. When the tribes gradually moved further away from one another, they transported this worship with them, the one to the banks of the Ganges, and the others to the Mediterranean. Afterwards, some learnt to worship Brahma, others Zeus, and others again, Janus; but all had preserved as a legacy the earlier religion which they had practised at the common cradle of the race.

It is remarkable that in all sacrifices, even in those offered to Zeus or to Athene, it was always to the fire that the first invocation was made. At Olympia assembled Greece offered her first sacrifice to the hearth-fire, and the second to Zeus. Similarly at Rome, the first to be adored was always Vesta, who was nothing else but the Fire. And so we read in the hymns of the Veda: "Before all gods, Agni must be invoked. We will pronounce thy holy name before that of all the other immortals. O Agni, whatever be the God we honour by our sacrifice, to thee is the holocaust offered." It was not that Jupiter and Brahma had not acquired a much greater importance in the minds of men, but it was remembered that the fire was much older than those gods.

When the populations of Greece and Italy had learnt to represent their gods as persons, and had given each a proper name and a human shape, the old worship of the fire was similarly modified. The sacred fire was called Vesta.[1] The common noun was made a proper name, and a legend by degrees attached to it. They even went so far as to represent the fire in statues under the features of a woman, the gender of the noun having determined the sex of the deity.

---

[1] Ἑστία, originally, altar, from ἵστημι.

[NOTE.—When the above was written, in 1869, I wished to put before the English reader the opinion of French savants, such as Mons. E. Burnouf, as to fire being the earthly representative of the Sun, the Sun himself standing for Light, Heat, and Motion. I now think that a savage people would at all events begin by worshipping sun and fire separately, as objects on which their comfort depended. There is a period in man's history when the objects of out-door nature are all worshipped together, as Sun, Dawn, Light, Twilight, and so on. Only later could one of these stand for another, and that other for certain abstract notions. De Coulanges would have done well to dwell more on those other hymns in the Rig-Veda, to Dyaus, Indra, Varuna, and not solely on those in honour of Agni.—T.C.B.]

CHAPTER II.

WORSHIP OF THE DEAD.

The worship of the sacred fire was not the only one known and practised by the Aryas. They worshipped also their buried ancestors. Before Tartarus and Elysium had been imagined in Europe, or the transmigration of souls in India, those early peoples had a ruder and simpler notion as to the condition of the dead. They were firmly persuaded of the continued existence of their friends beneath the earth. It seemed to them that the soul was laid in the tomb as well as the body, and Virgil rightly represents their belief in the words he attributes to Æneas: "animamque sepulchro condimus." Hence the objects which the buried person might be expected to need—as clothes, vessels, arms—were unfailingly interred with him. Wine was spilled upon his tomb to quench his thirst, and victuals were placed above it to appease his hunger. Horses and slaves were killed to be useful after death, and even women sometimes; as, for instance, when each of the Greeks, returning from Troy, took home his fair captive, the buried Achilles claimed his share also, and received Polyxena.[1]

This belief in the connexion of soul and body after death appears also from a story preserved in Pindar.[2] When Phryxus had died in exile, and was buried in Colchis, his soul appeared to Pelias and demanded removal to Greece, as supposing it to be known that if the body were not transferred, the soul would remain in exile also.

---

[1] Eur., *Hec.*, passim.; *Alc.* 618; *Iphig.*, 162; *Iliad*, xxiii., 166; *Æn.*, v., 77; vi., 221; xi., 81. Plin., *His. Nat.*, viii., 40. Suet., *Aes.*, 84. Lucian., De luctu, 14,
[2] *Pythic.*, iv., 284. Heyne., see Scholiast.

Many indications remain of the absolute necessity, according to ancient notions, of being buried. Most likely this religion of the ancient Aryas derived much of its influence over them from the common fear of ghosts, and the natural shrinking of mankind from all contact with the supernatural world. When we think how much terror may be inspired even in these days by stories and representations of this nature, it is easy to believe that in the infancy of society a most powerful influence was exerted by the dread of disembodied spirits and the powers they were supposed to possess.

It was believed that the souls of unburied men[1] flitted about, as phantoms or larvæ, haunting the living, sending sickness, or spoiling the harvest. And not only might unburied men re-appear, but those also at whose burial the proper forms had not been used. In a play of Plautus (the Mostellaria), a ghost wanders restlessly about, because it had been interred without proper rites. And the soul of Caligula, according to Suetonius, for the same reason, haunted the living till they determined to disinter the body and bury it again according to rule. Hence, also, persons still alive were very anxious both about their own burial and that of their friends. The Athenians put to death their generals who, after a great victory at sea, neglected to bury the dead. These generals, who were pupils of philosophers, made a distinction between body and soul, and no longer thought that the felicity of the one depended on the locality of the other. They did not, therefore, risk their ships in a tempest to pick up the dead for burial. But the common people of Athens, who remained much attached to old beliefs, accused the generals of impiety, and put them upon trial for their lives; because, although by their victory they had saved their country, yet by their negligence they had destroyed many souls. Hence, deprivation of burial was a punishment only inflicted on the worst offenders, because the soul itself then received chastisement; and it was thought that justice followed the offender through the ages.

A further belief was that the buried man needed food.

---

[1] *Odyss.* xi. 72. Eurip., *Troad.*, 1085. Hdtus., v., 92. Virgil, vi., 371, 379. Horace, *Odes*, i., 23. Ovid., *Fast.*, v., 483. Plin., *Epist.*, vii., 27. Suet., *Calig.*, 59. Serv., *Od. Æn.*, iii., 68.

Ovid[1] and Virgil describe the ceremonies with which the yearly offerings were made, for these forms long out-lasted the belief in them. The tombs were surrounded with garlands; cakes were placed beside, with fruit, and salt; and milk was poured out, and wine, and sometimes the blood of a victim.

Nor were these offerings a mere commemoration. The food was exclusively for the dead man. Not only were the liquids poured upon the earth of his tomb, but a hole was made in the ground by which the solid food[2] might reach him. When there was a victim, all its flesh was burnt, and no living person had a share. Certain formulas handed over the victuals to the deceased, and it would have been thought a most impious thing for any living person to touch what was intended for the dead.

We may mention the following proofs of these customs. Iphigenia is made to say in Euripides[3]: "I pour upon the soil of the tomb, milk, honey, wine; for with these we please the dead." Again, before every Greek tomb was a place, called a πυρά, destined for the immolation of the victim and for cooking the flesh. The Roman tomb, in like manner, had its culina[4] or kitchen, of a peculiar sort, for the sole use of the dead. Plutarch tells us respecting those who were slain at the battle of Platæa, and buried on the spot, that the people of the city engaged to offer them ever afterwards the yearly funeral repast; and this was still done in his time, nearly six hundred years after the battle. The unbeliever Lucian mocks at these opinions, but cannot help revealing to us at the same time how deeply rooted they were in the minds of men. Though other beliefs arose, yet these ceremonies lasted till the triumph of Christianity.

From believing that the dead existed, the ancients went on to make them sacred beings. Cicero says, "Our ancestors would have it that men who have left this life should be counted as gods." It was not even necessary to have been virtuous in order to be deified. A bad man might be

---

[1] Ovid., *Fast.*, ii., 540. Virg., *Æn.*, iii., 300, et ssq.; v., 77.
[2] Hdtus., ii., 40. Eurip., *Hec.*, 536. Paus., ii., 10. Virgil, *Æn.*, 5, 98. Ovid., *Fast.*, ii., 566. Lucian, *Charon.*
[3] Æsch., *Choeph.*, 476. Eurip., *Iphig.*, 162.; *Orest.*, 115, 125.
[4] Festus, v. *Culina.* Eurip., Elect., 513.

a god as well as another, only that he retained as a god the evil propensities of his manhood. The Greeks called their dead subterranean gods. In Æschylus, a son addresses his dead father as one that is a god beneath the earth; and Euripides, speaking of Alcestis,[1] says, "The traveller will pause beside her tomb and say, 'She is now a happy goddess.'" The Romans called their dead men the gods Manes, and Cicero writes: "Give what is due to the gods, the Manes; they are men who have left this life; look upon them as divine." The tombs were their temples, and bore inscriptions, *Dis Manibus*, or, in Greek, θεοῖς χθονίοις, and there was altar for sacrifice before each sepulchre, as before the temple of a god.[2]

This worship of the dead prevailed also among the Hellenes, the Latins, the Sabines, and the Etruscans. We find it also in existence amongst the Aryas of India. The hymns of the Rig-Veda mention it, and the Laws of Manou[3] speak of it as the oldest religion which man ever had. In this last book one can see indeed that the idea of transmigration of souls had prevailed over the old belief, and that even still earlier the worship of Brahma had been established. Yet the worship of the dead subsists in spite of them, living and indestructible; so that the compiler of the Laws of Manou is obliged to admit its ordinances into his book, of which it is not one of the least singularities to have preserved the laws relating to old beliefs, though evidently written when a newer creed prevailed.

According to these laws, then, the Hindoo was to procure for the departed the repast called sraddha: "Let the householder make the sraddha with rice, milk, roots, and fruit, that he may gain the good-will of the Manes." Thus the Aryas of the East, like those of the West, thought originally that the human being existed after death, invisible but immaterial, and claiming from mortals food and offerings. It was believed, also, as in Greece, that if these offerings were not

---

[1] *Alc.*, 1005. Æsch., *Choep.*, 469.　Soph., *Antig.*, 451.　Plutarch, *Solon.*, 21; *Quest. Rom.*, 52.; *Quest. Gr.*, 5.　Cicero, *De Leg.*, ii., 9. Varro, in S. August., *Civit. Dei*, viii., 26.

[2] Virg., *Æn.*, iv., 34.　Aulus.-Gellius, x., 18.　Plutarch, *Quest. Rom.*, 14.　Eurip., *Troad.*, 90.; *Elect.*, 513.　Sueton., *Nerva*, 50.

[3] Laws of Manou, i., 95; iii., 82, 122, 127, 146, 189, 274.

regularly presented, the soul would leave its dwelling-place and wander about to harass the living; whilst, on the contrary, if regularly honoured, the dead man was a protecting deity, who would still take part in human affairs, and benefit his offspring. Dead though he were, he could yet be active, and make it worth while to offer up the common prayer: " O god beneath the earth, be propitious to me."[1]

We may judge of the power attributed to the dead when we find that moral gifts are demanded of them, and that Electra[2] prays thus to the Manes of her father: " Pity me and my brother Orestes. Bring him home to his country. O my father, hear my prayer, and receive my libations." And she adds, " Give me a heart more chaste than my mother, and purer hands," by which it appears these gods were thought capable of granting more than material blessings. So the Hindoo prays to them." for more good men in his family, and much to give away."

The human souls thus rendered divine in death were what the Greeks termed *demons* or *heroes*, and the Latins *Lares, Manes, Genii*. The word 'hero' properly means dead man,[3] and is used in this sense in many inscriptions, which were generally written in the language of the vulgar. The Manes, according to Opuleius, if benevolent were called Lares, if ill-disposed, Larvæ.

---

[1] Eur., *Alc.*, 1004. Porphyr., *De Abstin.*, ii., 37. Plato., *Laws*, ix., 926, 927.
[2] Æsch., *Choeph.*, 122, 135.
[3] Böckh., Corp. Inscrip., Nos. 1629, 1723, 1781, 1784, 1786, 1789, 3398. See Ph. Lybas., *Monum. de Moree*, p. 205. Theognis., edit. Welcker., v., 513. Dion. Halic. Translates., *Lar familiaris.*, by ὁ κατ οἰκίαν ἥρως. *Antig. Rom.*, iv., 2.

CHAPTER III.

CONFUSION OF THE TWO RELIGIONS.

THE two worships which we have thus described, viz., that of the sacred fire and that of the dead, distinct as they seem to have been in their origin, yet were very early confounded and mingled into one. It will be found that these worships are almost undistinguishable in classical writings. There is a passage in Plautus,[1] and another in Columella, which show how, in common parlance, men said indifferently hearth-fire or domestic Lar. Also from certain expressions of Cicero, we conclude that the fire was not distinguished from the Penates, nor the Penates from the gods the Lares. "By the hearth-fire," says Servius, "the ancients meant the gods the Lares."[2] So Virgil writes indifferently sometimes fire for Penates, and sometimes Penates for fire.[3] In a famous passage[4] of the Æneid, Hector says to Æneas that he is about to commit to him the Trojan Penates, whilst it is but the fire of the hearth that he hands over to him. And, in another passage,[5] Æneas, invoking these same gods, calls them at once Penates, Lares, Vesta. When there was any one ancestor more distinguished than another, the hearth-fire is called after his especial name, as Orestes bids his sister come and stand by the fire of Pelops,[6] that she may hear his words; and in like manner Æneas designates the fire he is carrying over the sea as the Lar of Assaracus.

---

[1] Plaut., *Aulul.*, ii., 7, 16: *In foco nostro Lari*. Columella, xi., 1, 19: *Larem focumque familiarem*. Cicero, *Pro domo*, 41; *Pro Quintio*, 27, 28.
[2] Servius, in *Æn.*, v., 84.; vi., 152. Plato., *Minos.*, v., 315.
[3] Servius, in *Æn.*, iii., 134.
[4] *Æn.* ii., 293—297.
[5] Virgil, ix., 259; v., 744.
[6] Eurip., *Orest.*, 1140—1142.

If we are asked what causes may have led to this confusion of two originally distinct religions, two or three considerations occur as worthy of attention. In the first place both worships at first had one and the same local centre, since, as we learn from Servius, until the number of the dead became too great, they were buried in the house itself. We shall have to notice by-and-by that at a later period the family tombs are found outside the house in the fields; but still if a generation or two had been brought up seeing the grave and the altar as one material object, confusion would arise in the mind.

Secondly, this confusion would be increased, if the fire on the altar were used to burn the victims and the offerings presented to the dead. It would then seem to be no longer a separate sacred object, but, perhaps, a symbol of the dead, or their means of consuming the offering. It might be kindled in their honour, or it might be a representation of the ancestors' ever watchful souls.

Thirdly, the true notions at the bottom of fire-worship were somewhat abstruse. They are metaphysical notions attempting to explain the phenomena of the universe. The fire is the earthly representative of the Sun, who is to be worshipped as the chief example of motion in the world, and heat and light. All this might easily be lost sight of, as perhaps still higher truths had perished, among a simple people of shepherds and husbandmen. Great truths need unceasing discussion, that the possessors of the truths themselves may keep their notions clear; as water is bright in the running brook, but becomes thick when made to stand in little pools. We are speaking of a time when the Aryas were spreading abroad through unpeopled countries, and when each family, both by its position and also on account of its peculiar ancestral worship, was isolated in a high degree from others. So the ancient meaning of fire-worship became obscured, and its rites, though still practised, bore quite another signification.

CHAPTER IV.

IMPORTANT CHARACTERISTICS OF THE UNITED DOMESTIC WORSHIP.

THIS old religion was singularly different from all that have been founded in more modern times. In these days no religion can flourish which does not preach one God alone, and allow every one access to Him. But this primitive worship fulfilled neither of these two conditions. Not only did it fail to put before man one sole God, but the numerous gods whom it presented instead were not accessible to all. These deities made no claim to be the gods of all mankind; they did not even resemble Brahma, who was, at all events, the god of a caste, nor Zeus Panhellenius, who was worshipped by a nation. In this primitive religion, each god could only be adored by a particular family; so purely domestic was it.

There is a sort of resemblance in this primitive religion to the Christian doctrine of communion of saints, according to which, also, the living and the dead are bound together by a common sacrifice and a common repast. But there was an exclusiveness in the Aryan notions which we find it impossible to sympathise with. Their cult was only paid to their male relations in direct line. In the first place, the funeral ceremony could only be conducted by the nearest relative, and none but the family could assist at the feasts of the dead, which were renewed from time to time at the grave. Strangers were carefully excluded, because the dead would accept no offering but from the hands of relations. If any one else approached the sacred things, they were rendered profane and useless. A tomb might not even be touched by the foot of one not in the family, for even if it were done accidentally the dead must be appeased and the person who had touched it purified. The sacrifice and the prayer were exclusively addressed to the worshippers' forefathers,[1] whence the terms πατριάζειν, parentare; and Lucian tells us mockingly (but it was the popular belief) that the man who left no sons was exposed to perpetual hunger.

In India, as well as in Greece, the same rule prevailed that no one could make an offering to a dead man but a blood relation. Thus the Laws of Manou represent the dead as continually praying that sons may be born of their line to offer the milk, the honey, and the ghee.[2]

In Italy and Greece, therefore, as well as in India, a son who failed to make the proper libations and sacrifices was regarded as impious in the highest degree; for such negligence destroyed utterly the happiness of the dead, and was a parricide multiplied as many times as a man had forefathers. But if, on the contrary, the sacrifices were always duly accomplished, and the food carried to the tomb on the proper days, then each ancestor became a protecting deity. He repaid his descendant the aid he had himself received, and was invisibly at hand to succour him in distress. As the living could not do without the dead, nor the dead without the living, so the family was indissolubly bound together with the closest ties. Something even stronger than the communion of saints subsisted for them, for their saints were at once a man's relations and his gods.

Unfortunately, in proportion as the family, whether alive or dead, was united in itself, so was it leagued against the stranger; for in those days the anybody (ὅστις, hostis) was a foe, and no one had yet preached the golden rule of loving one's neighbour as one self. Hence the prayers, the hymns, and the ceremonies of this worship were kept carefully secret, as a peculiar family property to be shared with no one else; and all in Greece and Italy acted in the spirit of the Brahmin who says in the Rig-Veda, I am strong against my foes by reason of the hymns that I have learnt from my father.[3] Later ages, which were compelled by asso-

---

[1] At least, at first. We shall see that cities afterwards, as well as families, had their local and national heroes.
[2] Laws of Manou, iii., 138; iii., 274.
[3] Rig-Veda, tr. Langlois, i., p. 113. Laws of Manou, viii., —; ix., 7.

ciation in cities to feel more interest in their fellow creatures, marked the exclusive spirit of this old worship by the expression ἑστιᾷ θύεις, "thou sacrificest at the hearth," that is, you care only for your own family.

With a view to keeping the worship thus secret, the hearth-fire, where the service of the dead was conducted, was placed not only within the house, but not near the door, lest it should be too easily seen. Hence the gods themselves were termed gods of the recess (θεοὶ μύχιοι), or of the interior (Penates), and Cicero styles their sacrifices occult.[1]

It followed from this secrecy there was no common ritual or similar customs in the different families, but, on the contrary, that every one was completely independent. The head of each family was its priest alone, and he had no superior in religion. The Archon of Athens and the pontiff of Rome might ask that the ceremonies should be duly performed, but they could not make him alter any rite, or act otherwise than on the well-known maxim, *suo quisque ritu sacrificia faciat*.[2]

This religion possessed no temples, and was the invention of no priests, being much more probably the spontaneous production of the human mind. Probably the sight of death aud thoughts of its mysterious nature led on from the visible to the invisible, from the transitory and human to the eternal and divine.

Another cause which must have helped to make men deify their ancestors was certainly the ancients' peculiar ideas about generation. They believed that the reproductive power resides solely in the father, who alone can transmit the spark of life. It is observed that generally in the beginnings of society generation is an incentive to worship. The Chinese to this day pay divine honours to their forefathers; so did the ancient Getæ and Scythians, and so do certain tribes in America. When an African savage begets a son, he changes his name in honour of the fact; and we find even Homer, when he wishes to honour Ulysses, designating him as the father of Telemachus. No doubt, when the ideas of creation and a Creator are forgotten, or have never been grasped, those of generation and paternity assume

---

[1] Cic., *De nat. deor*, ii., 27; *De arusp. resp.*, 17.
[2] Varro, *De lingua Lat.*, vii., 88.
[3] Mitakchara, trad. Orianne, p. 139.

greater proportion. At all events, an important consequence resulted, namely, that as none but fathers were deified, so only those on earth who might hereafter be gods themselves seemed fit to be priests and conduct the worship of the family. Hence the direction of the service and the right to offer sacrifice passed from male to male, and a woman could only participate in the worship through her husband or father.

We shall see that still further results, also of great importance, with respect to the rights of property and the constitution of the family, are to be derived from these rules.

NOTE.—According to Sir J. Lubbock, the progress of the mind in religious ideas is from (1) a total absence of any definite idea on the subject, to (2) Fetichism, when man supposes he can force the Deity to comply with his wishes, and makes his likeness for this purpose: thence (3) to worship of stones and fire; 4thly, to the conception of superior deities of a different nature from man; 5thly, to Idolatry or worship of gods, *like* men, only more powerful. They are a part of nature, not creators; and are represented by images. 6. In his next stage, the Deity is regarded as the author of nature, and not merely part of it, becoming for the first time supernatural.

Such, perhaps, is the Law of Progress, but does history shew no retrogression?

CHAPTER V.

THE PRIMITIVE FAMILY WAS A RELIGIOUS ASSOCIATION.

THE family, as it existed in earlier days than those described by Homer, will be found, on examination, to be a more important institution than it can possibly be in modern times. When the Aryas had as yet no larger association than a hamlet, the family was the first home of religion, and, in consequence, the source of political organization. Society was united in no other form, and beyond the limits of the household religious practices were unknown. Each family was church and state as well, and the head of it was at once priest, judge, and king.

It might be thought from what has been said that generation, thus regarded in an exaggerated way, was the constituent principle of the primitive family. Indeed, the idea of paternity went for much, but we shall find even this principle over-ridden and subdued by a stronger one, no other, in fact, than the worship of the sacred fire and men's dead ancestors. The ancient family became even more of a religious association than one of nature, since in the most important matters we find both the principle of generation and the voice of natural affection altogether set aside and disregarded. If generation had been all, would not the sister have had equal consideration in the family with the brother? and would the emancipated son or the married daughter have ceased to retain any connexion with their former family? If natural affection had been of any account in comparison with religious principle, would not the father have been able to bequeath his possessions to a beloved daughter? and would a stranger adopted into a family, if only he continued the worship, be preferred in succession to the nearest relatives by the female line? Writers on the history of the Roman Law, having perceived that neither birth nor affection was the basis of the Roman family, thought they had discovered the true principle in the superior physical force of the father and the husband. But the father's superiority in strength was no less in their day than it had been in the early days, when the grown-up son still remained subject to the father, and when the younger sons on the father's death treated the elder brother as they had done their sire. Something stronger than either physical force or even than birth or affection was required to bind the members of the primitive family into that wonderful institution which we find it to have been. It was religion that wrought this great work. Thoughts of a life after this present one formed part of this power; the dread of supernatural beings increased its influence, and the community of worship was the present bond of union.

It is true that the religious principle, which was the strongest at first, faded away in after times before the others. Natural affections by degrees asserted its power, and the old laws were altered so as to favour the females. The daughter eventually inherited property, and the power over a son was limited. Physical force began to gain on religious authority, and sons, whether elder or younger, assumed an independence once unknown. Thus, in the Iliad, Achilles expects that Peleus, through age will be no longer able to maintain himself; and in the Odyssey, Laertes has ceded all power to Ulysses. But, if we consider how it must have been in times before those, we find religion to have been the main-spring of society; and there is no understanding Greek and Roman history unless we are thoroughly embued with the idea that the primitive family was what Herodotus calls ἐπίστιος (ἐφέστιος), that is, those who are about the hearth, or in other words, those who presented offerings to the same ancestors.

NOTE.—According to Sir J. Lubbock, the following is the march of ideas in regard to relationship :—First, a child is related to a tribe generally, all women being common to the tribe ; secondly, to his mother and not to his father ; thirdly, to his father and not to his mother (as proved by that state of things in some tribes when a man is careful as to what he eats, &c., during the pregnancy of his wife). Lastly, and lastly only, is the child considered related to both.—Orig. Civiliz., p. 113.

CHAPTER VI.

CONTINUITY OF THE FAMILY.

MEN who were convinced that their happiness in the next world depended on the continuity of the funeral repasts, esteemed it needful above all things that sons should be born regularly to each generation, for the purpose of offering those repasts. The perpetual wish of the dead, according to Hindoo belief, was that sons might be born of their line to bring rice, and milk, and honey. The Laws of Manou style the eldest son "him who is begotten to perform the duty." At Athens, in like manner, the chief magistrate was to see that no family became extinct. And Isæus[1] says in one of his speeches: "No one who knows he must die can have so little regard for himself as to leave his family without descendants, for then there would be nobody to render him the worship due to the dead. Celibacy, therefore, was not merely considered a misfortune for the man himself, but forbidden as impious. Dionysius,[2] of Halicarnassus, who had examined the old laws of Rome, says he found one which obliged young men to marry. Cicero,[3] who in a philosophic form always reproduces the old Roman laws, gives one to the same effect. At Sparta[4] a man who did not marry was deprived of the rights of a citizen; and this was the case also in other Greek states.[5]

Nor was it enough to beget a son. To be able to perpetuate the worship, a son must be born of a religious marriage, that is, of a woman who had been initiated into

---

[1] Isæus, vii., 30.
[2] Dion. Halicar., ix., 22.
[3] Cicero, *De leg.*, iii., 2.
[4] Plutarch, *Lycurg.*; *Apophth. Laced.*
[5] Pollux, iii., 48.

the family worship; and this son must be accepted by the father. The father alone, as the priest of the family and the representative of the dead, could pronounce whether or not the new-born boy belonged to the family. Moreover, when received, the male child needed a sort of initiation. This took place soon after birth, on the ninth day at Rome, on the tenth in Greece, and in India on the tenth[1] or twelfth. Then the father called together the family, summoned his witnesses, and sacrificed to the hearth-fire. The child was presented to the domestic god; a woman ran several times round[2] the fire with it; and this ceremony not only purified him, but initiated him into the worship. After that he was a member of this small church, so to speak, called the family. He took part in its worship, repeated its prayers; he honoured its forefathers, and eventually would become himself also a deified ancestor.

---

[1] Aristoph., *Birds*, 922. Demosth., *Contra Bœotos.*, p. 1016. Macrob., *Sat.*, l., 17. Laws of Manou, ii., 30.
[2] Lysias, in Harpocration, v. ἀρψιδρομια.

CHAPTER VII.

MARRIAGE.

WITH the Aryas and their descendants the birth of a son was more important than the marriage of a woman, for a man did not marry except for children. The Romans declared with an oath that this was their object in marriage: ducere uxorem liberorum quœrendorum causâ; and with the Greeks no less it was παίδων ἐπ' ἀρότῳ γνησίων.[1]

But for a bride in those times marriage must have been even a greater change than it can possibly be at present; for in those days, as it was an unheard of thing to worship at two hearths, she was compelled to adopt new gods with her new home. In Greece, the ceremony which effected this was often called τὸ τέλος, to indicate its peculiarly religious character; and its special object was to set free the bride from one worship and to initiate her into the other. It follows that this ceremony was not performed in the temples of the Olympian gods; even when their worship in after times had so completely prevailed over the other as to compel the bride and bridegroom to go and ask a blessing in the temple of Jupiter or Juno, yet all this did but constitute the prelude of the marriage. The ceremony itself took place at home, in the houses of the father and of the bridegroom, because the domestic deity was the one most nearly concerned in it, and because its chief object was originally that the bridegroom's forefathers might have another son to continue their service.

---

[1] Menander., fr. 185, ed. Didot. Alciphron, i., 16. Æsch., *Agam.*, 1166.
[2] Pollux, iii., 3, 38.

There were three parts in the ceremony.

1. The first was called ἐγγύησις, or *Traditio*,[1] and took place in the house of the father, who, after offering a sacrifice, set his daughter free from serving her own ancestors, and made declaration that he gave her away to her husband.

2. The second part of the ceremony (which was called πομπή, or *deductio in domum*) has less concern with our present purpose than the other two. But it gives interesting evidence, in passing, both of the religious nature of the ceremony and of its very high antiquity. The former point is proved not only by the white robe which was borne by the bride, but also by her crown; for though in later times this last became the symbol of power, it was at first purely religious; and we discern the antiquity of the ceremony from the fact that in classical times neither Greeks nor Romans understood the meaning of the words they shouted in the procession: (Ὀ' ὑμὴν, ὦ ὑμέναιε, and Talassie), as also by a show of violence which was kept up in introducing the bride to her new home. This points to a stage in the world's history when brides could only be gained by measures of force.

3. In the third part of the ceremony, the bride was brought before the hearth of her husband; lustral water was applied, and she touched the sacred fire. Then, after a few prayers had been said, both partook of a cake or of some bread, and this act associated them in the sacred worship. As the Roman lawyers expressed it, the wife became the associate of her husband in all things, human and divine. Uxor socia humanæ rei atque divinæ. Nuptiæ sunt divini juris et humani communicatio. All religious connection with her own family and her own ancestors was considered to be broken off; but she was, so to speak, born again into her husband's family, and became unto him as a daughter; for the legal phrase is *filiæ loco*.

---

[1] Varro, *De lingua Lat.*, v., 61. Dion. Hal., ii., 25, 26. Ovid., *Fast.*, ii., 558. Plutarch, *Quest. Rom.*, 1 and 29; *Romul.*, 15. Plin., *Hist. Nat.*, xviii., 3. Tacit., *Annal.*, iv., 16; xi., 27. Juven., *Sat.*, x., 329, 330. Gaius, *Inst.*, i., 112. Ulpian., *Digest.*, xxiii., 2, 1. Festus, Verb., *rapi*. Macrob., *Sat.*, i., 15. Serv., *Ad. Æn.*, iv., 168. For Etruscan customs, which were the same, see Varro, *De re Rust.*, ii., 4. For Hindoo, Laws of Manou, iii., 27, 30; v., 152; viii., 227; ix., 194. Mitakchara, trad. Orianne, p. 166, 167, 236.

This primitive religion had the merit of teaching that the union of husband and wife is something more than a sexual relation, or a transitory passion. It united the two by the powerful bond of the same worship and the same belief; and the ceremony of the wedding was so solemn, its end was so high, and so intimately connected with hereafter, that we are not surprised to find men believing it permissible only to one woman in each house. Polygamy could never have been permitted by the old worship of the Aryas.

In the same spirit, the divorce of a woman who fulfilled the end of marriage by having children was very difficult[1] to procure; perhaps at first it was impossible. In times when it could be done, a new religious ceremony was needed, as though those whom *confarreatio* or the eating of the sacred cake had bound together could only be sundered by a formal rejection of the same (diffarreatio[2]). On such occasions, husband and wife met together for the last time before the sacred fire, accompanied by a priest and witnesses. Then instead of prayers fearful formulas were pronounced, and by a sort of curse[3] the woman renounced her husband's gods. So the religious tie was broken, and after that all other.

Where there were no children, a divorce was not only attainable, but needful. The Hindoo woman who was barren was to be replaced at the end of eight years. Herodotus tells us of two kings of Sparta who were obliged to put away their wives for the same reason; and a Roman named Carvilius Ruga, though tenderly attached to his wife, thought it his duty to put her away for barrenness, seeing that he had sworn he married her to have children.

And in the same way, if it were the fault of the husband that there were no children, a brother or other agnate might be substituted for him to raise up seed that would be accounted his.

---

[1] Dion. Hal., ii., 25.
[2] Festus, v., diffarreatio. Pollux, III, c. 23, ἀποπομπή. We read in a certain inscription: "sacerdos confarreationum et diffarreatiorum." Orelli, No. 2648.
[3] Φρικώδη, ἀλλόκοτα σκυθρωπά. Plutarch, *Quest. Rom.*, 50.

CHAPTER VIII.

ADOPTION AND EMANCIPATION.

THE duty of perpetuating the domestic worship was the reason for adoption with the ancients. Just as a man must marry to avoid the extinction of his family, as the barren wife was replaced by another, and the impotent husband by a brother, so, as a last resource, extinction might be avoided by adoption.[1] Isæus, in pleading for an adopted son, whose adoption had been contested, says, "Menecles would not die without children, that some one might bury him, and perform the funeral rites. . . . If you annul this adoption, no one will offer him his feast, and he will be without worship."[2]

Since adoption had no other end but to prevent the extinction of a worship, naturally it was only permitted where a man had no sons. The Hindoo law is explicit upon this point, and the Athenian no less; all the pleading of Demosthenes against Leochares proves it.

That the same held good in ancient Roman jurisprudence there is no precise text to prove. We even know that in Gaius' time a man might have both natural and adopted sons, yet this would not have been allowed in Cicero's time. For Cicero speaks as follows:—"What is the right that regulates adoption? Must not he—who adopts—be too old to beget children, and must he not have tried to have them before he can adopt? To adopt is to ask of religion and law what nature does not grant"[3]; and he attacked Clodius' adoption on the principle that it was unlawful to be adopted by a man who had a legitimate son.

---

[1] Laws of Manou, ix., 10.
[2] Isæus, ii., 10—46; li., 11—14.
[3] Cicero, *Pro domo*, 13, 14. Aulus-Gellius, v., 19.

The ceremony of adoption consisted of initiation into a new worship. It resembled that which took place at the birth of a son. The person to be adopted was admitted to the fire of his new father, and entered upon this fresh religion. The gods, and prayers, and ceremonies of the adopting parent became also his. It was said of him, in sacra transiit[1]: he has passed over to new rites; and of course at the same time he renounced the property and religion of his natural sire. He could not even inherit from this latter, or take a place at his burial. He was allowed to go back to his own family only on condition that he left a son behind him in the new family; and then he had broken off all ties with this son.[2]

Emancipation, or *sacrorum detestatio*, was the renunciation of the family worship in which a man had been born, and necessarily preceded adoption.[3]

---

[1] ἐπὶ τὰ ἱερὰ ἄγειν. Isæus, vii., *Venire in sacra.* Cicero, *Pro domo*, 13, *in penates adsciscere.* Tacitus, Hist., i., 15, *est heres sacrorum.* Cicero, *amissis sacris paternis.* Coc.

[2] Isæus, vi., 44; x., 11. Demosth., *Leoch.* Antiphon., *Frag.*, 15. Laws of Manou, ix., 142.

[3] Consuetudo apud antiquos fuit ut qui in familiam transiret prius se abdicaret ab eâ quâ. natus fuerat. Servius, *Ad. Æn.*, ii., 156. Aulus-Gellius, xv., 27.

CHAPTER IX.

RELATIONSHIP, AGNATIO.

RELATIONSHIP, according to Plato, consisted in having the same domestic deities, and Demosthenes proves that men are akin by shewing that they had the same worship, and presented offerings at the same tomb.

As funeral repasts were only offered to male ancestors, so at first relationship was only by the father's side. The mother had renounced all connexion with her own family, and no longer sacrificed to her own ancestors; much less, then, had her son anything to do with that family.

Hindoo customs throw much light on this. In India, the head of a family twice a month offers a cake to his father's manes, the same to his grandfather by the father's side, and great grandfather; but to his fourth, fifth, and sixth ancestors in the ascending line he offers only a few grains of rice[1] and a libation. Two men are related if one of these ancestors is common to both. They are[2] *sapindas* if this ancestor is one who receives a cake, and *samanodacas*, if he only has the water and rice. No relationship through women is accounted of.

This will explain to us what was *agnatio* at Rome. Agnation was that relationship which had been originally established by domestic worship.

---

[1] Laws of Manou, v., 60.
[2] Mitakchara, tr. Orianne, p. 213.

Thus, in the following table:—

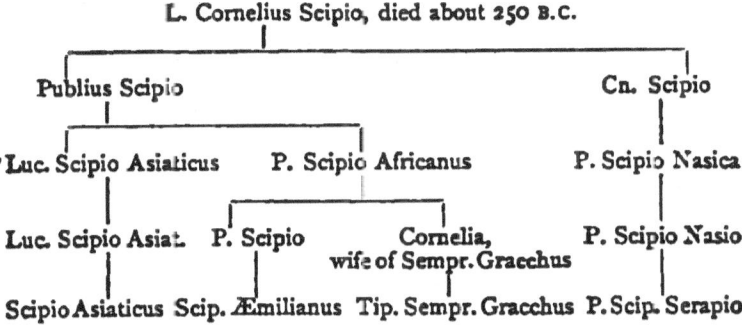

the fourth generation is represented by four persons, who would all have been relations according to modern notions.[1] A Hindoo would call Asiaticus and Æmilianus *sapindas*, and Asiaticus and Serapio *samanodacas*. But Sempronius Gracchus is no agnate at all, being only akin through the mother. They had a different worship. A person adopted into the family was nearer to Asiaticus than a cousin by the mother's side. If a son had been emancipated, he was no longer an agnate of his own father.

No doubt there came a time, for India as well as Greece and Rome, when relationship by worship was no longer the only one admitted. The old worship was less honoured, and the voice of blood spoke louder; and then relationship by birth was recognised in law. In reading the works of lawyers, from Cicero to Justinian, we see these two systems of relationship existing as rivals, so to speak, and disputing the domain of law. But at the time of the Twelve Tables agnation alone was known, and conferred the rights of heritage. We shall see by-and-by that the same was also the case in Greece.

---

[1] Gaius, i., 156; iii., 10. Ulpian, 26. Instituta, iii., 2; iii., 5.

CHAPTER X.

THE RIGHT OF PROPERTY.

THERE are races which have never succeeded in establishing a right to the soil, and others which have only done so with great difficulty, and after the lapse of many generations. And indeed it is not easy in the commencement of society to know whether an individual may appropriate to himself a portion of the soil and say, "This belongs to me and to no one else." Wandering tribes, like the Tartars, can conceive of property when it is a question of flocks and herds, but do not comprehend the idea when applied to the soil. With the ancient Germans, the land belonged to no one; each person received his lot to cultivate for the year, and next year had a different one. He owned his harvest, but not the soil which had grown it. And so it is still with some portions of the Semitic race, and with certain Slavonic peoples.

But with the populations of Greece and Italy ownership of land at the most remote period was a familiar thing. No territory was common except what had been conquered. Amongst them we find nothing resembling that yearly distribution of soil which prevailed in Germany; for whereas the tribes which acknowledged no ownership of land did allow each cultivator the fruits of the harvest, the citizens of many Greek states were obliged to store their harvests together, and to eat it in common, whilst all the time they were absolute owners of the soil; the land belonged to them more absolutely than its fruit. It seems that the idea of property in the Greek mind followed an unnatural order, and was not applied to the harvest first, and the soil afterwards, but, on the contrary, attached itself first of all to the soil, and then appropriated the harvest. In point of fact, it was religion inspired the idea of property, as it had constituted the family; and those three things were inseparable: the altar[1] with its sacred fire, the family who erected it, and the soil on which it was built. The altar and the tomb connected the family with the soil, and the soil was only conceived of as appropriated because there the dead were interred, and there the living made offerings to their shades.

That religion first gave rise to the possession of property is proved by another circumstance. According to the belief of the ancients, each hearth represented divinities so distinct that a marriage between two of their descendants did not at all bind these families together. Moreover, neither these gods nor their worshippers on the occasion of any feast could look upon the face of a stranger without profanation. Hence an enclosure of some sort, whether a hedge, a partition of wood, or a stone wall, was absolutely necessary for privacy, as well as to mark out each several domain. From this sacred enclosure, which it was deemed impious to pass over, the deity who protected it, and who was screened by it, received the name of ἑρκεῖος, or god of the precinct.[2] No houses in the present day possess any sign or symbol of appropriation nearly so sure and reliable as this enclosure thus marked out and protected by religion.

If we pass down the stream of time and follow the Aryas from their folds and flocks in the East to their villages and cities in Europe, we find the enclosure[3] as sacred as ever. The houses are nearer, but not contiguous, and the sacred enclosure still exists, though in reduced dimensions. Most frequently the fence is but a little wall, or a ditch, or a simple space of some feet wide. A party wall is an unheard of thing, for the household deities must not be without their precinct. The Roman law fixed two and a half feet as the free space by which houses must be separated, and this was consecrated to the domestic god. From these ancient rules

---

[1] Ἑστία, from ἵστημι, an altar. See Plut., *de primo frigido*, 21. Macrob, l., 23. Ovid, *Fast.*, vi., 299.

[2] The domestic god afterwards gave place to Ζεὺς ἑρκεῖος, but it was not so at first. Dion. Halic., i., 67; also of Paus., iv., 17. Eurip., *Troad.*, 17. Virgil, *Æn.*, ii., 514.

[3] Festus, v. *Ambitus*. Varro, *De lingua Lat.*, v., 22. Servius, *Ad Æn*, ii., 469.

of religion community of property was rendered impossible. Pythagoras tried in vain to establish institutions on such a principle; it was revolting to men's habits of thought. Ancient society never presented anything like the promiscuous life which was general in French villages of the twelfth century. Every family that had gods and a worship must also possess its own locality, its own house, and its own property.

This was the meaning of that saying of the Greeks that the fire on the hearth had taught men to build houses. The tent and the waggon would not suffice for families that were to inhabit successively the same abode. The wooden hut was followed by the house of stone, and this was not intended to endure for one life alone, but for generations.

When the Greeks built a house, they divided the sacred enclosure into two parts, of which the first was the court, the second was the site of the house. The sacred fire was placed near the middle of the whole precinct, at the bottom of the court, and near the entrance of the house. At Rome the arrangement was different, but the principle the same. The fire remained in the midst of the precinct, but the buildings were so raised about it that it was shut within a small court. It is evident that the object of all this was to protect and isolate the fire, and to make the house a sort of temple for the gods, whose presence consecrated it. Cicero says, "What is more sacred than the dwelling place? There is the altar; there burns the sacred fire; there is the religion and the sacred objects." According to Roman tradition, the domestic god drove off the thief and the enemy; and it would have been sacrilege to enter the house with malevolent intention.

If we pass on to that other object of worship, the family tomb, we shall find the same ideas attached. The offerings must be made where the dead reposed, and that repose must be disturbed by the presence of no strange[1] corpse; for, as

---

[1] Cicero, *De Leg.*, ii., 22; ii., 26. Gaius, *Jus.*, ii., 6. *Digest.*, liv., xlvii., 12. Clients and slaves *were* buried in the family tomb, for they had been initiated. When the State ordered a public burial, the rule did not hold good; ἀνδρῶν γὰρ ἐπιφανῶν πᾶσα γῆ τάφος. See Lycurgus, *Cont. Leocrat.*, 25. The pontiff's leave was required at Rome before a tomb could be displaced. Plin., *Lett.*, x., 73.

it had been in life, so also in death religion separated each family from all other. In later times the dead were buried in cemeteries, or along the great highroads, but at the period of which we speak the tomb was always in the field of each family. The laws of Solon[1] and many passages of Plutarch attest this custom, which lasted down to the time of Demosthenes. A law of the Twelve Tables at Rome speaks to the same effect, as also do the writings of lawyers, and the following passage in Siculus Flaccus[2]: "There were anciently two modes of placing the tomb; some put it at the border of the field, and some near the middle." Thus the departed members of a family had a hold on the soil, as well as the living; and their resting-place was inalienable. The Roman law exacted that, when a family had sold its field, it should still remain owner of the tomb, and have a right of way to perform the necessary worship.

From the tomb the idea of property extended to the whole field[3] in which the tomb was placed. The Italian labourer prayed that the Manes would watch over his field, keep off the robber, and bestow a good harvest. The form of this prayer is found in Cato. Thus the souls of the departed extended their tutelary influence, and with it the right of property to the limits of the domain. Burial had established an indissoluble connexion of the family with the soil; in fact, had constituted property.

In like fashion, religion gave Abraham a right to the soil of Canaan. "The Lord appeared unto Abram, and said, 'Unto thy seed will I give this land.' And he said, 'Whereby shall I know that I shall inherit it?'" Then Abraham is directed to offer a sacrifice, so that a local worship is established, after which the burial of the patriarchs confirmed the possession.

In fact, the ancient religion of the Greeks and Italians could not have dispensed with the right of property. With-

---

[1] Laws of Solon, cited by Gaius, *Digest.*, x., 1, 13. Demosth., *Cont. Callicles.* Plutarch, *Aristides*, 1. See also Cicero, *De Leg.*, 11, 24. *Digest.*, xviii., 1, 6.
[2] Sic. Flacc., edit. Goez, p. 4, 5. See also *Fragm. terminalia*, edit. Goez., p. 147. Pompon., cited in *Digest.*, xlvii., 12.5; also viii., 1.14.
[3] Lares agri custodes. Tibull., i., 1, 23. Cicero, *De Leg.*, ii., 2.; 2 Cicero, *De Leg.*, 1, 21. Cato, *De re Rust.*, 141. *Scrip rei agrar.*, edit. Goez., p. 308. Gen., xii., 7; xv., 8. Ovid, *Fast.*, ii., 639. Strabo, v., 3.

out it the hearth-fire would have had no fixed place, families would have been mixed up, and the dead neglected. By this religion, then, were surmounted the first difficulties in the way of civilization, and the path of progress was entered upon. Men were not slow to labour on the land to which they felt they had a right; and in improving the soil, their own habits and character, and condition were ameliorated also.

In fact, in the earliest times it was not the law which guaranteed the right of property, but religion; and this is proved by the way in which each family's possessions were marked off. Each separate property was surrounded by a strip of land, some feet in width, which was held sacred and must remain uncultivated. On certain days, the father of the family walked all round his field, following the sacred line. Victims were driven before him; he sang hymns, and sacrifices were offered to arouse the benevolence of his gods, and to mark out the inviolable boundary of his land. Further, at certain distances along this line, certain great stones or trunks of trees were placed, called *termini*. What these were, may be seen from the manner in which they were deposited in the earth. "After a hole had been dug, the Terminus was raised on the brink, and crowned with garlands. Then a victim was slaughtered in such a way that the blood ran into the hole. Embers (perhaps from the sacred fire) were thrown in, and cakes and fruit, with honey and wine; after which the block of wood or the stone was fixed in the hole." It is evident that the ceremony was intended to constitute the Terminus[1] a representative of the domestic worship. The sacred act was renewed every year, with libations and prayers; and the religion thus implanted in the soil attested for ever what was the family property. Afterwards, by dint of imagination and poetry, the Terminus became a god.

The use of sacred land-marks, being derived from a very early period, had been spread by the Aryan race into all lands. The Hindoo ceremonies differed little from those we have described, and the Etruscans and Sabines had termini before Rome existed.

---

[1] Laws of Manou, viii., 245. Vrihaspati, cited by Sice, *Legislat. Hindom.*, p. 159. Varro, *De lingua Lat.*, v., 74. 3, Pollux, ix., 9. Hesychius, ὅρος. Plato, *Laws*, viii., 842. Ovid, *Fast.*, ii., 677.

When a Terminus had once been planted according to the rites, no power in the world could displace it. It was to remain there to all eternity. Hence the legend at Rome that, when Jupiter wished for a place on the Capitol, he could not displace the god Terminus.

This tradition proves, at all events, the sacredness of property, and the inviolable character of the right to the soil. It became sacrilege to move a landmark. At Rome the man and the oxen that had touched a Terminus were devoted to death; and the Etruscan law[1] cursed such a transgressor as follows:—"His house shall disappear, and his race be extinguished; his land shall produce no fruit; his harvest shall be destroyed by hail, mildew, and drought; and his limbs shall be covered with sores, and wither away." The few remaining words of the Athenian law, "Pass not the landmark," are filled up by Plato, who completes the legislators' thought: "Let no one move the stone which separates friendship from enmity, and which a man's oath obliges him to respect."[2] It seems evident from all these practices and laws that it was the domestic religion of the ancients which taught them to appropriate land and maintain their right to portions of the soil. And it will not be hard to understand that the right to property thus conceived and established was much more complete and absolute in its effects than it can be in modern society, where it is founded upon other principles. The land of a family was so intimately connected with its religious worship, that its members could no more give up one than the other.

Everything inclines one to believe that in ancient times property was inalienable. Plato, in his treatise on laws, is not inventing any novelty, but only recalling an old law, when he forbids the landowner to sell his land; for we know that it was unlawful at Sparta to do so, and the same prohibition held good at Locri and Leucas. Phidon, of Corinth, in the ninth century before Christ, ordained that no alteration should be made in the number of families and properties. And it is evident this prescription could only be observed so long as the sale of land, and even its partition was forbidden.

---

[1] *Scrip. rei agrar.*, edit. Goez, p. 258.
[2] Plato, *Laws*, viii., 842.

Again, seven or eight generations after Phidon, though Solon no longer prohibits a man selling his property, yet it is ordered that he shall only do so at a terrible cost, viz., that of losing his right of citizenship. Finally, Aristotle tells us in a general manner that in many cities the old laws forbade the sale of land.[1]

These regulations ought not to surprise us when we reflect on what principle the right of property was founded. For if this right be founded only upon the principle of toil and work, then a man may part with his own acquisition. But found his right upon religion, and then there is something far stronger than the mere will of man to bind him down to it. Besides, the field where the ancestors are buried is not the property of the individual who may happen to be the head of the family; for it was not he who established his right to it, but the domestic deity. The living representative of the family may have enjoyment for the few years he remains on earth, but the land is the property of the dead who are buried in it, and of the future generations who shall bring offerings to the tomb.

Property, therefore, amongst the ancient Hindoos, could not be sold. It is not so easy to prove this for Rome. But before Rome existed there is reason to think that the soil of Italy was inalienable, seeing that the Roman laws which do exist on the subject seem to be successive and gradual relaxations of the old principle. In the laws of the Twelve Tables, we find that the tomb must always remain in the family, whilst the land about it is freed from this restriction. The next relaxation consists in the permission to divide a property between brothers, instead of its remaining entirely in the hands of the elder. But this amelioration was not effected in defiance of religion. On the contrary, new religious ceremonies must be performed, and the partition effected by a priest;[2] because religion alone could divide what itself had made indivisible. And the same was also the case when at length the unreserved sale of estates was

---

[1] Aristot., *Polit.*, ii., 4, 4; ii., 5; ii., 3, 7; ii., 6, 10; and vii., 2. Plutarch, *Lycurgus Agis.* Æsch., *Cont. Timard.* Drog., *Laert.*, i., 55.
[2] *Agrimensor.* See *Scrip. rei agrariæ.* Cp. Mitakchara, trad. Orianne, p. 50; but the rule disappeared with the rise of Brahmanism. Stobæus, 42.

allowed. A ceremony called *mancipatio* must be effected in the presence of a priest, denominated *libripens;* and it may be remarked generally of Greece that every change of property must be authorised by religion, no house being sold, or parcel of land disposed of, unless the gods were first appeased by sacrifice.

If a man found it hard to get rid of his land by sale, much harder was it to take it from him in spite of his will. In those days expropriation for the public benefit was unknown, and confiscation[1] was only practised as a consequence of exile, that is to say, when a man, having been deprived of his title to citizenship, could no longer exercise any right upon the city's soil. Neither is the right of expropriating for debt ever found in the laws of ancient cities. The Twelve Tables are not certainly lenient to the debtor; but they do not permit property to be confiscated for the profit of the creditor. A man's person may be answerable for his debt, but not his land, for that is inseparable from the family. Consequently, it was easier to make a slave of a man than to take away his property. However, when the debtor was delivered over to his creditor, after a certain fashion the land followed him into slavery; for the master who might profit by a man's physical strength, at the same time enjoyed the fruit of his land. But he never became the owner of this land, so paramount and inviolable was the right of property.

---

[1] In democratic days things became different. Mortgage was unknown in ancient times.—*Polit.*, vii., 2.

NOTE ON INSOLVENT DEBTORS.

In the clause of the Law of the Twelve Tables which concerns insolvent debtors, we find the words, *si volet suo vivito:* let him live if he likes on his own property; whence it appears, that, even when he had become almost a slave, the debtor still retained some property. Expropriation for debt was a thing unknown. And this is indirectly proved by the contrivances to which the Roman law was obliged to have recourse in order to assure the creditor that he should be paid. These were *mancipatio cum fiducia* and *pignus*. When, afterwards, personal slavery was abolished, it was needful to devise some other means of laying hold of the debtor's possessions. And this was not an easy thing; but a distinction was drawn between *property* and *possession*. The creditor obtained leave of the prætor to sell the debtor's goods, *bona,* not his property, *dominium*; and only in this way by a disguised expropriation, the debtor lost the enjoyment of his property.

CHAPTER XI.

THE LAWS OF INHERITANCE.

1. *The principle of the laws of inheritance.*—It was the rule without exception, in both Greek and Roman law, that a property could not be acquired without worship, nor a worship without property. According to Cicero, religion prescribed that the two should be inseparable, and that he to whom the estate had fallen should also perform the sacrifice.[1] At Athens, we find an orator[2] claiming an inheritance in the following terms:—Think well, O judges, and say whether my adversary or I ought to inherit Philoctemon's goods, and sacrifice upon his tomb." The care of the worship seems most clearly from this passage to accompany the inheritance. And so it was in India also, where the laws[3] of Manou provide that whoever inherits must make the offering at the tomb.

From this religious principle, therefore, and from no convention of men, every rule of inheritance was easily derived. Since the worship went from male to male, and never in the female line, so also, without any need of a testament or will, the son succeeded to his father's goods and was called *heres ipso jure*, or even *heres necessarius*.[4] For he had no choice of accepting or refusing the inheritance; like the care of the worship, it was an obligation as much as a right. Whether he would or no, he must accept the succession, even if it were charged with debt; the benefit of abstention and of public sale being only very late inventions of Roman law, and in Greek law unknown at all times.

---

[1] Cicero, *De Leg.*, ii., 19, 20. Festus, V°. *everriator*.
[2] Isæus, vi., 51. Plato calls the heir διάδοχος θεῶν, *Laws*, v., 740.
[3] Laws of Manou, ix., 186.
[4] *Digest.*, xxxviii., 16, 14.

Another technical form for the son at Rome was *heres suus*, as though they had said *heres sui ipsius*. In fact, between father and son there was neither donation, legacy, nor change of property, only on the father's death the estate is continued, *dominium continuatur*,[1] and the son inherits of himself, having been even in his father's life-time part-owner of the house and land.

Therefore, in order to form a right notion of inheritance among the ancients, we must not picture to ourselves a fortune passing from hand to hand; because the property is as immoveable as the tomb and the hearth to which it is attached. It is not the property, but man, which passes away. The family unrolls its endless generations, and each individual head of it comes in his turn to the hour when he must continue the worship, and take care of the domain.

2. *A daughter could not inherit.*—By Roman law a daughter could not inherit if she were married, and by Greek law in no case. This is explained by what we have said of the religious duty accompanying the property as a necessary condition to its possession. Of course, a married woman could not take the property of her forefathers, whose worship she had renounced in order to adopt that of her husband's.

The laws of Manou order the patrimony to be divided among the brothers, but recommend a dowry to be given to the sisters, as they had no right to the inheritance. And we see that the same rule held good at Athens, where the speeches of Demosthenes shew that daughters[2] could not inherit. Demosthenes styles himself the sole heir, since only a seventh part had been reserved by their father for his sister.

That daughters were excluded by the ancient law of Rome there are not precise texts to prove; but we gather that such must have been the case from marks remaining in more recent legislation. Even so late as Justinian's[3] time the daughter was excluded from the number of natural heirs, if she had ceased to be under the father's power, that is, if she had passed by marriage into the power of her husband. And if this were the case so late as the times[4] of Justinian, it is

---

[1] *Institutes*, iii., 1, 3; iii., 9, 7; iii., 19, 2.
[2] Demosth., in *Bæoticus*. Isæus, x., 4. Lysias, in *Mantith.*, 10.
[3] *Institutes*, ii., 9, 2.
[4] *Institutes*, iii., 2, 3.

easy to suppose that by the earlier law the principle was applied in all its rigour, and that a daughter, who was not yet married, but only *might* be, was excluded also; for the Institutes mention the disused but not forgotten rule that the heritage should pass in all cases to the males. As we go further back, we come nearer to this old rule. In Cicero's[1] time, a man, who had a son and a daughter, could only leave the daughter a third; and if he had an only daughter, she could but inherit the half of his property. And in these cases the father must make a will, since the daughter has nothing by full right. Finally, a century and a half before Cicero,[2] Cato, whose great object was always to revive ancient manners, carried the Voconian law, which prohibited a woman, first, from being constituted an heiress, whether or not an only child, whether married or single; secondly, from receiving as a legacy more than a fourth of the patrimony. This law was a restoration of ancient rules that had fallen into disuse; for it would never have been accepted by the contemporaries of the Scipios if it had not been founded on principles that were still respected. Let us add that nothing is said about the case of a man dying without will, because, most likely, there was no infringement of old custom to withstand. We conclude then, that at Rome, as well as in Greece, the primitive laws forbade a daughter to inherit, and that this was but a natural consequence of the principles which religion had laid down.

But a way was early found for reconciling this religious prescription with the natural desire of a father to leave his daughter his fortune. She might marry the heir.

Athenian legislation pushed this principle to the extreme. If the dead man left a son and a daughter, the brother, who was sole heir, was to marry the sister, unless he preferred giving her a dowry.[3] If the dead man left but one daughter, his nearest relation was the heir, but this relation, nearly

---

[1] Cicero, *De Rep.*, iii., 7.

[2] Cicero, in *Verr.*, 1, 42. Livy., xli., 4. S. Augustin, *Civitas Dei*, iii., 21.

[3] Demosth., in *Eubul.*, 21. Plutarch, *Themist*, 32. Isæus, x., 4. Corn. Nep., *Cimon*. Mark that the law allowed her not to marry a uterine brother, nor one who was emancipated, only the brother by the same father, whose heir he was.

allied as he would be to the daughter, must marry her. And what is even more remarkable, if this daughter were already married, she was to quit her husband in order to marry her father's heir. Nor was it an obstacle that the heir himself had a wife; he must quit his wife to take as bride[1] his near relation. We see how very little respect these old laws had for natural feeling, when it was a question of conforming to religious belief.

Another contrivance must be mentioned whereby the need of satisfying religion was reconciled with the interest of a daughter; and it is a point on which the Hindoo law is wonderfully in accord with the Athenian. A man who had no son, but a daughter, might give her away in marriage, with the condition that the male child born should be considered his own son, and continue *his* worship, and not that of the husband. This child was called the "son of the daughter" at Athens, θυγατριδοῦς.[1]

3. *Of collateral succession.*—When a man died without children, all that was required, in order to know who ought to inherit his property, was to see who ought to continue the worship.

As the worship was transmitted in the male line, so also was the inheritance, and the son of a daughter could not inherit. If direct descendants failed a man, his brother succeeded him, but not his sister; and the son of his brother, not the son of his sister. So, if there were neither brother nor nephew in existence, the nearest relation by the male line succeeded; with the Hindoos the nearest sapinda[2] or samanadaca, at Rome the nearest agnatus. The law at Athens ordained that if a man had died without children, the brother of the dead man should be his heir, if of the same father; and failing him, the brother's son, *since the succession must always pass to males, and to the descendants of males.*[4] This old law was still quoted in Demosthenes' time, though it had

---

[1] Isæus, iii., 64; x, 5. Demosth., in *Eubul.*, 51. Ἐπίκληρος means, not heiress, but the daughter who goes with the inheritance. There was not such a thing as an heiress, properly speaking.

[2] Cp. Laws of Manou, ix., 127, 136. Vasishta, xvii., 16. Also see Isæus, vii.; viii., 31; x., 12. Demosth., in *Step.*, ii., 20.

[3] Laws of Manou, ix., 186, 187.

[4] Demosth., in *Macart.*; in *Leoch.* Isæus, vii., 20.

been already modified, and although relationship through women had begun to be admitted.

In like manner, the law of the Twelve Tables decided that if a man died without an heir in his own right, the nearest agnatus or relation by the males must succeed to the estate. It was further specified that the nephew inherited from his father's brother (patruus), and not from his mother's (avunculus).[1] Thus, in the table of the Scipios cited above, the property of Scipio Æmilianus, dying without children, could pass neither to his aunt Cornelia, nor to C. Gracchus, who, according to our modern ideas, would be his cousin-german, but to Scipio Asiaticus, who was really his nearest relation.

In Justinian's time these old laws were no longer understood, and the Twelve Tables are accused of excessive rigour for always giving preference to male posterity, whilst relations through women were always excluded from inheriting.[2] And unjust they doubtless are, if one has regard alone to natural feeling, but very logical, if we start from the principle that the inheritance went with the worship; since those only, who could not continue it, were set aside.

4. *Effects of emancipation and adoption.*—The son who had been excluded by emancipation from the paternal worship, lost all right to inherit. But, on the other hand, an inheritance might be gained by an adopted son, upon initiation into the new family worship. For the religious tie was held of more account than the tie of birth.

In the pleadings of Athenian orators, we often meet with men who have been adopted into another family, and yet desire, notwithstanding, to inherit the property of their own original family. But the law is always opposed to this, and compels a man to renounce one or other. If he prefers to join once more his original family, he must give up also the patrimony of his adoptive family, leaving behind him his son to continue that worship, and not his own. But this father and son can no longer inherit from one another; they no longer are of the same family, nor even relations.[3]

---

[1] *Institutes*, iii., 2, 4.
[2] *Institutes*, iii., 3.
[3] Isæus, x. Demosth., *Passim.* Gaius, iii., 2. *Institutes*, iii., 1, 2. The prætors' laws afterwards modified all this.

5.—*Wills were not known originally.*—It was against the belief on which the rights of property and of inheritance had been founded for a man to make a will, that is, to dispose of his goods after his death otherwise than to his natural heir. Could men think of making wills, when the property went with the worship, and the worship was hereditary? Besides, the property did not belong to the individual but to the family; the men had not acquired it by the right of toil, but by that of domestic worship. It belonged to the family and passed from the dead to the living, not by virtue of the dead man's choice, but by the force of superior rules which religion had established.

The ancient Hindoo law knew no testament. At Athens it was absolutely forbidden down to Solon's time, who only permitted it to those who left no children.[1] At Sparta, it was long forbidden or ignored, and was only authorized after the Peloponnesian war.[2] We have traditions, also, of a period when the same rule held good at Corinth and Thebes.[3] It is certain that the arbitrary disposition of a man's property was never recognised at first as a natural right, the constant principle of early times being that all property should remain in the family to which it was attached by religion.

Plato[4] clearly expresses the thought of the ancient legislators in his treatise on Laws, which is, in a great measure, a commentary on the laws of Athens. He supposes a dying man to claim the right of making a will, and saying: "Is it not hard, O gods, that I cannot dispose of my property as I will, giving more to this and less to that person according to the affection they have shewn me?" But the legislator replies: "Is it for thee, who canst not make sure of another day on earth, to decide on such matters? Thou art neither master of thy goods nor of thyself; all belongs to thy family, *i.e.*, to thy ancestors and to thy descendants."

It is probable that there was a period in Roman law also when a man could make no will. This appears from the formula *hæres suus, et necessarius*, which was still employed by Gaius and Justinian, though no longer in accordance with

---

[1] Plutarch, *Solon*, 21.
[2] Plutarch, *Agis*, 5.
[3] Aristot., *Pol.* ii., 3, 4.
[4] *Laws*, xi.

the legislation of their time. In the earliest days a son could neither refuse an inheritance nor be disinherited. And yet we have no law before those of the Twelve Tables, which either allows or refuses right of testament. The Twelve Tables certainly allow the right of willing, uti legassit, ita jus esto. But this fragment is too short and incomplete for us to be sure we can know the true provisions of the legislator in this matter. In granting this right of willing, we cannot say what reserves and what conditions he might have attached. Suppose we had no words left of Solon's law except διαθέσθαι ὅπως ἂν ἐθέλῃ, *to will as he likes,* we might suppose that the right of testament was accorded in every case; but the law adds ἂν μὴ παῖδες ὦσι, *if there be no children.* Therefore, when there were no children, to make a will was not absolutely an unknown thing at Rome, but it was extremely difficult, and needed great formalities. In the first place, the intentions of the testator could not be kept secret during his life-time. He must be made to feel all the odium attaching to the disinheritance of his family, and the thwarting of the law. Furthermore, his wishes required the approval of sovereign authority, that is, of the people assembled by curies under the presidence of the [1]pontiff, which would be no idle form in times when the comitia curiata were the most solemn meetings of the Roman people. It is even probable enough that a vote was necessary, on the principle that a general law which regulated inheritance in a very rigorous manner could only be modified by another law; so that in point of fact a testament amounted to a new law. We conclude, then, that the right of making a will was neither fully recognized as existing, as a matter of course, nor could possibly have been so, as long as men remained under the influence of the old domestic religion.

6. *The right of primogeniture.*—In the ancient codes of the Hindoos, Greeks, and Romans, certain flagrant inconsistencies are frequently found, and often two laws are recorded on the same subject completely contradicting one another. The reason of this is, that, all laws being based on religion, it would have been an act of impiety to abrogate

---

[1] Ulpian, xx., 2. Gaius, i., 102, 119. Aulus-Gellius, xv., 27. The *testamentum calatis comitiis* had gone out of use by Cicero's time. *De Orat.*, 1, 53.

any. Thus, at the period when the Laws of Manou were written, certain clauses were in being which authorized the partition of an estate between brothers. And yet it is made as clear as possible that originally the eldest son took all the estate, along with the performance of the religious duties. " He was born for this duty ; the rest of the brothers are but the fruit of love." *He* repeated the hymns, and presided at every ceremony. His brothers were subject to him as to their father. It was he who paid the debt to the ancestors, and who, therefore, ought to possess all.[1]

As the Greek law proceeded from the same religious beliefs as the Hindoo, it is not surprising to find in it also the right of primogeniture. It subsisted longer at Sparta than elsewhere, from the very conservative character of that city. With the Spartans the patrimony was indivisible, and the younger son debarred from all share in it.[2] And this was no less the case in many other cities whose laws Aristotle had studied. We learn from him that at Thebes the number of the allotted lands was unalterable ; whence it is evident that the younger brothers could have had no share in the inheritance. An old law of Corinth also ordained that the number of the families should remain unchanged ; but this could only have been the case so long as the right of primogeniture presented an obstacle to the natural dismemberment[3] and division of the family.

At Athens, we cannot expect to find that this law lasted down to the days of Demosthenes, yet there is a relic of it[4] in the πρεσβεία or privilege of the elder, in virtue of which, besides his equal share, he took the house with the hearth-fire and the ancestral tomb, and retained alone the family name.

By way of compensation for his hard lot at home, a younger son was sometimes adopted into another family, whose worship he inherited ; sometimes he married an heiress ; and sometimes received the lot of an extinct family. All these resources failing, he might join a colony.

---

[1] Laws of Manou, ix., 105—6—7, 126. Of course this rule was modified with the increasing disbelief in the old religion.
[2] Fragments of Hist., Grec. Coll. Didot, ii., page 211.
[3] Aristot., *Polit.*, ii., 9 ; ii., 3.
[4] Demosth., *Pro Phormione*, 34.

There is no Roman law in favour of the right of the elder, yet primogeniture must have been known in ancient Italy. We cannot otherwise explain the existence of the Roman and Sabine Gens. How could a family have come to contain several thousands of free men, like the Claudian family, or several hundred combatants, like the Fabian, unless the right of primogeniture had preserved it united for many generations, adding to its members from century to century, and preventing its dismemberment? Here the right of primogeniture seems to be proved by its consequences, or, so to speak, by its works.[1]

This opinion is confirmed by comparing the etymology of the word *consortes*[2] with its application. It is derived from *sors*, which Festus explains as equivalent to patrimonium, a domain or lot of land. Consortes, then, must be those who dwelt together on the same plot of ground. But in the old language the word designates brothers, and even distant relations. Surely this bears witness to a time in Italy when patrimonies and families could not be divided.

---

[1] Demosth., *in Bœot. de nomine.*
[2] Festus, Vº. *Sors.* Cicero, *in Verr.*, ii., 3, 23. Livy, xli., 27. Velleius, i., 10. Lucretius, iii., 772; vi., 1280.

CHAPTER XII.

PATERNAL AUTHORITY.

1. *Principle of it.*—Paternal authority must have been in existence when the city was formed. The city would never have allowed a father to sell or even to kill his son (which he might do both in Greece and Rome), if it had been able to give laws to the family. The city would rather have said, "The life of thy wife and of thy child are not thine; nor yet their liberty; I will protect them, even against thee. If they have done wrong, I will be their judge." And if the city says not so, it is simply for want of power. No doubt paternal authority, like the laws of property, existed before the city came into being. So, also, it was against the city's interest for land to be inalienable, and the patrimony indivisible. But when the city began to write down her laws, she found those rights already established, rooted in the manners of men, and strong in general adhesion. She accepted them because she could do no otherwise, and only dared to modify them after a lapse of time. The system of ancient laws was not the work of any legislator, but rather was imposed upon the legislator against his will. It came into being in the family, originating in the principle that constituted that family. It was the result of religious beliefs universally admitted in a primitive age, and which ruled the minds and wills of a very early people.

Legal commentators are probably in error when they derive the power of the father over his son, or of the husband over his wife, from nothing but mere physical force. The expression *manus* at first sight might seem to imply it, but this power itself originated in religious belief, which raised man above woman. What proves it is the fact that only after initiation into the religious rites was a woman subject to her husband.

A concubine's son was not subject in the same way as the legitimate son, because he had no share in the worship. And when a son renounced the family rites in order to be adopted into another worship, he was free from his father's power.

Had it not been religion, but only physical force, which was at the bottom of paternal authority, the son would have left his father's roof when he became of age, and the younger brothers would never have respected the elder, as they did, after the father's death. But this we know was the case at first. That the authority of the father was very great in the earliest times is shewn by the substitution of the word *pater* for *genitor* before the separation of the eastern and western Aryas. There is no notion of progenitorship in the word pater, etymologically considered. It is rather a title of dignity, being applied to gods who were not the fathers of men, as well as to those who were; just as *mater* was said of virgin goddesses, as of Minerva and Diana. Perhaps pater is connected with pastor, and implied a shepherd-king, or great owner of flocks, such as Abraham; at all events it was a title of great dignity; and that this title should have been so continually bestowed on every father of a family as at last to be substituted for genitor in every Aryan language, proves not only the great power that fathers had, but also that they enjoyed this power at a very early period.

2. *Enumeration of the rights which made up paternal authority.*

The various and important rights conferred by primitive religion on fathers of families may be summed up under three heads, according as we consider them in their capacity of (1) priests, (2) owners of property, or (3) judges.

1. As responsible for the worship of the family and the perpetuity of his line, the father had the right, by Greek[1] as well as Roman law, to acknowledge and receive the new-born child, or, if he thought fit, to reject it. Even when the paternity of the infant was undisputed, before it could become a member of the family, it must be associated in the sacred cult with his consent, by the ceremony of initiation.

In like manner he could, again, exclude from the worship and from the family the son whom he had himself received

---

[1] Hdtus., i., 59. Plutarch, *Alcib.*, 23; *Ages*, 3.

into it; and by the process of adoption he could introduce a stranger to a place before the sacred hearth.

He could repudiate his wife, if she were barren, lest his family should become extinct, or in case of adultery on her part, in order that his race might be preserved pure from all intermixture of other blood.

It was he who gave his daughter in marriage, because no other could yield up to the husband the power which he possessed over her; and it was he who chose a wife for his son, because that was a matter which concerned the perpetuation of the line. Finally, at his death, he could nominate a guardian for his wife and children.

And these rights were exclusively the father's. For the wife (at all events in the earliest times) had no right to divorce her husband; whilst if divorced herself, she did not even retain possession of the daughters. As a widow she could neither emancipate nor adopt, and was never appointed guardian of her children. Her consent was not asked to the marriage of her daughter.

2. As property had not been conceived of at first as an individual right, but rather as belonging to a whole family, including dead ancestors and unborn descendants, so this property by its nature was incapable of division, and could be enjoyed by one person alone, viz., the head of the family for the time being.

Neither the wife nor the son had any share in the property. The dowry of the former belonged without reserve to her husband, who not only administered it but owned it himself. She did not even recover it on becoming a widow, and all that she might gain in her life-time fell into the hands of her husband.

In like manner the son could possess nothing, and therefore could give away nothing, and could gain nothing for himself. If a stranger bequeathed him a legacy, it was the father who received the money. Hence the Roman law declared there could be no sale between father and son, for if the father sold to the son it was selling to himself.

Moreover as the son could only gain for the father, and as his toil was a source of income, he might himself be regarded as a sort of property and handed over, if the father thought good, to another person. This was termed selling the son;

but although the nature of this contract is not clearly described in the texts that remain, nor yet the reservations that may have been made, still it seems certain that the son did not become the slave of the buyer. It was only his toil, and not his liberty, that had been sold; and he remained a member of the family, subject to his father's will. Probably the sale only temporarily ceded possession of the son by a sort of contract to hire. Afterwards, this so-called sale was only made use of as a contrivance for emancipating a son.

3. In times much later than those of which we have been speaking, women could not appear in a court of justice even as [1]witnesses; and from the following expressions of a Roman lawyer, it results that neither son nor wife could become plaintiff or defendant, accuser or accused, but that the father alone could appear before the city tribunal with a rightful claim to justice at its hands. "It should be known that nothing can be granted in the way of justice to persons under power, that is to say, to wives, sons, and slaves. For it is reasonably concluded that, since these persons can own no property, neither can they reclaim anything in point of justice. If a man's son, subject to his father's will, has committed a crime, the action lies against the father; nor has the father himself any action against his son;[2]" because, in fact, the justice which took cognizance of wives and sons was not in the city, but in the house; and the head of the family was their judge,[3] placed on the judgment-seat in virtue of his authority as husband, father, or master, in the name of the family, past or future, and under the eyes of the domestic deity. Livy relates that, when the Senate wished to destroy the worship of Bacchus at Rome, and had sentenced to death all who had taken part in it, although the sentence was easily carried into execution upon the citizens themselves, yet a great difficulty arose with respect to their wives, because their families only and not the state had right to do justice upon them. In the end the Senate did not set aside the old-established principle, but left to the husbands and fathers the duty of pronouncing sentence of death upon the guilty women.

---

[1] Plutarch, *Publicola*, 8.
[2] Gaius, ii., 96; iv., 77, 78.
[3] Afterwards the father consulted the rest of the family. Tacit., xiii, 32. *Digest.*, xxiii., 4, 5. Plato, *Laws*, ix.

In fact, the head of a family exercised justice in his house as completely as the magistrate in the city. There was no appeal against him, nor any means of modifying his decrees. "The husband," says Cato Senior, "is judge of his wife. His power has no limit. He can do what he likes. If she has drunk wine he punishes her, if she has committed adultery he puts her to death." Nor was his power less over his children. One of Catiline's fellow-conspirators was put to death by his own father for sharing in the conspiracy, and a certain Atilius, according to Valerius Maximus, slew his daughter for unchastity.

But we must not suppose that any father had an absolute right to kill his son or his wife, or that he did so except as judge. His power was founded on the belief which was entertained by all alike. In his right to exclude his son from the family he was checked by the fear of extinguishing the family and depriving his ancestors of their offerings. Though he had a right to adopt a son, religion forbade his doing so whilst his own was alive; and similarly, if he was the sole proprietor of the family possessions, yet he could not (at all events originally) sell them. And against the wanton repudiation of the wife there was an obstacle in the solemn union which religion had established between the two. So if the primitive worship conferred many rights upon the father, it did not entail fewer obligations.

The family long remained as we have described it. Without the exercise of outward force or of any social power, the beliefs at the bottom of men's hearts were enough to give it a regular constitution, a discipline, a government, and a system of private and criminal jurisprudence.

CHAPTER XIII.

MORALITY IN THE PRIMITIVE FAMILY.

IT is evident that the religion of the ancient family, if it were really such as we have described it, must have highly fortified whatever moral sentiments it found in the heart of man. Only as the religion of those early days was exclusively domestic, so also its morality did not extend beyond the narrow circle of the family hearth. When religion pointed out one man to another, it was not to say to him, "Behold thy brother," but "Behold a stranger: thy gods are not his gods, and would reject his adoration. Reject him likewise, and regard him as thy foe." So in this religion charity literally commenced at home, and taught no one to pray for other than himself and his.

But as, in the Aryan race, the god began by being very small, and was gradually conceived as greater and more powerful; so morality, which was at first narrow and incomplete, insensibly became enlarged, until at length it arrived at proclaiming man's duty towards all his fellows. Duty began with the family, and was first revealed beside the hearth.

If, then, we try to bring before our eyes this religion of the fire and of the tomb in the period of its full vigour, we find men inhabiting their houses under a deep sense of the presence of their deities. Their minutest actions were surveyed by witnesses as all-pervading as conscience, and supernatural beings seemed continually at hand both to sustain their toils and to punish their delinquencies. For "the Lares," said the Romans, "are formidable divinities charged to watch over what passes in the interior of houses, and to punish mankind."

A common epithet bestowed upon the hearth-fire was that of chaste, and it was believed to enjoin this virtue upon men; for in sight of the fire no act either materially or morally impure could be committed. Thus the man who was stained with blood-shed could no more approach his hearth to offer sacrifice, libation, or prayer. His god repelled him, admitting no excuse as to intention, nor any distinction between voluntary and involuntary crime. Hence we see that this race entertained at a very early period just ideas of sin and its consequences; and even, moreover, that these were not without means of alleviation, for the religion had expiatory rites which effaced the stains of the soul and consoled man for his errors.

It was perhaps in the first instance from fire-worship that the foregoing lesson in morality was derived. The worship of men's forefathers seems to have given rise to a no less valuable one. It must have been this which traced out so clearly all the family duties. Not only did the need of continuing the family render celibacy a crime and marriage obligatory, but the union of the husband and wife, taking place with the sanction of the household deities, was sacred and indissoluble. It was impossible for a man and woman in those early days to do what was so often done in the last period of Greek and Roman society, when marriage was made a mere contract during pleasure; at all events the penalty was very great. For the male offspring of such an union, so far from being able to accomplish what was expected of a son, was esteemed a bastard, and having no share in the religion could neither pray, nor sacrifice, nor have any place beside the hearth.

Again, according to this religion, adultery was a crime of the most heinous nature; because it disturbed the order of birth and prevented transmission of worship in the direct line. By it every sacred offering was made an act of impiety, and the sacred tombs of the forefathers, when the son of the adulterer was buried there, were polluted by his presence. Nay, the family might be extinct without men knowing it, and the forefathers robbed for ever of their happiness.

Hence it was that the head of a family might reject a newborn infant; and hence the laws against adultery were so severe that at Athens the injured husband might slay the adulterer, and was obliged to repudiate the guilty wife, whilst at Rome he could condemn her to death.

This religion, then, acted very powerfully in favour of family purity. A man and woman were united for life, and clearly saw that any failure in their conjugal duty would entail grave consequences, both in this world and the next. Hence they felt a restraint which produced the best effects, and we are not surprised that this state of things lasted a long time.

In no less a degree was it a source of other domestic duties; of obedience, for instance, on the part of wife and children to the father, and also of respect towards all in their several positions. For the wife had her place at the hearth, and the domestic worship was not complete without her. Amongst the Greeks it was felt to be the greatest misfortune to have a "hearth without a wife,"[1] and the Romans thought her presence at sacrifices so necessary that a priest lost his office on becoming a widower. The wife was termed materfamilias, οἰκοδέσποινα, grihapatni, as the husband was termed paterfamilias, οἰκοδεσπότης, grihapati; and the Roman formula, "ubi tu Caius, ego Caia," shews that if there was not equal authority in a house there was at all events equal dignity.

The son, also, had so needful a function to fill in the sacred worship that on certain days the Roman, who had no son, was obliged to adopt one for the day alone; and we can conceive of no stronger bond of union between father and son than the thought that the future repose of the elder would depend upon the attention of the younger, who also himself would have to invoke the other as a protecting deity.

In this way the domestic duties were so exalted as to assume the name of piety; and we find duty, affection, and piety all confounded into one quality, which, whether it was *erga parentes* or *erga liberos*, was still always *pietas*.

The simple love of home, in like manner, was exalted into a positive virtue. Virgil represents Anchises as unwilling to leave his old abode even when Troy was burning around him, and in Homer Ulysses scorned uncounted wrath and

---

[1] Xenophon, *Govt. of the Lacedæmonians.*

immortality itself as a bribe to keep him from his home. Even in later days, Cicero[1] could write in prose: "Here is my religion, here is my race, and here the traces of my forefathers. I find here an indescribable charm that pervades my heart and senses." Probably only a strong effort of imagination can bring vividly before our minds the love of the old Greek or Italian for his paternal abode. Habit and association is all that connects *us* with the place in which we have lived; for our God is the God of the universe, and we can find him everywhere. But the penetralia of the ancient Greek or Italian contained his chief divinity, his providence, which protected him individually, which received his prayers and answered his vows. Therefore man loved his house in those times as now-a-days he loves his Church; because beyond the walls of his own house he found no deity, or only the hostile one of his neighbour.

So ancient morality, if it ignored charity, at all events taught home-duty, and in the isolation of the family the virtues bloomed. Civil society, also, we shall find, was affected with this narrowness; for the city sprung from the family, and inherited the faults of its parent. Its greatest merits also had the same source, and whatever greatness and duration it had are to be attributed to this cause.[2]

---

[1] *De Leg.*, ii., 1; *Pro Domo*, 41.

[2] The foregoing remarks are to be understood as applying to the ancestors of the Greeks and Romans; since even so early as the times described in the Odyssey we find a modification of sentiments and manners.

CHAPTER XIV.

THE GENS AT ROME AND IN GREECE.

THE *gens* or γένος was an institution which flourished in its greatest vigour in pre-historic times, which is decaying when cotemporaneous documents begin to exist, and which in the times best known is barely traceable. Its constitution was entirely aristocratic, and gave the patricians at Rome, and the Eupatrids at Athens, so strong an internal organization that they maintained their great privileges intact for many generations. When the popular party got the upper hand they did their utmost against it, and had they been strong enough to destroy it utterly, doubtless not a trace would have remained. But the gens was singularly tenacious of life, and profoundly rooted in men's manners; and the democratic party were obliged to be content with a partial extermination of it; that is, with taking away its power and leaving the exterior forms which did not interfere with their new systems. Thus at Athens the old γένη were overthrown, mingled together and replaced by demes; whilst at Rome the plebeians established other gentes for themselves, alongside and in imitation of the patrician ones. In speaking of the revolutions of old society we shall have to revert to this point. It may be enough to remark just now that in consequence of the profound alteration which democracy effected in the constitution of the gens, it is enough to puzzle all who seek to understand it, since all the information that has reached us about it belongs to a period posterior to the transformation, and nothing is visible but what the Revolutions have left.

It is as if we had to find out what was the nature of the feudal system in the middle ages without any history of the period, or any contemporary documents, from nothing but its remains in the present day, that is to say, from a nobility in some countries deprived of political power, from a few expressions in modern languages, from some law terms, and from many vague recollections and sterile regrets.

1. *What we are told of the gens after its modification.*

Instances might be cited to prove that the gens was an institution universal in Italy and Greece, but the following may suffice for our present purpose. In a certain law-suit Demosthenes produces seven witnesses, who all depose that they belong to one and the same γένος, that of the Brytidæ. And yet it is remarkable that these seven members of the same γένος are enrolled in six different demes; which leads us to conclude that the γένος was not exactly a deme, nor yet another mere division for government purposes.[1] In Roman history, we find at the time of the Punic wars three persons, named Claudius Pulcher, Claudius Nero, Claudius Centho, all alike belonging to the Claudian gens.

There were, therefore, gentes at Rome and γένη at Athens. It appears, further, that each *gens* had a peculiar worship, with fixed ceremonies, and place, and day of sacrifice. As for Greece, Plutarch[2] speaks of the place where the Lycomedidæ sacrificed; and Æschines mentions the altar of the Butadæ. At Rome, when the Capitol was besieged by the Gauls, a [3]Fabius was seen, in religious robes and with sacred objects in his hands, to cross the enemies' lines and proceed to the altar of his gens on the Quirinal. The absolute necessity of his offering at that time and place accounted for his running the risk. And another Fabius, when his policy was saving Rome, to our astonishment leaves his army under the orders of the imprudent Minucius, and risks its destruction by Hannibal in order that on the proper day he might offer the sacrifice of his gens at Rome.

---

[1] Demosth., in *Near.*, 71. Plutarch, *Themist.*, 1. Æschines, *De falsâ leg.*, 147. Boeckh, Corp. Inscrip., 385. Ross, *Demi Attici*, 24. In Greek gens is sometimes called πάτρα. Pindar, *Passim.*

[2] Plut., *Themist.*, 1. Æsch., *De falsâ leg.*, 147.

[3] Livy, v., 46; xxii., 18. Valer. Max., i., 1, 11. Polyb., iii., 94. Dion. Halic., ii., 21; ix., 19; vi., 28. Plin., xxxiv., 13. Macrob., iii., 5.

That the worship of the gens must be continued from generation to generation, and that it was a duty to leave sons after one to perpetuate it, we gather from Cicero's reproach to his enemy Clodius, who had left his own gens to become member of a plebeian one: "Why exposest thou the worship of the Claudian gens to be extinguished by thy neglect?"

It seems, further, that the Dii Gentiles, or gods of the gens, protected no other than their own, and would be invoked by its members alone. They were offended with all alike if any stranger were present to partake of the victim that was offered.

So, also, each gens had a common tomb, which must receive the corpse of no stranger. This appears from two speeches[1] of Demosthenes, in one of which he tells us that a certain "man, having lost his children, buried them in the tomb of his fathers, the tomb which was common to all those of his gens;" whilst in the other he describes the place where the Buselidæ buried its members and offered a yearly sacrifice as being "a good large field, enclosed with a fence according to custom." So also, for Rome, we have mention of the *tomb of the Quintilian gens, and it may be gathered from Suetonius that the tomb of the Claudii was on the slope of the Capitoline.

By a law of the Twelve Tables, the members of a gens could inherit from one another in default of sons and of agnates. In fact, on this system the *gentilis* was more akin than the nearest relation by the females, that is, the nearest *cognatus*.

No possible union could be closer than that of a gens, who, because they had communicated in the same ceremonies, afterwards assisted one another in all the necessities of life. Thus, if one of them was made a magistrate, all the others contributed their quota towards his expenses;[2] and similarly the whole body was responsible for the debt of one of its members, and ransomed him if taken captive, or paid his fine if he were condemned.

The accused was accompanied to the court of justice by

---

[1] Demosth., *in Macart.*, 79; *in Eubul.*, 28.
[2] Velleius, ii., 119. Sueton., *Tiber*, i.; *Nero*, 50.
[3] Livy, v., 32. Dion. Halic., *Fragm.*, xxii., 5. Appian., Annib., 28.

all the members of his gens, so close was the legal connexion between them; and it would have been an act of impiety either to plead or to bear witness against a member of the same gens. In this spirit Appius Claudius the Decemvir, when another Claudius, his personal enemy, was in danger of being condemned to death, came forward to defend him, and used earnest entreaties in his favour, not from any affection, as he said, but because it was his duty to do so.[1]

No member of a gens could be cited by another before a city tribunal, because justice was administered within the gens itself, the gens possessing in the person of its chief at once a judge, a priest, and a general.[2] Thus, when the Claudian gens became Roman instead of Sabine, the three thousand persons, who composed it, all obeyed a single chief. And, afterwards, when the Fabii alone undertook the Veientine war, one chief spoke in their name before the Senate, and led them against the foe.[3]

That in Greece also each γένος had its chief, commonly called ἄρχων,[4] we are led to believe from inscriptions, by which also it appears that they met together and made decrees,[5] which the members obeyed and the city respected. Such are the laws and customs that we find still flourishing in times when the constitution of the gens had been so transformed that it was scarcely any longer itself. They may be called the relics of that ancient institution.

2. *Examination of certain opinions on the Roman Gens.*

Two passages of Cicero, in whose times the gens was not understood, and who, therefore, gives but an unsatisfactory explanation of it, have rendered still more difficult the right comprehension of the matter. The facts which we have just enumerated render it impossible for us to believe that the gens is a "mere similarity of name," or a "sort of factitious relationship," or that it expresses the "relation between certain families who act as patrons and certain others who act as clients." Nor yet can we agree in the following more

---

[1] Dion. Halic., xi., 14. Livy, iii., 58.
[2] Dion. Halic., ii., 7.
[3] Id., ix., 5.
[4] Boeckh., Corp. Inscr., 397, 399. Ross, *Demi Attici*, p. 24.
[5] Livy, vi., 20. Sueton., *Tiber*, 1. Ross, *Demi Attici*, 24.

plausible explanation, that the "gens is a political association of several families originally unconnected, but who in default of blood-relationship have been bound together by the city into a feigned union of religious relationship." Because, if the gens is but a fictitious association, how can we explain the right of its members to inherit property from one another? Why should the *gentilis*, if he has no connexion, be preferred to the *cognatus* who has? The rules of inheritance, as we have proved, were strict; and, for religious reasons, property could only go to relations in the male line. Would the law in early times have so far transgressed this fundamental principle as to grant succession to *gentiles*, if they had been totally unconnected with each other?

Now the most striking and best-proved feature of the gens is, that it possessed a worship of its own like that of the family. And if we examine what sort of god the gentes adored, we find that it was almost always a deified ancestor, the offering being made at a tomb. Thus, at Athens, the Eumolpidæ worship Eumolpus; the Phytalidæ adored Phytalus; the Butadæ, Butes; the Buselidæ, Buselus; the Lakiadæ, Lakios; the [1]Amynandridæ, Cecrops. At Rome, the Claudii are descended from a Clausus; the Cœcilii pray to a hero Cœculus; the Calpurnii to a Calpus; the Julii to a Julus; and the Clœlii to a Clœlus.[2]

It may be allowed that many of these genealogies were a later invention; but, as now-a-days false coats of arms are only borne by pretenders, because true ones exist, so the invention of these genealogies would be without motive if true gentes had not recognized and worshipped a common ancestor.

Besides, as the primitive worship was by no means a vain show, this deception could not have been so easily conceived and carried out. The feelings of the early Greeks and Italians revolted from the idea of worshipping a stranger. No doubt afterwards when no one cared for the old family religions such a fiction might have been possible. But if we go back to early times, when this belief was still strong, we cannot imagine that several families would have agreed

---

[1] Demosth., *in Macart.*, 79. Pausan., i., 37. Inscr. quoted by Ross, 24.
[2] Festus, V^{is}. Cæculus, Calpurnii, Clœlia.

together to perpetrate a great falsehood, to erect a pretended ancestral tomb, and establish feasts in honour of someone whom they did not really care for. This would have been to mingle deceit with the most sacred things, and to make a mockery of religion.

The etymology of the word gens, which is identical with genus (since the Latins said indifferently Fabia gens and Fabium genus), affords another glimpse of the real truth. These words are connected with gignere and genitor as γένος corresponds to γεννᾶν and γονεύς. The ideas of paternity and sonship are contained in all of them; and another word which was applied to members of the same gens, ὁμογάλακτες, those of the same milk, is in perfect agreement. If we compare these words with those others which are habitually translated family, namely, οἶκος and *familia*, and of which the original idea is merely property, slaves, house and money, (for the Law of the Twelve Tables, speaking of the heir, says *familiam nancitor*, let him take the property), it will seem very unlikely that, whilst these words, whose true sense is house and chattels, are continually used to designate a family, those other words, whose meaning is rightly connected with paternity and sonship, should never have meant anything but an artificial association of people who are not connected by blood. Surely the ancients acted more logically. We cannot doubt that the idea of a common origin was attached to the word gens; and, although this notion may have perished when the constitution of the gens was altered, yet the word remains to attest the original fact.

Three arguments, then, seem to militate against the explanation of gens as a factitious association, viz., 1st, that taken from the right of the gentiles to inherit from one another; 2nd, the primitive objection to worship any stranger; 3rd, the etymology of the word gens, which implies a common origin. Lastly, this explanation is not in accord with experience or the science of history when it would make us believe that society began with convention and artifice.

3. *Gens is the family still possessing its primitive organization and unity.*

Everything tends to show us the *gens* as a body united by the bond of birth.

In the first place, the names of the *gentes* both in Greek and Latin are patronymics, as Butadæ, sons of Butes, Claudius, son of Clausus; and it seems most sensible to understand from this that the members of the gens were descended from the founder.

Next, an examination into the periods when the different family names arose will shew that the families did not unite to make up a gens; but that the gens was split up into the families. The Cornelian gens contained indeed Scipios, Lentuli, Cossi, and Syllæ, but there were Cornelii long before the others were heard of. All the Cornelii are at first called Maluginenses, and afterwards Cossi. It was only in the time of the dictator Camillus that one branch of the gens took the name of Scipio. Afterwards another branch assumed the name of Rufus, which it replaced with Sylla. The Lentuli only make their appearance at the period of the Samnite war, and the Cethegi in the second Punic war. So the Claudii remained long united in one single family, surnamed Sabinus, or Regillensis, in token of their origin. We can follow them for seven generations without being able to distinguish any branches in this family, numerous as it was. It is only in the eighth generation, whilst the Punic war is raging, that we remark its separation into three branches, who adopt surnames that become hereditary. Of these the Centhos very soon became extinct, the Pulchri lasted for two centuries, and the Neros prolonged their existence into the times of the empire.

Again, the family names, such as Scipio and Lentulus, were called agnomens or additional names, as though the other name, such as Cornelius, were prior in point of time, and not assumed by a number of associated families.

Finally, many gentes never had but one line of descent, as, for instance, the Mareii and the Lucretii, as also the Quintilii for a lengthened period. And certainly we should find it hard to say which families made up the Fabian gens, since all the Fabii known to history evidently belong to one stock, being all called at first Vibulanus, afterwards Ambustus, and at last Maximus or Dorso.

It is clear, then, that the gens was not an association of families, but the family itself. It might indifferently comprise but one single line or numerous branches, but whether ramified or not, it was never anything but one family.

It is, however, by no means difficult to account for the formation of the ancient gens, if we do but follow out to their consequences the old beliefs and institutions already described. For what were the prescriptions of this primitive religion and the results of the laws regarding property in those times? Around the tomb of the first man buried in it were gathered year by year an increasing number of descendants to honour him as a god, and offer the funereal repast. To this centre all the branches of the family, however numerous, would repair, and it would gather them in a single band. We shewed before that the sons of each family remained subject to their father's authority as long as they lived, without ever quitting his roof, and that even after his death the younger brothers paid the same deference towards their elder. The property was at first indivisible, and the tomb and the hearth inalienable, and consequently the family likewise remained stable and undivided. Retaining the unity which its religion enjoined, and perpetuating its worship from century to century, it developed itself to the extent permitted by its ancient laws of property, and became what is known as a gens.

When this is once admitted, all that the classical authors tell us about the gens becomes clear. Then there is nothing surprising in the strict union of all these persons, because we see that they are relations by birth. The worship which they practised in common is no fiction, but the legacy of their forefathers. As they are but one family, they have but one burial ground, and can inherit property from one another. Hence, also, their common surname, and, as a consequence of there being but one patrimony for all, the custom, nay the absolute need of all being responsible for the debt of one, as also that any member who might be taken prisoner or fined should be assisted by the rest. These rules, which had been established when the gens was entire and united, could not suddenly disappear in its decay. Persistent traces of its true nature remained in the annual sacrifice which gathered together its scattered members, in the laws which permitted *gentiles* to inherit, in their common name, and in their habits of mutual aid.

4. *Slaves and Clients.*

Another element was introduced into the primitive family by the mutual need which the rich have of the poor, and the poor of the rich. But a service entirely voluntary, and capable of ceasing at the will of the servant, was not in accordance with the state of society in those times. As the family lived in much isolation, and could admit of no strangers, the slave must be initiated into the family worship, and become a member of it also himself.

The ceremony of initiation for slaves had much resemblance to what took place on the occasions of adoption and marriage. Lustral water was poured upon the head of the future slave, and he partook of some cakes[1] and fruit with the family. After this he was allowed to be present when prayers and sacrifices were offered; he shared in the family feasts[2]; he was supposed to be protected by the family[3] deities, and, when he died, he was buried with his master.

When the slave was raised, as continually happened, from the condition of lowest service and treated as a freedman, his liberty was not such as to enable him to quit the family altogether, because the name of piety and the worship of the household gods retained him. Even then he could only marry by permission of the patron whose client he had become, and the children that were born to him remained in the same dependent position. Hence every great family had several subordinate ones attached to it, and a vast number of persons were sometimes united under one head.

This institution was attributed by the Romans to their first king, just as many old customs and laws of the English are attributed to Alfred. But it clearly sprung spontaneously from the natural wants of men who followed a peculiar religion. Its date is much older than that of Romulus, and the Italians and Greeks had it established amongst them quite as much as the Romans. Moreover it was not an institution likely to find favour with the kingly founder of a city, being naturally suited rather to a patriarchal or aristocratic state of society, and found by experience to be inconsistent with civil institutions.

The client of early times, far from resembling the client of Horace's day, was for a long time a servant attached to his patron, but yet a servant dignified by association with the

---

[1] Demosth., *in Stephan.*, i., 74. See especially Schol. Aristoph., *Plutus*, 768.
[2] Ferias in famulis habento. Cicero, *De Leg.*, ii., 8; ii., 12.
[3] Quum dominis turer famulis religio Larum. Cicero, *De Leg.*, ii., 11.

family religion, and bound to be protected by his master in every possible way, and especially in the courts of justice; indeed, so closely was he connected with the patron that the latter was accursed if he wronged[1] him at all, and whilst he could bear witness against his own cognates, could give no testimony that would be received against a client.

5. *The family was once the only form of society.*

What we have already observed of the family with its religion and laws, will incline us to believe it was once an independent institution subject to no superior power. Its gods were purely domestic; and it had its own priesthood, with separate government and administration of justice. The city had not yet been organized when these institutions were set on foot. This narrow and uncharitable religion with its petty gods, tending to isolate and separate society, had never been designed or favoured by the founders or legislators of any more extended society. For what can be more contradictory than for men to live together in civil society and yet have separate gods for each family? Doubtless this contradiction was maintained for long; because beliefs and practices once established are tenacious of existence, and because the city could not dissolve them at once. But there had been a time when the contradiction did not exist. Then the narrow religion and the family administration of justice corresponded exactly to men's social condition, and all the Aryan race was living in a sort of patriarchal state (most likely for many centuries) in many groups of isolated families, having little connection with one another, but each independent and self-sufficing. Further, it may be remarked that a comparison of the *political* institutions of the Eastern Aryas with those of the West, shews scarcely any analogy between them, whilst if we compare, on the other hand, the *domestic* institutions of these several peoples, we perceive that the family was constituted on the same principles in Greece and India; and these principles were of a nature so singular that we cannot suppose the resemblance accidental; and not only are the institutions analogous, but the words which designate them are the same throughout the languages which

---

[1] Cato, in Aulus-Gellius, v., 3; xxi., 1.

this race made use of from the Ganges to the Tiber. Two conclusions may be formed from this; one is, that the birth of domestic institutions in this race is anterior to the period when the different branches separated; and the other is that, on the contrary, the birth of political institutions is posterior to this separation. The first were fixed when the race was still dwelling in its home in Central Asia; the second were gradually formed in the different countries to which their emigrations conducted them.

One can obtain a glimpse, then, of a state of things, wherein for a lengthened period men knew no other form of society than the family. Then it was that the domestic religion arose, adapted only for such a condition of society, and itself an obstacle to progress; a religion which gave rise to laws of property in perfect harmony with itself, but which were afterwards, from change of opinion, obliged to be disused. Perhaps the Aryan race for some centuries was composed of a number of such societies, of a thousand isolated groups that had but little connexion with one another, and no political or religious bond of union, but each its own gods, a separate domain, and an independent government.

CHAPTER XV.

THE PHRATRIA, OR CURIA.

WE have not been able hitherto to specify any date, nor can we do so now; for in the history of these ancient forms of society, periods are more easily marked by ideas and institutions than by succession of years.

We are now to pass from the age of the family or gens to that of the phratria or curia. For the old limits of human association were too narrow, both for men's material wants, since the family by itself could scarcely suffice against the various chances of life; and also for the moral wants of human nature, seeing how circumscribed was its knowledge of the divine, and how incomplete its moral teaching.

The littleness of society answered completely to the littleness of the gods, and man, becoming discontented with the one, must expand the other at the same time. Many centuries were to elapse before the Aryan race could attain or recover the knowledge of one true God, incomparable and infinite, but at all events they could insensibly approach the ideal by enlarging their conception from age to age, and by extending the horizon-line that shut in their narrow view.

It was so, that human society and religious ideas grew together.

The domestic religion forbade two families to mingle into one, but it seemed possible for several families, without any of them giving up anything of their particular worship, to unite for the celebration of another newer worship. A certain number of families united to form a group called in Greek a phratria, in Latin a curia.[1] We cannot affirm for

---

[1] *Iliad*, ii., 362. Demosth., *in Macart.* Isæus, iii., 37; vi., 10; ix., 33. There were φράτραι at Thebes; Pindar, *Isth.*, vii., 18, and Scholiast. Dion. Halic., ii., 85. Dion. Cass., translate curia by φρατρία. At Sparta, the word was ὠβή'.

certain that there was any tie of birth between them, though the etymology of the words, φρατρία, band of brothers, κουρία, band of sons, may be in favour of such a view. But what seems clear is that the new association was not formed without a certain enlargement of religious views. At the moment of their union, these families conceived of a divinity, superior to their domestic divinities, who was to be common to all and to watch over the entire group. They raised to him an altar, kindled a fire, and instituted a worship. No curia or phratria was without an altar and a protecting deity, to whom libations and prayers were offered, and whose worshippers held themselves to be in communion with one another, when they had partaken of the meat offered to the idol.

The repasts of the curia lasted so long and so persistently at Rome, that even in the days of Augustus they had lost none of their formality. Besides referring to the description of them given in Ovid's[1] Fasti, we may quote the following words of Dionysius of Halicarnassus: " I have seen in these sacred abodes the feasts set forth before the gods; the tables were of wood, and the dishes of earthenware, according to the usage of our forefathers. The food consisted of bread, and cakes of flour, and some fruits. I saw them make libations, not out of gold and silver cups, but from earthen mugs, and I [2] admired my contemporaries for their fidelity to the customs of their fathers.

At Athens, these repasts took place during the feast which they called Apaturia.[3]

Certain customs which endured down to the latest days of Grecian history, throw some light on the nature of the ancient phratria; as, for instance, in the time of Demosthenes, for a person to belong to a phratria it was needful for him to have been born in lawful wedlock of one of the component families. For the worship of the phratria, like that of the family, was only transmitted by blood, and the young Athenian was

---

[1] Cicero, *De Orat.*, 1, 7. *Fasti* of Ovid, vi., 305. Dion. Halic., ii., 65.
[2] See, however, Plaut., *Aulularia*. The feasts of the curia became a vain formality, which some neglected; and which were replaced by a distribution of victuals and money.
[3] Aristoph., *Acharn.*, 146. Athenæus, iv., p. 171. Suidas, ἀπατούρια.

presented to the phratria by his father, who swore that he was his son. At the admission, which was a religious ceremony, all the members of the phratria must be present, whilst a victim was slain and cooked upon the altar; then if they refused to admit the candidate, as doubting his legitimacy, they must remove the flesh from the altar; but if, on the contrary, they partook of the flesh in company with the new comer, his admission was good, and he became irrevocably a member of the association.[1]

Each phratria or curia had its chief called *curio, magister curiæ* or φρατρίαρχος, whose principal function in historic times was to preside[2] at sacrifices, but perhaps he had originally fulfilled more extensive duties; for the phratria had its own assemblies and tribunal, and could pass its own decrees. Being modelled exactly on the gens it had a god, a priesthood, an administration of justice, and a government.

---

[1] Demosth., *in Eubul.*; *in Macart.* Isæus viii., 18.
[2] Dion. Halic., ii., 64. Varro, v., 83. Demosth., *in Eubul.*, 23.

CHAPTER XVI.

THE TRIBE.

THE tribe was a union of several curiæ or phratriæ, just as these were made up of gentes; and the union was no less formed upon a religious principle, since every tribe had its altar and protecting deity, who was a hero, or deified man, and gave his name to the tribe. He had his yearly feast-day, when all the members of the tribe partook of a sacrifice in common.[1]

It seems evident from what remains to us of the institutions of the tribe, that it was originally constituted to be an independent society without any social power above it; for it had its meetings, where decrees were issued, to which every member must submit for fear of penalties which it had the right to inflict.

The head of the tribe was called φυλοβασιλεύς[2] in Greek, and tribunus in Latin. Small traces remain in history of the religious and political organization of the three primitive tribes at Rome. They were too powerful for the city to have allowed them to remain in independence any longer than it could help, and the plebeians besides strove their best to effect their disappearance. Of course we are speaking here of religious tribes, and not of the local ones, which belong to a much later period.

In Greece, the universality of the religious tribes is proved by passages in Homer, Herodotus, and Thucydides.

---

[1] Demosth., *in Theocrinem*. Æschines, iii., 27. Isæus, vii., 3, 6. Paus., i., 38. Schol., in Demosth., 702.
[2] Æsch., iii., 30, 31. Aristot., *Frag*. Quoted by Photius, V°. ναυκραρία.

CHAPTER XVII.

THE GODS OF OLYMPUS.

WHEN the ancestors of the Greeks and Romans had quite forgotten that the fire which they worshipped was a representation of heat and motion, and, consequently, as was thought, of the origin of life, then they no longer possessed anything to adore as a power of outward nature. The sacred fire, as it consumed the victims offered on it, had come to be looked upon as a symbol of the ancestral ghosts receiving their offerings; and its entire connexion with the sun, and therefore, much more with other outward powers, was ignored. Consequently, men seemed to be left without means of appeasing the powerful material influences of the world in which they were placed. But the ancient Aryas, living an out-door life and being an impressionable people, felt very keenly these powers, and could not banish from their minds the terrors of darkness and storm, and the cheering loveliness of dawn.

The tradition having been lost that sun, earth, and stars were made by one sole Being, these things seemed to them a confused mixture of jarring forces, each having a will, a power, and a nature like their own. And so the air, and the sea, and even rivers, seemed to be persons like themselves, only more powerful, and able to do with them as they chose. Therefore they acknowledged their dependence, and falling down before them in adoration, made of them their gods. We have, then, two orders of belief giving rise to two distinct religions, which lasted as long as Greek and Roman society. According to one of these, man attributed divinity to what he could perceive of the soul in himself; according to the other he applied his idea of the divinity to the exterior objects which he loved or feared, as masters of his happiness and life. Yet these two religions, though their practices were different, and their dogmas not only distinct but sometimes even contradictory, still subsisted together in amity amongst the same people, sharing the empire over man, without at all becoming confused. The worship of the dead having been fixed at a very early period, remained unchangeable to the last, but the other, being newer and more consistent with progress, was freely developed from generation to generation, modifying its doctrines from time to time, and up to a certain point increasing its authority over man.

The new religion, owing nothing to divine revelation properly so called, was entirely the work of observation and fancy. It sprung from no priestcraft, but from a thousand different minds working in the same direction. For a long time the greatest confusion prevailed, but as there was resemblance amidst variety some degree of order was gradually introduced.

The objects that could be deified were not many, to wit, the sun which warms and fecundates, the cloud with its rain and its storm, and the earth and the sea; yet out of these elements a thousand gods originated; because men gave different names to each of these physical agents, according to the point of view from which they viewed them. Thus the sun was called in one place Heracles, the glorious, in another Phœbus, the brilliant, elsewhere Apollon, the driver away [of night], by others Hyperion, who goes aloft; and it came to pass in the end that the persons who had given these names to the same object did not at all perceive that they were worshipping the same god.

In fact, each individual did but adore a very small number of divinities; but since those of one man were not those of another, the total number of gods in existence at first was infinite. Many of the gods, indeed, might have the same names; as they received for appellations adjectives in common use, such as Heracles, Phœbus, or Apollo. But yet their different adorers had not realized it as possible that all the deities designated by the same name could be generalized into one God; because each conception had been worked out by an individual mind, and seemed to be its own property. Whence it happened at last that there were thousands of Jupiters, Junos, and Minervas, each independent of the other, and with a separate legend and worship.

As these beliefs arose at a period when the Aryan race was still living in the state of separate families, the new gods had at first, like the Lares, the condition of family deities. Each little group retained for itself the gods whom it had invented, and would allow their protection to be shared by no stranger. This thought appears frequently in the hymns of the Vedas, and there are traces enough remaining in Greek and Roman religion to prove it once reigned also in the minds of the Western Aryas. As fast as a family had personified a physical agent and made it a god, it gave him a place beside the hearth-fire, and, counting him among its penates, added some words in his honour to the general form of prayer. Hence the expressions found in ancient authors; as, "the gods who sit beside my fire," "the Jupiter of my hearth," and "the Apollo of my fathers." So, in Sophocles, Tecmessa beseeches Ajax by the name of "the Jupiter who sits at his hearth;" and in Euripides, the enchantress Medea swears by Hecate, "her goddess mistress, whom she adores, and who inhabits the sanctuary of her hearth." Also, when Virgil wishes to put before us the very commencement of Roman religion, he describes Hercules as one of Evander's household gods, sharing adoration with the Penates.

The result of this was a thousand petty religions, of which the greater part could never be generalized or united; and Polytheism swarms with hostile gods, whose existence depended on the varying success in warfare of the villages and districts that supported their claims. Of these only the smallest part can be known, so many having perished, without leaving a trace, along with the families who invented them; whilst of those which we are aware of, the greater part were very long in emancipating themselves from the adorers who would have retained them to themselves. Some only partly extricated themselves from the domestic tie, as, for instance, the Demeter of Eleusis remained the particular deity of the Eumolpidæ, and the Athene of the Acropolis belonged to the family of the Butadæ. The Politii of Rome had a Hercules, and the Nautii a Minerva,[1] whilst there is

---

[1] Livy, ix., 29. Dion. Halic., vi., 69.

great probability that the worship of Venus was long confined to the family of the Julii.

When the deity of a family had acquired considerable reputation, and, from the prosperity of his worshippers, was judged to be both benevolent and powerful, then it often happened that a whole city would wish to adopt it, and by diligent service win its favour. This was the case with the Demeter of the Eumolpidæ, the Athene of the Butadæ, and the Hercules of the Politii. But it is to be remarked that when a family thus consented to share its god, it reserved to itself the office[1] of priest, and the circumstance of a priesthood to some particular god remaining long in a single family seems to bear witness, when it occurs, to a time when the god himself was the property of this family, and protected no others.

It may be safely affirmed, then, that from the beginning this second religion was in unison with the social state of men, and though each god was long shut up in the family who invented him, still the religion was not so ill adapted to the future progress of human society as the worship of the dead had been. For by their very nature ancestors and heroes were gods who could not be adored but by a very small number of men, and they established for ever impassable lines of demarcation between families. But there was no stern law forbidding the propagation of the worship of the gods of physical nature, nor was it of the essence of these gods to be adored by a family and to reject the stranger. Finally, men were compelled at length to conclude that the Jupiter of one family was at bottom the same being or the same conception as the Jupiter of another, which they could never have believed of two Lares, of two ancestors, or of two fires.

Let us add that this new religion had a wider spirit of charity, not confining itself to teaching man his domestic duties. For Jupiter was the god of·hospitality, and it was in his name that strangers, the "venerable suppliants," pre-

---

[1] Hdtus., v., 64, 65; ix., 27. Pindar, *Isthm.*, vii., 18. Xenophon, *Hell.*, vi., 8. Plato, *Laws*, 759; *Banquet*, 40; *De Divin.*, i., 41. Tacit., *Ann*, ii., 54. Plutarch, *Thes.*, 23. Strabo., ix., 421; xiv., 634. Callim., H. ad Apoll., 84. Pausan., i., 37; vi., 17; x., 1. Apollodorus, iii., 13. Harpocration, v., Εὐνίδαι. Bœckh., Corp. Inscr., 1340.

sented themselves to be treated as brothers. Also these gods, if they sometimes assumed the shape of men to join in human conflicts, yet also very often did it to prescribe concord, and to teach men to aid one another.

In proportion as this second religion developed itself, society must necessarily be growing, and, feeble as it was at first, it evidently, afterwards, assumed great proportions. Originally it had been, as it were, sheltered under the protection of its elder sister beside the domestic hearth. There the new god had obtained a little space, a narrow *cella*, besides and in front of the venerable altar, in order that a little of the respect paid to it might be shared by him. But by degrees the god, assuming more influence over the soul, renounced this sort of tuition, and leaving the family hearth, had a dwelling and sacrifice to himself. This dwelling (ναὸς, from ναίω to inhabit) was indeed built after the fashion of the ancient sanctuary, and continued to be a *cella* in front of a fire. But the cella, growing larger and handsomer, became a temple. The fire remained at the entrance of the god's house, but seemed very small in comparison of him. That which had been at first a god and the principal object of adoration, was reduced to a mere accessory, became, in fact, a mere fire on the altar, whose work it was to consume victims for some newer deity, and bear aloft to him the prayers of men.

CHAPTER XVIII.

THE CITY FORMED.

AS the tribe had a special worship from which all aliens were excluded, and into which no new members, whether individuals or curiæ, could be admitted, it seems to have been intended, like the gens and the curia, to subsist as an independent body. But though two tribes might not be mixed up into one, yet, as was the case with gentes and curiæ, they might be united to form a larger body, on condition that their several private worships were respected. And as soon as this had been effected, the City was constituted.

The determining cause might be sometimes the superior power of one tribe, and sometimes the ambition of a single individual; or it might be for the interest of all alike; but it seems certain that the bond of union was once more a worship, since the tribes, who thus bound themselves together into one, never failed to kindle a sacred fire and to give themselves a common religion. And so in the Aryan race society did not spread after the fashion of a tree which enlarges its circumference outwardly, as we see in its section. The growth of the ancient state was rather like those inferior plants which join many tubes together by aggregation. Or we may compare it to the work of the woodman, who first binds many sticks into a bundle and then many bundles into a faggot, and finally puts many faggots into a load. Certain families made up a phratria, certain phratriæ a tribe, and certain tribes a city; but in uniting not one of these groups lost its independence or individuality. Each family and phratria and tribe remained as in its days of isolation; and neither worship, priesthood, nor laws of property were changed. The curia and tribes when united retained their own festivals, sacrifices, and chiefs. In matters of religion there remained a multitude of smaller services; with one great worship over all; and in politics a crowd of smaller governments under one greater one.

The city, then, being but a confederation, was obliged, for some centuries at least, to respect the civil and religious independence of the tribes, curiæ, and families, and refrain from interfering with the interior affairs of each of these lesser bodies. For instance, the father of each family continued to possess the right of condemning wife or son or client, subject to no inspection or prohibition. And although the laws of private property were disadvantageous to the interests of the city, they subsisted long without modification.

That this was the mode in which ancient cities were formed is attested by some customs which lasted to a comparatively late period. In the times of Homer, armies were arranged by tribes, by phratriæ, and by gentes, so that "each warrior fought next the man who in peace stood beside the same altar with him to make libations and offer sacrifices."[1] At Rome it was by [2]gentes and curiæ that the public assemblies voted in early times, and in religious matters the number of the Vestals (two for each) indicates the three tribes; whilst at Athens, in like manner, when the Archon offered sacrifice for the whole city, he was assisted by as many officers as there were tribes.

The progress of each Athenian from being a member of his family to being accepted by his phratria, and afterwards by the city, presents an illustration of the steps by which society advanced in the Aryan race. For an [3]Athenian was not born a member of each association, as an Englishman at his birth belongs at once to a family, a parish, and a county. But on the tenth day he was initiated into the family; after some years into the phratria; and finally, at sixteen or eighteen, he might present himself for admission to the city.

There was a time when the families, so well known afterwards[4] at Athens, the Eumolpidæ, the Cecropidæ, the Gephyræi, the Phytalidæ, the Lakiadæ, lived up and down

---

[1] *Iliad*, ii., 362. Varrò, *De Lingua Lat.*, v., 89. Isæus, ii., 42.
[2] Aulus-Gellius, xv., 27.
[3] Demosth., *in Eubul.* Isæus, vii., ix. Lycurgus, i., 76. Schol., *in Demosth.*, p. 438. Pollux, viii., 105. Stobæus, *De Reput.*
[4] Plutarch, *Thes.*, 24; *Ibid*, 13.

the territory in the completest independence of patriarchal state. And each family had its separate religion; the Eumolpidæ, who were settled at Eleusis, revering Demeter; and the Cecropidæ, who dwelt on the rock afterwards called Athens, having Poseidon and Athene for protecting deities. Not far off Ares was a guardian power, on the hill called after his name, Areopagus. Marathon had its Hercules, Prasiæ her Apollo, Phlius another Apollo, Cephalus its Dioscuri; and so on for the other districts.

There was a tradition pervading all Attica, when Pausanias visited it, and it was a tradition handed down with the worship, that every little burgh had had its king at the time when Cecrops reigned at Athens. What can this be but a recollection of the distant period when every patriarchal family or clan had a hereditary chief, who also was priest and judge? A great number of societies then lived in a state of isolation throughout the country, each on its own land, sometimes at war with one another, and having no religious or political bond of union, but being, in fact, so separate that marriage between members of the two was not permitted.

However, necessity or a more generous sentiment brought them together after a time, and insensibly they became united in little groups of four or five or six. Thus we learn that the four burghs of the plain of Marathon united to worship the Delphinian[1] Apollo; whilst the men of the Piræus, Phalerum; and the neighbouring districts joined in building a common temple to Hercules.[2] By this means the numerous petty states were reduced to a dozen confederations in the sixteenth century before Christ, at the time of Cecrops, to whom the change is commonly attributed; although in point of fact he only reigned over one of the twelve[3] associations, the other eleven having been completely independent, each with its proper[4] chief, altar, and god.

As generation after generation passed by, the group of the Cecropidæ insensibly acquired more importance, and successfully maintained a bloody struggle against the Eumolpidæ of Eleusis, who were obliged to submit with the sole reserve

---

[1] Plutarch, *Theseus*, 14.
[2] Pollux, vi., 105. Stephen of Byzant., ἐχἰλιδαι.
[3] Philochorus, quoted by Strabo., ix.
[4] Thuc., ii., 16. Pollux, viii., 111.

of keeping the hereditary priesthood of their divinity.[1] It is easy to conceive that there were many other contests, of which all record has perished; the end of them was that the rock of the Cecropidæ, on which the worship of Athene had gradually developed itself, and which assumed her name, acquired the supremacy over the other eleven states. Afterwards came Theseus, to whom all traditions give the credit of uniting the twelve groups into one city. In fact, he caused the worship of Athene Polias to be adopted in all Attica, so that henceforth the whole country joined in celebrating the sacrifice of Panathenæa. Thucydides[2] and Plutarch must be wrong, when they say Theseus destroyed the local prytanea and magistrats of the burghs; for the simple reason that we find these in existence long afterwards. Doubtless all that he attempted was to make the prytaneum of Athens the religious centre of all Attica, with a view to constituting Athenian unity; so that each district preserved its peculiar worship, and its political rights under its own officers, but with the central government of the city over every local one.[3]

Two important truths, then, seem to have been established by all these recollections and traditions thus faithfully preserved at Atticus; one, that the city was a confederation of groups constituted before itself, and the other, that society was not developed without a simultaneous enlargement of religious views. One can hardly say that religious progress brought on social advancement, but it is certain the two were produced at the same time with a remarkable agreement.

We have one reservation to make as to this origination of ancient cities; which is, that, when the construction of this state-system had once been discovered, it was not necessary

---

[1] Pausan., i., 38.
[2] Thuc., ii., 15. Plut., *Thes.*, 24. Pausan., i., 26; viii., 2. With which compare Bœckh., Corp. Inscrip., 82; Demosth., *in Theocr.*: and Pollux, viii., 111.
[3] We cannot believe that the Eupatridæ were the aristocracy founded by an Ionian invasion, for there is no tradition of such an invasion. Strabo says that Attica was called Ionian from the earliest time, and the word is doubtless older than Hellenic. It is true the date assigned to Ion, son of Xuthus, is much more recent; but this genealogy was merely invented in later days to express an old relationship of peoples.

to go over again the same long and hard route for every new town. Indeed, the inverse way was sometimes followed; for a chief who left a constituted city to found another, often only took with him a small number of fellow-citizens, and associated with himself a great number of other men who came from different countries, and might belong to different races. But this chief never failed to form the new city on the model of the one which he was leaving, dividing his people into phratriæ and tribes, each of which had its altar, feasts, and sacrifices, with an ancient hero whom it worshipped, and whom at last it regarded as a forefather.

Again, it often happened that some people or other would be living without laws or order, either because social organization had failed to be established (as in Arcadia), or it had been spoilt by too violent revolutions, as at Cyrene and Thurii. If, then, any legislator took in hand to put these men in order, he would be sure to begin by dividing the people into tribes and phratriæ, as if no other type of society existed. To each he assigned a hero eponymus, establishing sacrifices and inaugurating traditions. Nor could Plato himself, when he wished to set up a model city, imagine any other system of constituting a regular society *(Laws,* v., 738; vi., 771; and Hdtus., iv., 161).

CHAPTER XIX.

URBS. THE CITY BUILT.

THE word city has two separate significations in our language, for which the Latins had two words, (1) *civitas*, or the religious and political association of families, and (2) *urbs*, the place of meeting and the domicile of the association.

The way in which a modern town is built, insensibly, house by house, for a great number of years perhaps, till the village is large enough to receive municipal institutions, is very different from the suddenness with which an ancient city was founded at once, and in a single day.

Only it was needful that the association should have been agreed on first, and the families, curiæ, and tribes united in one worship. That was often a long and difficult process, but when it was once effected, then a city would be built immediately, to be the sanctuary of the common religion.

As an example of the religious act which took place at the foundation of the city, we shall first take Rome itself, notwithstanding the general incredulity attaching to this real piece of ancient history.

Many writers have represented Rome as the work of a captain of adventurers, who gathered a people to his side by inviting vagabonds and robbers, with the inducement of shelter for themselves, and protection for their booty. But, unfortunately, the accounts we find in ancient writers are quite of another sort, and the witness which antiquity gives of itself induces a totally different belief. It is true that Romulus, after the example of many other founders of cities, opened an asylum, or sacred enclosure, to which he admitted all those that presented themselves; but this asylum was so far from being the city, that it was not even open till after the city had been founded and completely built; and then it did not constitute a part of the city, which occupied the platform of the Palatine, but was merely an addition placed on the slope of the Capitoline.

It is important to distinguish clearly the double element of the Roman population. In the asylum were adventurers without home or hearth-fire. On the Palatine were the men from Alba, that is, men already organized into a society, distributed into gentes and curiæ, with laws and domestic worships. The asylum is but a sort of hamlet or suburb where lawless cabins have been run up at random; whilst upon the Palatine are reared the habitations of a religious and sacred city.

Antiquity abounds in information as to the way in which the city was founded. Dionysius of Halicarnassus had gathered some from authors older than himself; and we find more in Plutarch, in Ovid's Fasti, in Tacitus, and in Cato Senior, who had thoroughly examined the old annals of the city, besides two other writers partly preserved to us by Festus, and in whom we may repose the greatest confidence, the learned Varro, and the learned Verrius Flaccus, both deeply imbued with Roman antiquity, lovers of the truth, not at all credulous, and aware of the rules of historical criticism. All these writers concur in handing down to us the tradition of the religious ceremony that marked the foundation of Rome, a tradition too uniform and too strongly attested for us to have a right to reject it.

Things that surprise us in ancient history are not for that reason to be called fabulous, especially if the circumstances that are opposed to our notions are in accordance with the belief of the people of those times. We have been examining in detail a religion which regulated every action of their private life; and we have seen besides that this religion was the very foundation of their society; what is there to astonish us after that, if the foundation of the city also was a sacred act, and if Romulus himself observed rights which were customary elsewhere?

The choice of a site was the founder's first care, and as the people's future destiny would much depend upon the wisdom of this choice, the decision was always referred to the gods. If Romulus had been a Greek, he would have consulted the oracle at Delphi ; had he been a Samnite, he would have followed one of those sacred animals, the wolf or the [1]wood-pecker. But, as a neighbour of the Etruscans, being initiated into the science of augury, he begs the gods to reveal their will by the flight of birds ; which, we are informed, they did, making answer to his request by sending a number of eagles in such a way as to indicate the Palatine.

On the day appointed for the ceremony a sacrifice was offered, and a fire of brush-wood lighted, in order that the founder and his companions, by leaping through the flame,[2] might purify themselves, as they supposed, from all physical or moral stain.

When this preliminary ceremony had prepared the people for the great act of foundation, Romulus dug a round hole in the ground, and threw into it a clod of earth brought from the town of Alba.[3] Each of his companions approached in turn, and after his example threw in a little earth from the country he had just left. It seems that, as they were forbidden by their religion to quit the land and the hearth where their fathers had been buried, each man who established himself elsewhere must have recourse to fiction, and bring with him in the shape of his clod the sacred soil to which the souls of his ancestors were attached. The new settler must be able even in the land of his adoption to say, " This is my fatherland," terra patrum, terra patria ; for the real thought of the ancients was that by burying their clods they were shutting up their forefathers' manes, who would reassemble there and receive the service of their descendants. So the hole into which the clods of earth had been cast was called [4]*mundus*, that is, the region of the manes ; and another belief was that from that place the souls of the dead were allowed an exit thrice a year.

The altar placed by Romulus on this spot was the hearth[5]

---

[1] Cicero, *De Divin.*, i., 17. Plutarch, *Camill.*, 32. Plin., xiv., 2 ; xviii., 12.

[2] Dion. Halic., i., 88.

[3] Plutarch, *Romulus*, 11. Dion. Cass., *Frag.*, 12. Ovid, *Fasti*, iv., 821. Festus, V°. *Quadrata*.

[4] Festus, V°. *Mundus*. Servius, *Ad. Æn.*, iii., 134. Plutarch, *Romulus*, 11.

[5] Ovid, *Fast.*, iv. When the three towns of the Palatine, Capitoline, and Quirinal united in one, the common hearth or temple of Vesta was placed on neutral ground between the three hills.   G

of the city, around which the city itself must be built, as a Roman house surrounded its own sacred fire. There Romulus duly marked the enclosure with a brazen plough-share, drawn by a white bull and a black cow. He guided the plough himself in his priestly robes and with his head veiled, chanting prayers as he went. Behind him his companions in strict silence picked up the clods thrown out by the plough, and cast them within the furrow, that no portion of this sacred earth might be left to the stranger.[1]

This enclosure, once marked out by religion, was so inviolable that neither citizen nor foreigner might pass over it, and a well-known tradition relates that the brother of the founder, having leapt over the little furrow traced to mark out the walls, paid the penalty of the sacrilege with his life.[2] In order to allow an entrance and an exit to the city, the line of the furrow was interrupted in certain places, and as the plough was there lifted up and carried (porto) these intervals were called portæ,[3] gates. The walls being reared upon the sacred furrow, or at all events a little within it, they also were esteemed sacred,[4] and at no period could any one lay hand to them even for purposes of repair without permission from the pontiff. A space on either side this wall was given up to religion, and called the [5]pomœrium; no one might cultivate it or build there.

That such was the ceremony of the founding of Rome a crowd of witnesses assert; and if it be asked how the recollection of it could have been preserved down to the time of the writers who inform us of it, the truth is this ceremony was every year recalled to public memory by an anniversary festival, called the birth-day of Rome. Throughout antiquity it was celebrated from year to year, and even in modern times the Romans still keep it on the self-same day (April 21), with a singular fidelity to old customs.

It would not be reasonable to suppose that Romulus himself invented these rites on the occasion of his using them,

---

[1] Plutarch, *Rom.*, 11. Ovid, *Fast.*, 825—9. Varro, *De Lingua Lat.*, v., 143. Festus, V°. *Primogenitus*; V°. *Urvat*. Virgil, v., 755.
[2] Plutarch, *Quest. Rom.*, 27.
[3] Cato, in Servius, v., 755.
[4] Cicero, *De Nat. Deor.*, iii., 40; *Digest.*, i., tit. 8, 8. Gaius, ii., 8.
[5] Plutarch, *Quest. Rom.* Varro, v., 143. Livy, i., 44. Aulus-Gellius, xiii., 14.

and accordingly we are not surprised to learn that many cities before Rome had been founded in the same manner. Cato the elder, who, before writing his Origines, had consulted the annals of all the Italian peoples, informs us that similar ceremonies were practised by all founders of cities; and Varro assures us that such rites were common to the Latins and Etruscans, the latter possessing books[1] in which were written down the complete ceremonial.

The Greeks believed, like the Italians, that the site of a city ought to be chosen and revealed by the gods, and did not presume to found one without applying to the Pythia at Delphi. So it seemed an act of impious folly to Herodotus[2] that Dorieus of Sparta should have dared to build a town without either consulting an oracle or practising any authorized ceremonial; and therefore he was not surprised that a city thus built in opposition to all rule should have lasted but three years. Thucydides, in one passage,[3] mentions the pious hymns and sacrifices which were set forth when Sparta was founded; and in another says that Athens had a peculiar ritual, without which no colony was founded. There is, besides, in Aristophanes' comedy of the Birds, a pretty correct picture of the ceremony employed, since his jocular description of the founding of the birds' city is clearly founded upon practices actually in use amongst his countrymen; for he puts on the stage a priest kindling a sacred fire, with a poet singing hymns, and a soothsayer reciting oracles.

Pausanias,[4] who travelled through Greece in Adrian's time, relates the founding of the town of Messenia, with details, which he had from the priests. As the event took place as late as Epaminondas' time, there is more reason to believe him.

The Messenians had lived since their expulsion without country of their own amongst the other Greeks, but always preserving with pious care their customs and their national religion. The Thebans were desirous of bringing them home again to Peloponnese, in order to fix an enemy in the side

---

[1] Varro, *Ling. Lat.*, v., 143. Cato, in Servius, v., 755. Festus, V°. *Rituales*.
[2] V., 42.
[3] V., 16.
[4] IV., 27.

of Sparta, yet found it very hard to decide the Messenians themselves to take the step. Epaminondas, knowing he had to do with a credulous people, circulated an ancient oracle predicting a return of the Messenians to their ancient home. At the same time certain apparitions attested that the national gods, having repented of their former desertion, had again become favourable. Then the people decided upon entering Peloponnese behind the Theban army; only, as the sites of the former cities, from having been soiled by conquest had become useless, it was hard to determine where they should fix themselves. The ordinary resource of consulting the oracle of Delphi was out of the question in this case, since the Pythia was on the side of Sparta; but happily the gods had other means of revealing their will, and a priest of the Messenians was favoured with a dream, in which one of their gods invited him to follow him to Mount Ithome. The site having been thus fixed, a further difficulty occurred respecting the proper ceremonies to be observed in the foundation, since the Messenians had forgotten their own ritual, and could not lawfully adopt any other. A second dream opportunely directed another Messenian to proceed to Mount Ithome and search under a yew tree which grew near a myrtle. There an urn was discovered, containing leaves of tin with the whole ritual proper for the sacred ceremony engraved thereon. The priests took the opportunity of transcribing it into their books, not doubting that an ancient king of the Messenians had made the deposit before the conquest of the country.

The ceremony forthwith began with a sacrifice, and an invocation of the ancient gods of Messenia, the Dioscuri, Jupiter of Ithome, and the ancient heroes, their venerated ancestors. As these had quitted the country, according to ancient belief, on the day when the foe had become its master, they were now entreated to return. Formulas were pronounced with a view to effecting this all-important purpose, as though this were the main part in the founding of a city. "Come with us," they repeated, "O Divine Beings, and join us in inhabiting this city." A whole day having been occupied with the sacrifice and prayers, the enclosure was traced next day to the chanting of religious hymns by all the people.

At first it seems surprising that, according to ancient authors, no town was to be found, however old, which did not claim to know the name of its founder, and the date of its foundation. But the fact is, a city could not possibly lose the recollection of its birth-day ceremony, seeing it was renewed every year with a sacrifice. Athens had her birthday as well as Rome.

When it happened that colonists or conquerors were about establishing themselves in a city that was already built, although they had no houses to erect and might step at once into those of their predecessors, yet, all the same, the ceremony of foundation had to be accomplished, a sacred fire to be lit, and the national gods to be settled in their new abode. Hence it is we read in Thucydides and Herodotus that the Dorians founded Lacedœmon, and the Ionians Miletus, although those two peoples had entered upon towns already built, and in fact quite ancient.

These customs may serve to give us some idea what a city was in the minds of the ancients, viz., a sacred enclosure extending round an altar, and a religious abode of gods and citizens. Livy said of Rome that there was no part of it unimpregnated with religion, and where some divinity did not dwell. And any other ancient might have said the same of his own city; for if it had been founded with proper ceremonies it had received within its precincts protecting deities who were, so to speak, implanted in the soil never to leave it; so that it was, in fact, a holy sanctuary.[1]

Moreover, as the gods were for ever attached to the city, so the people also on their side, by a sort of mutual contract, must not desert the gods. After Rome had been devastated by the Gauls, and when it was nothing more than a heap of ruins, the tribunes of the plebs proposed that the people should remove to Veii, which was a large and well-built town, only five leagues off, and devoid of inhabitants on account of the Roman conquest. But the Romans decided on remaining in their own city, following the counsel of Camillus, who reminded them that the gods

---

[1] "Ἴλιος ἵρη, ἱεραὶ Ἀθῆναι (Aristoph., Knights, 1319). Λακεδαίμονι δίη, (Theognis, iv., 837). Theognis calls Megara ἱερὰν πόλιν; Neptunia Troja, θεόδμητοι Ἀθῆναι.

themselves had marked out its site when it was founded, and that, all in ruins as it might be, it was still their sacred dwelling-place.

CHAPTER XX.

THE WORSHIP OF THE FOUNDER: THE LEGEND OF ÆNEAS.

IT is easy to conceive how much respect was felt in an ancient city for the founder, who had fixed the gods within its walls and bestowed upon it existence. Alive, he was regarded as the father of his country, and dead he became a common ancestor of all succeeding generations, the city's Lar familiaris. Sacrifices and feasts were yearly[1] renewed at his tomb, and the town adored him as its providence. Thus Romulus himself, though he might be murdered by the senators, could not be deprived of his worship, and his temple and priests lasted down to the triumph of Christianity. Nor did any ancient city fail to adore the man to whom it owed its being. Cecrops and Theseus had each a temple at Athens, Abdera sacrificed to Timesius, Thera to Theras, Tenedos to Tenes, Delos to Anius, Cyrene to Battos, Miletus to Naleus, and Amphipolis to Hagnon.[2] In Pisistratus' time a Miltiades went out to found a colony in the Thracian Chersonese, and, "according to custom," as Herodotus says, was worshipped by the colony,[3] as likewise at a later date Hiero of Syracuse was adored by the citizens of the town of Ætna,[4] which he had built. There was not a town of Greece when Pausanias went through it in the second century of our æra, which could not give its founder's name, with his genealogy and history. They had not been able to forget what formed part of their religion, and what a sacred ceremony yearly called to mind.

---

[1] Pindar. *Pyth*, v. 129; *Olymp.*, vii., 145. Cicero, *De Nat. Deor.*, iii., 19. Catull., vii., 6.
[2] Hdtus., i., 168. Pindar, *Pyth.*, iv. Thuc., v., 11. Strabo, xiv., 1. Plutarch, *Quest. Græc.*, 20. Pausan., i., 34; iii., 1.
[3] Hdtus., vi., 38.
[4] Diodor., xi., 78.

It was natural, therefore, that a great number of Greek poets should have chosen the foundation of their city for the subject of their song. Philochorus sung the foundation of Salamis, Ion that of Chios, Crito that of Syracuse, and Zopyrus that of Miletus; and we may mention Apollonius, Hermogenes, Hellanicus, and Diocles as additional names of persons who had written poems or histories on this theme. Perhaps there was not a single town without a hymn, if not a poem, on the sacred act which had given it birth.

There is one poem of this nature which has not perished with the rest, because its beauty has rendered it precious to all ages and peoples. Æneas, being the founder of Lavinium, from which city sprung both Albans and Romans, was looked upon as the first founder of Rome, and a great mass of traditions and recollections had been gathered together about him, which Nævius and Cato the elder had already consigned to verse, when Virgil took up the subject and wrote the national poem of the Roman state.

The arrival of Æneas, or rather the transport of the Trojan gods to Italy, is the subject of the Æneid. The poet sings the man who crossed the sea to found a city and bear his household gods to Latium, *dum conderet urbem Inferretque Deos Latio*. And let not Æneas be judged, after modern ideas, as wanting in passion and force. Readers of Virgil become tired of the epithet pious, and of seeing a warrior so scrupulous in consulting his Penates upon every occasion, lifting up his arms to heaven when it is time to fight, and allowing himself to be sent backwards and forwards by the oracles; but what is wanted is not so much a warrior as a priest. The poet would represent Æneas as the divine founder, the head of a worship, the sacred hero whose mission it is to save the penates of the city. *Sum pius Æneas raptos qui ex hoste Penates Classe veho mecum.* His ruling quality must be piety, and the poet's commonest epithet suits him best. His virtue is to be of a cold and lofty impersonality, which makes of him what is no longer a man, but the instrument of the gods. *Multa gemens multoque animum labefactus amore Jussa tamen Divûm insequitur.*

Homer had already represented Æneas as a sacred personage and great priest, whom Jupiter preferred to Hector, and whom the people venerated like a god. In Virgil, he is the guardian and preserver of the Trojan deities, and it is no mere whim or ornament of the poet, when Hector appears in a dream and confides to him the sacred objects, the protecting statues, and the holy fire. In fact, this is the foundation on which the whole poem reposes, since by it Æneas is become the depositary of the gods, and has received his sacred mission. Though the material part of Troy has perished, yet, thanks to Æneas, its fire is still alight and its gods have still a worship. They cross the deep with him, and seek a country where it may be fated for them to stop, *considere Teucros errantesque deos agitalaque numina Trojæ*. However small it be, Æneas seeks for them a fixed abode, *Dis sedem exiguam patriis*. But the choice of this abode, to which the city's destiny shall be for ever bound, does not depend on men. Diviners and oracles must be consulted to know the will of the gods, who only can direct his course. He would have stayed in many places first; in Thrace, in Crete, in Sicily, or at Carthage with Dido; but the fates oppose. *Italiam non sponte sequor*, he says, the fates ever come between him and his wish to rest, or between him and his love.

Indeed, if it was doubted whether the true hero of Milton's poem was Adam, much more may it be doubted whether Virgil's true hero be not Æneas, but the gods of Troy, who were one day to be those of Rome. Is not the true subject of the Æneid the struggle of the Roman deities against obstacles of every description raised by a hostile goddess? The storm had almost destroyed them, and an ardent woman's love had nearly enslaved them, but they triumph over all and arrive at the wished-for end, *fata viam inveniunt*.

To Romans far more than to us must this poem have been replete with interest; for in the poem they saw themselves, they saw their founder, their town, their religion, their empire. For it was the history of their gods, without whom none of those things would have existed.

---

[1] The legend of Æneas represents a belief, if not a fact, which is enough for our purpose. Besides Rome, there were other towns in Thrace, in Crete, in Epirus, at Cythera, Lacynthus, in Sicily, in Italy, who looked upon Æneas as their *penatiger*, and worshipped him as founder.

CHAPTER XXI.

THE GODS OF THE CITY.

WE must not lose sight of the fact that the bond of all society amongst the ancients was a worship, and as the domestic altar grouped round it all the members of a family, so the city was the assemblage of those who acknowledged the same protecting deities and sacrificed at the same altar. The city altar was enclosed in a building called by the Greeks prytaneum,[1] and by the Romans the Temple of Vesta. There was nothing more sacred in the whole city than this altar, which duly-appointed persons were always watching, and on which the fire was never extinct. Even when Greece afterwards lost somewhat of her reverence, because her ardent imagination was led astray to finer temples and richer legends, yet this feeling was never diminished at Rome, whose inhabitants ever remained convinced that the destiny of the city was attached to the fire which represented their gods. An indication of this is the respect entertained towards the Vestal Virgins who tended the fire (for if a consul met one in the street his lictors lowered their fasces before her), as also the terrible punishment awarded if one of them allowed the fire to be extinguished, or defiled the worship by unchastity. One day, the temple of Vesta was nearly burnt in a conflagration of the neighbouring houses, and all Rome was in terror for its future prosperity. When the danger was over, at the Senate's in-

---

[1] Dion. Halic., ii., 23. Poll., i., 7. Scholiast on Pindar; Nem., 11. Scholiast on Thuc., ii., 15. See also Hdtus., iii., 57; v., 67; vii., 197. Polyb., xxix., 5. Appian., *Mithridat. War*, 23; *Punic War*, 84. Diod., xx., 101. Cicero, *De Signis*, 53. Bœckh., Corp. Inscr., 1193. The Temple of Vesta at Rome was but a fire-place: Cicero, *De Leg.*, ii., 8; ii., 12. Ovid, *Fast.*, vi., 297. Florus, i., 2. Liv., xxviii., 13.

stigation the consul sought the authors of the crime, and after search accused some Capuans sojourning in Rome; not that he had any proof to allege against them, but because it was likely that so great a danger could only have been caused by the most bitter enemies of the state; and Rome could not have a worse foe than Capua, who was then both Hannibal's ally and aspired to be the queen of Italy. The consul was so imbued with this superstition that he thought the enemies of Rome could find no better means of conquering her than to destroy her sacred fire. Such was the belief of the ancients. The public hearth was the city's sanctuary, nay, even the cause of its being and its constant preserver.

Strangers were not allowed to be present at the services before the public fire of the city, any more than at the fires of private families. Indeed, a mere look from a person foreign to the worship would profane a sacred act.[1]

Each city had its peculiar gods, generally such as those worshipped also in families, and termed Lares, Penates, Genii, Demons, Heroes,[2] being, in fact, men deified. For man first worshipped the immortal power which he found to exist in his own soul. These Genii or Heroes were generally such ancestors[3] of the people as had been interred in the city or its territory, this interment being a necessary condition, since the soul was believed to remain with the body. These heroes watched the city and protected the country from their sepulchres, being, after a sort, its leaders and masters, for so the Pythia called them in an oracle to Solon,[4] "Honour the chiefs of the country, the dead who dwell beneath the earth." This opinion was derived from the great power attributed by the ancients to the human soul after death. Every man who had rendered a great service to any city, whether its founder, or a victorious leader, or an improver of its laws, became a god to that city. Nor was it necessary to have been a great man or a benefactor: any one who had vividly struck the imagination of his cotemporaries seemed, when dead, a being whose protection was desirable, and whose anger was to be feared. For ten centuries the

---

[1] Ovid, *Fast.*, ii., 616.
[2] Virgil, iii., 408. Paus., v. 15. Appian., *Civ. Bell.*, i., 54.
[3] Plutarch, *Aristides*, 11.
[4] Plutarch, Solon, 9.

Thebans[1] continued to offer sacrifices to Eteocles and Polynices. The inhabitants of Acanthus worshipped a Persian, who had died in their country during the expedition of Xerxes. Hippolytus was revered as a god at Trazene, and Achilles' son was a god at Delphi, simply because he had died and was buried there. A hero was worshipped at Crotona merely for having been the handsomest man in the city. The Argive Eurystheus was one of the adored protectors of Athens, for a reason explained by Euripides, who makes him, when dying, beg to be buried in Attica, promising that if his request were granted he would be propitious to them from his grave as protector of the land. The whole tragedy of Œdipus Coloneus turns on this belief, in fact, on a dispute between Athens and Thebes for the body of a man who is about to die and become a god.

A city was esteemed fortunate which had some dead who were at all remarkable. Mantinea, for instance, spoke with pride of the bones of Areas, Thebes of those of Geryon, and Messena of those of Aristomenas.[2] Stratagem was frequently employed to get possession of precious relics, as, for instance, in the case of the bones of Orestes[3] treacherously stolen by the Spartans. And the first care of Athens, as soon as she had it in her power, was to take away the remains of Theseus from Scyros, and to erect a temple for them at home, in order to add one more to the number of her protecting deities.

Besides these heroes and genii, men had gods of another sort, such as Jupiter, Juno, and Minerva, whom the sight of nature had led them to invent. But, as we have seen, these creations of human intellect long retained the character of domestic or local divinities; and they were not at all regarded as watching over *all* the human race. Each of them seemed rather to belong to particular families or towns.

And so it was usual for every city, besides its heroes, to have a Jupiter, a Minerva, or some other deity, placed besides the altar amongst its penates.[4] Thus there were in

---

[1] Pausan., ix., 18.
[2] Pausan., i., 43. Polyb., viii., 30. Plaut., *Trin.*, ii., 2, 14.
[3] Hdtus., i., 68.
[4] Hdtus., v., 82. Soph., *Phil.*, 134. Thuc., ii., 71. Eurip., *Electra*, 674. Paus., i., 24; iv., 8; viii., 47. Aristoph., *Birds*, 828; *Knights*, 577. Virgil, ix., 246. Pollux, ix., 40. Apollod., iii., 14.

Greece and Italy a crowd of indigenous divinities, the greater part of whose names have perished, and others barely survived, such as Satrapes, god of Elis, Diudymene of Thebes, Soteira of Ægeium, Britomartis of Crete, Hybloea of Hybla. Nor is it to be supposed that the Jupiters, Heres, and Neptunes of all the separate cities were acknowledged to be the same gods. In the legend of Troy, we find a Pallas who fights for the Greeks, whilst there is another who protects the Trojans. The Here of Samos was represented with quite different attributes from the Here of Argos. Veii had a Juno as well as Rome; and these were so far from being the same deity that the dictator Camillus conjured the enemy's Juno to leave their camp for his own, and when he had mastered the town, devoutly removed the statue to Rome, not doubting that he was bestowing upon his country a second protecting goddess. A few years afterwards another dictator brought back a Jupiter from Prœneste,[1] when the city already possessed three[2] or four.

Any city which owned a deity was jealous of its protection being extended to others, and would allow no stranger to enter the temple. Thus no one but an [3]Argive could worship in the temple of Here of that city; and a man must be an Athenian to worship Athene at [4]Athens; and similarly the Romans, who had two Junos at home, could not sacrifice to a third Juno who inhabited the little town of Lanuvium, until they had conquered it.[5]

It must not be supposed that the ancients generally had any idea of the unity and greatness of God, notwithstanding the guesses of some philosophers and the revelations at Eleusis to the most intelligent of the initiated. Their notion of the Deity was that of a protector to a family or a town. Something of the same sort can be seen now-a-days in Greece itself, where it may be doubted whether the peasants, who pray so fervently to particular saints, have any idea of a general Providence. So, in Naples, every district has its Madonna, and the lazzarone, who is devout enough

---

[1] Livy, v., 21, 22; vi., 29.
[2] Varro says there were 300 different Jupiters at Rome.
[3] Hdtus., vi., 81.
[4] Hdtus., v., 72.
[5] Livy, viii., 14.

before his own, will insult that of the next street; nay, two facchini have been known to fight with knives for the merits of their respective Madonnas. Now these cases, which are exceptional at present, constituted the rule with the ancients.

We are not surprised then, in a tragedy of Æschylus, to find a stranger telling the women of Argos that he neither owes anything to the gods of their country, nor fears them. Each city looked to its own heroes for safety and success, and in case of neglect or adversity would sometimes desert the worship of a god or even overturn his altar. And it must be confessed that in general the gods were believed to take great pains and toil very hard on behalf of those who offered them sacrifices. In the Æneid, Juno strives energetically to win for Carthage the future empire of the world, and doubtless, like her, all the gods were thought to have at heart the greatness of their respective towns, their interests being the same as those of their human fellow-citizens. So in war they marched to battle with the army, and a warrior would say, as in Euripides, "The gods that are with us are more powerful than those of our foe."[1] The Æginetæ never entered upon a campaign without the statues of their national heroes the Æacidæ, nor the Spartans without those of the [2]Tyndaridæ. Gods and men mutually supported each other in the conflict, and, if the day was won, it was because all parties had done their duty.

When a town was conquered, it was believed that its gods were conquered with it; and if the town was taken, its gods themselves were captive also. But on this latter point opinions were very fluctuating, many persons being persuaded that a city could not be taken so long as the gods continued to reside in it. In Virgil's poem, when the Greeks were masters of Troy, Æneas exclaims that the gods have deserted their temples and are flying from the town; and in Æschylus a chorus of Theban women, animated by the same belief, entreats the gods to be faithful to the city.[3] A formula has been preserved by [4]Macrobius, which the Romans frequently employed to induce the enemy's gods to desert them: "Thee, O mighty one, who protectest this city, I

---

[1] Heraclid., 347.
[2] Hdtus., v., 65; v., 80.
[3] Æsch., *Sept. Cont. Theb.*, 202.
[4] Macrob., iii., 9.

worship, and earnestly beseech to abandon it, with its people, leaving their temples and sacred spots, to come to Rome to me and mine. Oh may our city and our temples be agreeable to thee. Take us into thy keeping. This if thou wilt do, I will found a temple in thine honour." And it appears from Thucydides[1] that in like manner the Greeks, on laying siege to a city, did not fail to invoke the gods of it, and beg permission to take it. But often, instead of making use of a formula, the Greeks preferred to shew their ingenuity in carrying off the statue of the god; as Ulysses had done at Troy with the statue of Pallas. At a later period, when the Æginetans were about to make war upon Epidaurus, they began by carrying off two images, which they transported to Ægina.[2] This same people were themselves robbed of the protection of Æacus in a slightly different way. For the Athenians[3] built him a chapel on their own soil, and for thirty years without intermission sacrificed and worshipped; after which, when war broke out, victory declared for them. The island of [4]Salamis was won from the Megarians in the same way. When Solon had consulted the oracle, he was informed that it was needful to gain the favour of the indigenous heroes who protected the isle. Sacrifices were consequently offered in the name of Athens to the chief heroes of Salamis, and they, unable to resist the temptation, espoused the side of Athens, and permitted the island to be taken.

In time of actual warfare, the besiegers strove to get possession of the city gods, and the besieged on their side did their best to prevent it. Sometimes the god was fastened with chains to prevent his desertion; and sometimes he was hidden, that the enemy might not find him. Sometimes the form of words by which the foe sought to debauch a god was opposed by other words which had power to retain him. But perhaps the Roman plan was the safest of all, for they kept secret the name of their chief and most powerful protector; imagining that if the enemy could never call the god by this name, he would not desert their cause or leave their city to be taken.[5]

---

[1] II., 74.
[2] Hdtus., v., 83.
[3] Hdtus., v., 89.
[4] Plutarch, Solon, 9.
[5] Macrob., iii., 9.

The priests of each city were entirely independent of all foreign authority; and there was no bond of union, or communication, or exchange of ritual between the priests of two cities. On passing from one city to another the traveller found other gods, other doctrines, other ceremonies. The ancients had liturgical books, but those of one town were different from those of another. And every city had its repertory of prayers and practices, which it kept quite secret, fearing to compromise its religion and its destiny by exposing them to strangers.

Thus every town was like a separate church, with its own gods, and rites, and worship.

The belief of the ancients may seem gross to us, but it was that of the most intellectual people of those times, and it exercised such influence that the greater part of their laws, their institutions, and history was deduced therefrom.

CHAPTER XXII.

PUBLIC REPASTS.

THE religion of the city, like that of the family, was symbolized by certain repasts, at which food, previously prepared on the altar, was partaken of by members of the association. These feasts, being held necessary for the [1]safety of the city, were universally celebrated in Greece and Italy.

On solemn occasions every member of the city was present, and tables were prepared for vast numbers in large halls or in the streets. Such a feast was that described in the Odyssey[2] as taking place at Pylos, when nine long tables were spread for five hundred citizens at each; and such also was that feast which was being celebrated at Athens on the day when Orestes arrived there from the murder of his mother.[3] The public meals at Sparta, of which so much has been said in history, were no ways different; for it is an error, though a common one, to suppose that all the Spartans ate[4] daily in public, whereas there are plenty of passages to prove they often took meals at home, whilst their public repasts only occurred twice a month, and on feast-days.[5]

But besides these banquets a religious meal took place every day in the prytaneum before the public altar, in the presence of the protecting deities, whose favour could not be

---

[1] Athenæus, v., 2, σωτηρία τῶν πολίων σύνδιπνα.
[2] *Odyss.*, iii., 5—9; 43—50; 339—341.
[3] Athen., x., 49.
[4] Athen., iv., 17; iv., 21. Hdtus., i., 57. Plut., *Cleom.*, 13.
[5] For Athens, see Xenoph., *Gov. Ath.*, 2. Scholiast on *Aristoph. Clouds*, 393. Athenæus, x., 49. For Crete and Thessaly, Athen., iv., 22. For Argos., Bœckh., 1122. For other towns, Pindar, *Nem.*, xi. Theognis, 269. Pausan., v., 15. Athen., iv., 32; iv., 61; i., 58; x., 24, 25; xi., 66.

H

retained without. At Athens, the duty of eating these meals was once fulfilled by certain persons chosen by lot, called parasites,[1] (then an honourable term), but in Demosthenes' time the prytanes had to fulfil the duty, and parasites were no longer chosen.

Lots were used, no doubt, in order that the gods might have the guests they preferred; and the whole feast was of a religious character. Every guest had a crown of flowers or leaves, as usual at religious ceremonies, for, as Sappho[2] sings, "More flowers please more the gods, who scorn the sacrifice of men uncrowned." And for the same reason all wore white robes, white being the colour which the deities liked best.[3]

The feast, having been commenced with prayers and libations, was accompanied from time to time with hymns in honour of the gods. In each city careful rules were laid down concerning the nature of the dishes, and the sort of wine to be used; and it would have been the gravest offence to deviate from the prescribed viands, or to alter in the least the sacred songs. Religion went so far as to fix the sort of vessels to be used both in cooking and on the table. In one town the bread[4] must be served in copper baskets; elsewhere on earthen ware. Also the form of the loaves had been irrevocably fixed. In fact, the primitive simplicity of these repasts lasted long after belief and manners and social state had quite altered; perhaps all the longer because it was not forbidden, after the religious banquet, to begin another more luxurious meal in private.[5]

In Italy the Œnotrians,[6] Oscans, and Ausonians had the same practices as the Greeks. Virgil has preserved us two examples in the Æneid, one, when Latinus receives Æneas's envoys, not in his dwelling, but in a temple where a festival is taking place after sacrifice; and a second, when Æneas

---

[1] Plutarch, Solon, 24. Athenæus, vi., 26.
[2] Fragm. in Athen., xv., 26.
[3] Plato, *Laws*, xii., 956. Cicero, *De Leg.*, ii., 18. Virgil, v., 70, 774; vii., 135. The Hindoos also, in religious ceremonies bore a crown and were clothed in white. Laws of Manou, iv., 66, 72.
[4] Athenæus, i., 58; iv., 32; xi., 66.
[5] Athen., iv., 19, 20.
[6] Aristot., *Pol.*, iv., 9. 3.

finds Evander sacrificing amidst his people, who are all crowned with flowers, and all, seated at the same table, sing a hymn to the god of the city. At Rome the Senators feasted in the Capitol, the representatives of the curiæ in the large hall of some temple, whilst on great occasions when all the people were to be entertained, tables were placed in the streets, which at first the pontiffs superintended, but afterwards certain priests called *epulones*.

CHAPTER XXIII.

THE CALENDAR.

AS the Italians and Greeks were people so eminently religious, it will seem natural that they should have set apart certain days as a respite from secular thought, and to be devoted to religion.

The following are the chief feast-days common to most ancient cities:—

1st, The birth-day of the city, when the ceremonies which had attached the gods to the soil were renewed and repeated.

2ndly, Amburbalia,[1] or feast of the city bounds, and ambarvalia, or feast of the territorial bounds, when the citizens, crowned with leaves and clad in white, formed a great procession and made the circuit of the city or its territory, led by priests who sang hymns and drove before them victims to be immolated at the conclusion of the ceremony.

3rdly, The Feasts of the Founder, and the Feasts of the chief heroes, who protected the city. Amongst the persons honoured at Rome we must reckon not only Romulus and Servius Tullius, but also Romulus's nurse and the mother of Evander. Athens held festivals in honour of Cecrops, Erechtheus, Androgeos, Theseus, and Theseus's guardian, with many others.

4. There were, besides, rural feasts for ploughing, seed-time, time of flowering, and for vintage. For every act of agriculture was accompanied with sacrifice and the singing of hymns. At Rome the priests yearly fixed the date for the commencement of vintage, as well as the day when the new wine might be drunk. The pruning of the vine in like

---

[1] Tibullus, ii., 1. Festus, Verbo *Amburbiales*.

manner was ordered by religion; and it was thought to be an act of great impiety to offer to the gods the fruit of a vine which had not been pruned.[1]

On these feast-days, besides ceasing from work, men were expected to be joyous and gay, to sing, and join in public games. A law of Athens added as a caution for such days that men should beware[2] of wronging one another, as though the better the day the worse the sin.

The calendar, being a mere list of feasts, was arranged and ordered by the priests. A long time elapsed before it was put into writing at Rome. Only on the first day of the month, the pontiff, after sacrifice, called the people and stated the festivals of the current month. This *calling* is signified in Latin by the word *calatio*, and from it the first day of the month was termed the Kalends.

The regulation of the calendar depended neither upon the course of the sun nor yet, as far as we can judge, upon that of the moon; but upon certain mysterious laws known only to the priests. For sometimes religion ordered the year to be shortened and sometimes to be lengthened; and some idea of what the primitive calendars were, may be formed from the fact that at Alba the month of May had twelve days and March thirty-six.[3]

Moreover, as the religion and the gods of one city were quite different from those of another, so also were its feasts and its calendar. The years were not of the same length, and the months had different names. The names of the months were taken from their chief festivals, and Athens had not the same feasts as Thebes, nor Rome as Lavinium. So also the commencement of the years did not agree, nor did they count the number of them from the same æra. In Greece, the feasts of Olympia at length afforded a common date, but that did not prevent each city having its own particular way of counting. In Italy the different cities reckoned their years from the day of their founding.

---

[1] Varro, vi., 16. Virgil, *Georg.*, i., 340—350. Plin., xviii., 29. Festus, V°. *Vinalia*. Theophrast., *Caract.*, 3. Plutarch, *Quest Rom.*, 40; *Numa*, 14.
[2] Demosth., *in Timoc.* Law of Solon.
[3] Censorinus, 22. Macrob., i., 14, 15. Varro, v., 28; vi., 27.

CHAPTER XXIV.

THE CENSUS.

ONE of the most important ceremonies in all ancient cities was what they called the purification. This took place yearly at Athens,[1] but at Rome every five years. Its name, as well as the practices observed, indicate that its object was to remove the guilt contracted by neglect of ritual, or involuntary error. For in those days purity of intention did not reckon for much, and religion consisting in the minute practice of innumerable rules, men were always in terror of having offended their gods by some omission or mistake. An expiatory sacrifice, therefore, was needful to give comfort to the heart of man, and was performed as follows:—

The officiating magistrate (at Rome it was the censor; before the censor, the consul, and before the consul, the king,) commenced by taking the auspices to see if the gods approved the ceremony. Then a herald convoked the people in a set form of words. When all were gathered together on the proper day, without the walls, the magistrate went three times round the assembly driving before him a sheep, a pig, and a bull (suovetaurile), which three victims both in Greece and Italy constituted an expiatory sacrifice.[2] The priests and slaughterers followed, and at the end of the third round the magistrate pronounced a set form of prayer and

---

[1] Diog. Sacrt., *Socrat.*, 23. Harpocrat., φαρμακός. For purification of domestic hearth see Æsch., *Choeph.*, 966.

[2] Varro, *Lingua Lat.*, vi., 86. Valer. Max., v., i., 10. Livy, I, 44; iii., 22; vi., 27. Propert., iv., 1, 20. Servius, *Ad. Æn.*, viii., 231. Livy attributes this institution to Servius; but the institution is older than Rome herself, and common to all old cities. What Servius did was to modify it, as we shall see.

slaughtered the victims; after which every stain was effaced, every neglect of worship repaired, and the city at peace with its gods.

The absence of all strangers and the attendance of every citizen were conditions necessary for the proper accomplishment of this act. For the presence of a stranger would have profaned it, and the absence of a citizen would have rendered it imperfect. The citizens, therefore, were counted with the greatest care both at Athens and Rome; and it is probable that their number was mentioned in the prayer which the magistrate pronounced, as we know it was afterwards inscribed in the written account of the ceremony. The penalty for absence was loss of citizenship, a very severe one no doubt, but explained when we remember that it was the favour of the gods which constituted the city, and those who had not been seen by the gods on this great day were not citizens in their eyes.[1]

At Rome men took rank as they were ranged by the censor on that day, as senators, knights, or simple citizens. Hence the great power of the censor.

Although none but citizens were present, yet each handed in a list of his family and dependents; and the women and slaves were purified in the persons of the patres familias.

Down to Augustus's time the purification was performed with the same scrupulousness, and with unaltered rites. The pontiffs still looked upon it as a religious act, whilst statesmen considered it at least a useful practice.

---

[1] Velleius, ii., 15. No reason was accounted sufficient to keep a citizen of Rome away from the lustration.

CHAPTER XXV.

RELIGION IN THE ASSEMBLY AND THE ARMY.

THERE were certain days on which no assembly was permitted to meet; because it was remembered that some disaster had happened on that day, and it was concluded that therefore on that day every year the gods would be unpropitious from absence or anger. Therefore no justice was administered, and in fact all public life was suspended on these *dies nefasti*.

Even on days when assemblies were permissible, the augurs must see first whether the gods were favourable, after which at Rome the consul, prompted by the augur, repeated a prayer.

At Athens, after sacrifice a large ring[1] was marked out on the ground with lustral water, and the citizens gathered together inside. The tribune from which the orator spoke was held to be a sacred place, a short prayer preceded the speech, and the orator bore a chaplet on his head.[2]

At Rome, the meeting of the senate always took place in a temple, and a decision arrived at in any other spot would have been null and void, from the absence of the gods. Every senator as he entered, poured out a libation and invoked the gods.[3]

At Athens, the senate met with equal regard to religion, every senator wearing a chaplet, and an altar being always at hand.[4]

---

[1] Aristoph., *Acharn.*, 44. Æschin., *in Timarch.*, i., 21; *in Ctesiph.*, 176; and Scholiast. Dinarch., *in Aristog.*, 14.
[2] Aristoph., *Thesmoph.*, 381. Ch. Scholiast.
[3] Aulus-Gellius (Varro), xiv., 7. Cicero, *Ad. Fam.*, x., 12. Sueton., *Aug.*, 35. Dion. Cassius, liv., p. 621. Servius, vii., 153.
[4] Andocides, *De Myst.*, 44; *De Red.*, 15 Antiphon., *Pro Chor.*, 45. Lycurgus, *in Lever.*, 122. Demosth., *Modias*, 114. Diodor., xiv., 4.

Courts of justice were only open, whether at Athens or Rome, on favourable days. At Athens it begun with sacrifice,[1] and was held in a sacred place, according to the tradition of Homer, who speaks of judges assembling in the holy circle.

Festus informs us that the rituals of the Etruscans laid down rules for the founding of a city, for the consecration of a temple, for the arrangement of tribes and curiæ in public meetings, and, lastly, how to dispose an army in order of battle.

In time of war religion was no less mixed up with men's doings than in time of peace. The Italian[2] towns had colleges of priests called *fetiales*, who, like the heralds of Greece, presided at all sacred ceremonies in which different cities were concerned. War was proclaimed by a fetialis, veiled and garlanded, and at Rome the consul in priestly robes, after having sacrificed, opened the temple gates of the most ancient and venerable Italian deity. Before starting upon an intended expedition, the general uttered a prayer and offered a sacrifice in the presence of his assembled army. And similar rules prevailed at Athens[3] and Sparta.

An army in campaign was an image of the city, its sacred fire[4] accompanying it and being kept up night and day. The Greeks carried with them the statues of their gods, and a diviner; and the Romans could not march without both augurs and sacred chickens.

No Roman general would begin a battle unless assured of favourable auspices, and it was the great principle of their military art not to be obliged to fight when the will of the gods was contrary. On this account their camp was daily made a sort of citadel.

The accounts of the battle of Plataeæ prove similar practices and beliefs in Greece, for then the Spartans could not begin the battle, notwithstanding the Persian advance, be-

---

[1] Aristoph., *Wasps*, 860—5. Homer, *Iliad*, xviii., 504.
[2] Dion. Halic., ii., 73. Servius, x., 14,
[3] Dion. Halic., 57. Virg., vii., 601. Xenophon, *Hellen.*, vi., 5.
[4] Hdtus., vii., 6. Plutarch, *Agesil.*, 6; *Public.*, 17. Xenophon, *Gov. Lac.*, 14. Dion. Halic., ix., 6. Julius, Obsequens, 12, 116. Stob., 42.

cause the entrails of the victims shewed unfavourable signs. Every man remained in his place crowned with garlands, and singing hymns to the sound of flutes. In vain the Persians shot their arrows and slew several men. As many as four victims were killed before a favourable sign allowed them to lift their bucklers from the ground, and only when the entrails at length were pronounced satisfactory did they handle their swords and begin to fight.

A vow had generally been made before the battle, similar to that in [1] Æschylus: "Ye gods who inhabit and possess our land, I promise, if our arms are victorious, to sprinkle your altars with the blood of sheep, to slaughter bulls, and to hang up in your temples the spoils won by our spears." As a result of this vow the conqueror owed the gods a sacrifice, which was offered in the presence of the whole army, who re-entered the city in procession singing the sacred hymn, θρίαμβος.

At Rome the corresponding ceremony and procession was no other than the celebrated triumph, so called from the refrain of the hymn which the soldiers sung as they marched, crowned with garlands, up the sacred hill. The words, Io triumphe, were never forgotten or omitted even when the rest of the words, having become unintelligible, were replaced by an unbelieving soldiery with barrack-songs or jokes upon their general.

But that was at a later period. Enough has been said to shew how thoroughly religion was mixed up with all the thoughts and doings of ancient men. Their souls and their bodies, their public as their private life, their meals, their feasts, their assemblies, their courts of justice, their battles, were all controlled and regulated by the religion of the city. Not an action or a habit was free from its influence; and human beings were governed with so absolute an authority that nothing was left free from it.

To believe that all this religion was a farce and a quackery would be to entertain a very mistaken idea of human nature. All the respect which we entertain for Montesquieu will never make us believe with him that the Romans adopted such a system in order to keep under the people. It may be

---

[1] *Sept. Cont. Theb.*, 252, 260. Eurip., *Phœn.*, 573.

doubted whether any religion ever existed which had such an origin, and no religion which has fallen so low as to be kept up merely for political reasons can last very long. Again Montesquieu is in error when he says that the Romans subjected religion to politics, for one cannot read many pages of Livy without being convinced that the contrary is true. If the Greeks and Romans knew nothing of those sad struggles which have been so common since between church and state, it was that religion had enslaved the state both at Sparta and Athens, and at Rome. Or rather the state and religion were so completely mixed up and confused, that it is hard not merely to conceive of their conflicting, but even to distinguish one from the other.

CHAPTER XXVI.

RITUALS.

WE can hardly expect to find in the religion of the ancients that grandeur and elevating tendency which belongs to Revelation. Indeed, the word religion had a different meaning in those days to what it has now; implying, as it did, not a body of doctrine concerning God, and a revelation of mysteries, but a mass of petty observances that made man a slave to the letter of a difficult ritual. There was more of terror than of love in their observances, and the principal object of all seems to have been to avoid the hatred or appease the anger of the gods.

The most useful method that their experience had discovered for effecting these objects was simply to employ the forms of words that had been successful in former time. If a certain prayer, composed of certain words, had in time past actually obtained what it asked for, doubtless it was a charm too powerful for the god to resist. Therefore the mysterious formula must be remembered, must be committed[1] to writing, must be repeated with exactitude. Not a syllable or word must be altered, nor the rhythm to which it should be chanted. The son must repeat it as his forefathers before him, else the prayer would lose its force, and this armour of man against the fickleness of heaven be all in vain. And not only the form of words, but the very gestures and dress of the sacrificer were regulated. Before one god the worshipper's head must be veiled, before another uncovered; whilst in adoring a third, the skirt of

---

[1] Dion. Halic., i., 75. Varro, vi., 90. Cicero, *Brut.*, 16. Aulus-Gellius, xiii., 19.

his toga must be over his shoulder. Sometimes a man must be barefoot; sometimes he must whirl rapidly round from left to right.

Again, the religion of each family or each city laid down very careful rules as to the colour of the victim, the way of killing it, the shape of the knife, and the sort of wood to be used in burning it. These minutiæ were esteemed of such importance, that the Athenians wreaked the direst vengeance on the priest who altered any point of ritual, and the senate of Rome would degrade a consul or a dictator who had made any mistake about a sacrifice.

In the course of time great quantities of forms had accumulated in the sacred books of Greeks, Romans, and Etruscans.[1] They were sometimes inscribed on wood and sometimes on canvas, but Athens had hers engraved on brass, that they might be imperishable. At Rome there were books of the pontiffs, books of the augurs, books of ceremonies, and the collection called Indigitamenta. Nor was there a town[2] that had not its repertory of old songs in honour of the gods, which remained unaltered with the universal change of manners and belief; the rhythm and the words remaining, long after all sense of their meaning had departed.

All these books and hymns were preserved with great care, as belonging to the essence of religion, but they were also carefully concealed from strangers. It was treason to reveal anything of this nature to an enemy. Most of the books, therefore, were kept hidden from the citizens themselves, and known only to the priests.

---

[1] Pausan., iv., 27. Plutarch, *Cont. Colot.*, 17. Pollux, viii., 128. Plin., *H. N.*, xiii., 21. Val. Max., i., 1, 3. Varro, *Lingua Lat.*, vi., 16. Censorinus, 17. Festus, V°. *Rituales*.

[2] Plutarch, *Thes.*, 16. Tac., *Ann.*, iv., 43. Ælian., H. V., ii., 39.

CHAPTER XXVII.

ANNALS.

THEIR ancient history was of greater importance to the people of Greece and Italy than ours can be to us, because of its connexion with their religion, and because many of their sacred rites were only to be explained in this way. So their history began with the birth of each city, and the sacred name of the founder. The legends of the city's gods and of her protecting heroes were then related. The date and origin of each of these worships was set forth, and explanations added of obscure rites. Then would be declared the prodigies wrought by the gods to manifest their power, their goodness, or their anger. Descriptions were inserted of ceremonies by which the priests had cleverly diverted an evil omen, or appeased the rancour of the deities. The diseases by which a city had been smitten, and the forms of prayer which had cured them, were all written down, as well as the date of consecration of different temples, and the reason of certain sacrifices. Not less were inscribed the events which had any relation to religion, battles in which the gods were seen to fight, victories that proved their aid, and defeats which testified to their ire. All this was written for the instruction and advantage of posterity. It seemed to prove the existence of the national gods, and to teach a citizen all he should believe, and all that concerned his worship.

Of course it was written by the [1]priests. At Rome, the

---

[1] Dion., ii., 49. Livy, x., 33. Cicero, *Re Div.*, ii., 41; i., 33; ii., 23. Censorinus, 12, 17. Sueton., *Claud.*, 42. Macrob., i., 2; v., 19. Solin., ii., 9. Servius, vii., 678; viii., 398. Letters of Marc. Aurel., iv., 4.

pontiffs kept their annals; and so did the Sabine priests, and the Samnites, and the Etruscans. In Greece, we hear of sacred annals existing at Athens, Delphi, Naxos, and Tarentum[1]; and Pausanias heard many local histories repeated from the annals of many little towns by the priests who had studied them. These annals never went beyond the foundation of the city, and did not relate to any other part of the world than that particular city, or its enemies and allies. They were quaint enough, no doubt, and short, and dry; but even the beautiful narrations of Herodotus and Thucydides will not console us for the loss of what we should have learnt from them of the inmost life and belief of Greece and Rome.

It must be remembered that these annals were contemporaneous narratives of events, and that it was materially impossible to corrupt them, guarded as they were by the priests, and being of the utmost importance to religion. Pious frauds even are not to be suspected; for the ancients thought that every event, just as it happened, was an indication of divine will and a lesson to coming generations. For this reason, though, we can believe that there might be many involuntary errors, resulting from credulity, from love of the marvellous, from faith in the national gods, yet deliberate falsehood is inconceivable; it would have been so impious: it would have done so much to harm religion. Therefore we may be sure that, if all in these old books was not true, at all events there was nothing which the priest did not believe true. And it is a great thing for the historian, who would penetrate the darkness of early ages, to know that, if there are blunders, there are no frauds. The very mistakes, being contemporaneous with the period he is studying, may shew him what men thought, if they do not precisely state what actually occurred.

At length the time came when these annals were divulged. Those of Rome were published, and those of other Italian cities were known, nor did the priests of the Greek towns any longer scruple to relate the contents of theirs. All these authentic monuments were studied and examined; and a

---

[1] Plutarch, *Cont. Colot.*, 17. Athenæus, xi., 49. Plutarch, *Solon*, xi.; *Moral*, 869. Tac., *Ann.*, iv., 43.

school of learned men was formed, from Varro and Verrius Flaccus down to Aulus Gellius and Macrobius. Light being let in upon ancient history, many errors of tradition were corrected, which historians of the preceding period had repeated. For instance, it was known that Porsenna had taken Rome, and that gold had been paid to the Gauls. The age of historical criticism began; yet even those who went deepest did not reject the general historical whole constructed by such writers as Herodotus and Livy.

CHAPTER XXVIII.

THE KING.

WHEN an ancient city was founded, whether by union of tribes, or colonization from an older city, men did not sit down to deliberate what sort of government they should establish, nor what laws they would adopt. The city's institutions were already nascent in the religion and in the belief of each citizen, being the growth of seeds sown long ago in former history.

Each worship that we have described, whether that of the family, or that of the curia, or that of the tribe, had its chief, viz., the paterfamilias, the curio or phratriarch, and the tribe-king or φυλοβασιλεύς. And so the city also must have its chief-priest, who was called king, or archon, or prytanis, and whose duties were to maintain the public fire, to offer sacrifice and prayer, and to preside at religious feasts.

It is important to prove that the ancient kings of Italy and Greece were priests, for erroneous notions have prevailed on this point, perhaps, because in modern times kings have no religious functions, and priests no military or political ones. But Aristotle says, "The care of the city's public sacrifices belongs, according to religious customs, not to special priests, but to those men, whose dignity is derived from the sacred fire, and who are called in one place kings, in another prytanes, and in another archons."[1] And no one better understood the constitutions of Greek cities than Aristotle. That the three words king, prytanis, and archon were long synonymous is clear from this plain statement; but it is attested also by another fact, that an ancient

---

[1] *Polit.*, vii., 5, 11 (vi., 8). Cf. Dion, ii., 65.

historian,[1] Charon of Lampsacus, when he wrote a book about the kings of Lacedæmon, entitled it, "The Archons and prytanes of the Lacedæmonians." Further indications of the priestly character of ancient kings may be found in classical writings. The daughters of Danaus, in Æschylus, address the king of Argos as follows: "Thou art the supreme prytanis, and watchest over the fire of this city."[2] In Euripides, Orestes the matricide says to Menelaus, "It is just that I, being son of Agamemnon, should reign at Argos," to which Menelaus answers: "Art thou, O murderer, in a position to touch the vessels of purifying water for sacrifice, and to slay the victims?"[3] In fact, a king's chief function was to perform religious ceremonies. An ancient king of Sicyon was deposed because he was unfitted to offer sacrifice, by having soiled his hand with a murder.[4] As he could no longer be priest, neither could he any more be king. We know from Demosthenes that the ancient kings of Attica themselves offered all the sacrifices required by the city worship, and from Xenophon that the kings of Sparta were the heads of Lacedæmonian religion.[5] Homer and Virgil represent their kings as incessantly occupied with sacred ceremonies; and in like manner the Etruscan Lucumos[6] were at once pontiffs, magistrates, and military chiefs.

The kings of Rome were all likewise priests, if we examine the traditions respecting them. Romulus appears to have been instructed in the science of augury, and we have seen that he founded the city in accordance with religious rites. Livy says that Numa himself fulfilled the greater part of the priestly functions, but, foreseeing that his successors, having many wars on their hands, could not always be ready to sacrifice, he instituted pontiffs to take the place of kings, who might be absent from Rome." Wherefore the Roman pontificate was but a sort of emanation from the primitive royalty.

These king-priests were enthroned with religious ceremony.

---

[1] Suidas, V°. Χάρων.
[2] Æschy., *Supp.*, 361 (357).
[3] Eurip., *Orestes*, 1605.
[4] Nic. Damas., Frag. Hist. Grec., iii., 394.
[5] Demosth., *Cont. Neær.* Xenoph., *Gov. Lac.*, 13.
[6] Virgil, x., 175. Livy, v., 1. Censor., 4.

Having been conducted to the summit of the Capitoline hill, the new king seated himself on a throne of stone with his face towards the south. On his left was seated an augur, whose head was covered with sacred fillets, and who held an augur's staff in his hand. With this staff the latter traced some lines in the sky, repeated a prayer, and, laying his hand upon the king's head, besought the gods by some visible sign to make it evident that this chief was agreeable to them. Afterwards, as soon as lightning, or the flight of birds had proved the god's assent, the new king took possession of his charge. Livy[1] describes this ceremony for Numa, but Dionysius of Halicarnassus assures us it took place not only for all the other kings, but also for the consuls, and that it was practised in his own time. And there was good reason for such a custom, because, as the king was about to be supreme head of its religion, and the safety of the city was to depend upon his prayers and sacrifices, it was natural that men should wish to be assured he was agreeable to the gods.

Plutarch tells us that at Sparta the ephors took care to see that the kings continued in favour with the gods by a similar inspection. "Every nine years," he writes, they choose a bright night, but when there is no moon, and they sit in silence with their eyes fixed upon the sky. Then if they see a star shoot from one side of heaven to the other, it is an indication that the kings are guilty of some fault against the gods. The kings are then suspended from the exercise of their office until an oracle from Delphi relieves them of their incapacity.[2]

That political power in early times should have accompanied the priestly functions we need not be at all surprised to find, when we remember what has been said of the authority of the father in a family (an authority derived from religion), and when we compare the infancy of other peoples. Perhaps, in the beginning of a people's history religion is the only thing strong enough to enforce obedience; perhaps human nature will submit to nothing but a moral idea. When we see how religion was mixed up with everything, with government, justice, and war, we can understand how

---

[1] Livy, i., 18. Dion. Halic., ii., 6; iv., 80.
[2] Plutarch, *Agis*, 11.

the altar, as Aristotle says, conferred upon the king his dignity and power, and that he became at once magistrate, judge, and general. It was so, says the same writer, with the kings of Sparta,[1] and Dionysius expresses himself in the same terms about the kings of Rome.

As family priesthoods were hereditary, on account of the worship being ancestral, so also was the kingly; and the political power accompanied the sacerdotal functions. And of course, the man who had kindled the sacred fire of the city was its first priest.

These two truths are at once illustrated and proved by the history of the Ionian colonies, which were by no means purely Athenian, but composed of a mixture of Pelasgians, Æolians, Abantes, Cadmeans, and only called Ionian because the hearth was placed and the fire kindled by some descendant of the Athenian hero Codrus. These colonists never had a leader of their own race, but in every one of the twelve cities bestowed the royalty upon a [2]Codrid, whom they respected for religious reasons, and not at all because superior force compelled them to obey him. Yet the royalty long remained hereditary in these families.[3] In like manner, as Battos had founded Cyrene, there the Battiadæ were long in possession of the royal dignity, and at Marseilles the descendants of Protis, its founder, long filled the office of chief priest and enjoyed great privileges.

It was not, then, by force or violence that the chiefs and kings of ancient cities attained the position which they filled, nor could it be truly said of them that the first of their line was a soldier of fortune. Religion and the worship of the sacred fire gave the city her kings, as it had made the father head in the house. Faith taught obedience to "holy kings" (as Pindar calls them), and authority was conferred on *him* who was "most powerful to conjure the anger of the gods."[4] And it is curious to remark how free from all struggle and fluctuation (such as have marked the beginning of modern

---

[1] Aristotle, *Polit.*, iii., 9.
[2] Hdtus., i. Pausan., vi. Strabo.
[3] We are speaking here only of the early ages of cities. After a certain period royalty ceased to be hereditary, as at Rome; this will be explained further on.
Sop., *Œdip. Rex.*, 34.

society), was the origin of those ancient peoples. After the fall of the Roman Empire, centuries were occupied in finding once more the rules of regular society. Many contradictory principles were disputing amongst themselves for the government of the nation, and the people more than once refused to submit to any social organization. But no such sorrowful sights are discoverable at the beginnings of either Grecian or Italian history. The revolutions and the conflicts which we have to study appear only at the end. With them society formed itself slowly and gradually, passing gently from the family into the tribe, and from the tribe into the city, without shock or struggle. Royalty came into being as a matter of course, first in the family, and afterwards in the city. No man's ambition was to blame for its origin, but it arose spontaneously from a want discerned by every eye. It remained in peace, both honoured and obeyed, for many generations, needing no material force to sustain its pretensions, and having neither army or finances, but being supported only by the sacred and inviolable authority of general belief.

We shall have to speak shortly of a revolution which overthrew royalty in every city. But when it fell it left no hatred in the heart of men, and the mixture of contempt and dislike, so often attaching to fallen greatness, was never felt for it. Fallen as it was, the respect and the affection of men continually followed its memory. We even find in Greece (and it is a circumstance not usual in history) that in those towns where the family royal was not extinct, not only was it not expelled, but the very men who had deprived it of power persisted in honouring it. At Ephesus, at Marseilles, at Cyrene, the royal families when deprived of power yet preserved the respect of the population, retaining even the titles and insignia of their rank.

It is probably an error to suppose that, when the republican form of government was established, the title of king was hated and despised. If so, would the Romans have applied it, as they did, to their gods? If usurpers never dared to assume the title, it was because of its sacred character, and not for any odium attaching to it.[1] Often as monarchy

---

[1] Strabo, iv., 171; xiv., 632; xiii., 608. Athenæus, xiii., 576. Livy, iii., 39. Sueton., *Julius Cæsar*, 186. Cicero, *Rep.*, i., 33.

was re-established in the cities of Greece, the new monarchs never supposed they had a right to call themselves kings, but contented themselves with the name of tyrants. And the difference between these two names is not in the more or less of moral qualities to be found in the prince; for men did not call a good sovereign a king, and a bad one a tyrant. The distinction was a religious one. The primitive kings had derived their authority from the sacred hearth, and fulfilled the functions of priests; whilst the tyrants of a later period were merely political chiefs owing their power to force or election.

CHAPTER XXIX.

THE MAGISTRATE.

THE confusion of political and sacerdotal functions lasted after the period of royalty; and the republican forms of government that were established did not separate one sort of authority from the other.

Whether the annual magistrate of the republic was still called a king, as at Megara, and Samothrace, or archon as at Thebes, or merely prytanis as elsewhere,[1] his office differed but little from a priesthood. The archon of Thebes, for instance, bore a chaplet[2] like a priest, might not let his hair grow, or carry any article of iron upon his person, obeying rules very much like those which distinguished the Roman flamens. In like manner, the archon of Plataeae was obliged to be dressed in the sacred colour of white[3] during the whole period of his magistracy; and the first duty of the Athenian archons was to sacrifice on the Acropolis to the city deities. It was also usual for them in the exercise of their office to wear a crown[4] of myrtle on their heads, and we must remark again that the crown, though now it has become a symbol of power, was then a mere emblem of religion naturally accompanying prayer and [5]sacrifice. Of the nine Athenian archons, the one named king attended specially to religious matters, but every one of his colleagues had some function to fulfil and some sacrifice to offer the gods.[6] Pindar tells us that

---

[1] Bœckh., 1845. Pindar, *Nem.*, xi.
[2] Plutarch, *Quest. Rom.*, 40.
[3] Plutarch, *Aristides*, 21.
[4] Demosth., *Midias*, 33. Æsch., *in Timarch.*, 19.
[5] Plutarch, *Nicias*, 3. Phoc., 37. Cicero, *in Verr.*, iv., 50.
[6] Pollux, viii., ch. ix. Lycurgus, Coll. Didot, ii., p. 362.

the magistrates, by the offerings they make at the altar, assure the safety of the city; and the common Greek expression for public officers, οἱ ἐν τέλει, those who are in sacrificing,[1] shews what was the idea originally entertained of these personages.

In addition to what we have said above of the inauguration of the consuls at Rome, it may be remarked that their first duty on entering office was to offer solemn sacrifice in the forum, the people preserving a religious silence, and a flute-player accompanying him with a sacred air.[2] A few days afterwards he had to go to Lavinium, whence the Roman penates originally came, and there offer a similar sacrifice.

Everything shews that the ancient magistrate had a sacred character unknown to modern times. He was the intermediary between gods and man, and the public fortune was attached to his lot. So we understand the extraordinary anxiety of the Romans on such occasions as that when Claudius Nero left his army to succour his colleague; for they thought that the army, without a consul and therefore without auspices, was practically without divine protection.

The other Roman magistracies, being, so to speak, successive emanations from the consulate, united in the same way political and priestly attributes. Thus the censor was seen, on certain days, to offer victims in the name of the city, the prætors and the curale ædiles presided at religious feasts; nor was there any magistrate but had some sacred act to perform, all authority being religious, in the opinion of the ancients. The tribunes of the people, whose power was of a very exceptional nature, as we shall explain by and bye, were the only ones who had no sacrifice to offer; and therefore they were not reckoned as true magistrates.

The priestly character of the magistrate was further shewn in the mode of his election. Mere voting was originally deemed quite insufficient to constitute one whose principal function it was to please the gods. And therefore when primitive royalty ceased to be, and hereditary succession went with it, no better way of choosing the head of a state presented itself to the Athenians and other Grecian peoples

---

[1] Thuc., i., 10; ii., 10; iii., 36; iv., 65. Cf. Hdtus., i., 133; iii., 18. Æsch., Per., 204; Agam., 1202. Eurip., Trach., 238.
[2] Cicero, De Leg., Agr., ii., 34. Livy, xxi., 63. Macrob., iii., 3.

than to draw lots. We must remember that with them the drawing of lots was not merely having recourse to chance, but, on the contrary, it appeared to be the best method of penetrating the thoughts of the gods. Lots were regularly used in the temples to discover the divine will in other matters. And therefore this way of election is not to be a matter of accusation against the Athenian democracy, as if they wished in this way to arrive at a sort of equality. It was, indeed, no invention of the democracy, but flourished most when the aristocracy[1] were in power. When the Athenian democracy got the upper hand, it left in being the election by lot for the office of archon, but abolished it for the strategi, who had the real power. Plato says in his "Laws," "We reckon that the man designed by lot is dear to the deity, and we think it fair that he should command. In whatever magistracy religion is concerned, we allow the gods to choose those who please them best, and therefore we have resort to drawing lots."[2]

A very similar principle prevailed at Rome for the election of consuls. A magistrate who was already in office (that is to say, some one who had the auspices, and who was invested with a sacred character) appointed a lawful day for the nomination; and himself on the night before kept watch out of doors on the sky, waiting for the signs that the gods might send as he mentally pronounced the names of the several candidates for the office.[3] On the morrow he presided at the meeting in the Campus Martius, and called aloud the names of the candidates for whom the auspices had been favourable, omitting[4] the names of those for whom the presage had been adverse. And the people could only vote for the names which the president had pronounced.[5]

This mode of election explains much which might otherwise surprise us in Roman history, as for instance, why the people sometimes could not succeed in making consuls of two men in favour of whom they were almost unanimous;

---

[1] Plutarch, *Peric.*, 9.
[2] Plato, *Laws*, iii., p. 690; vi., 759. Cf. Demosth., *in Aristog.*, 832. Dem. Phal., fr. 2.
[3] Val. Max., i., 1, 3. Plutarch, *Marcell.*, 5.
[4] Vell., ii., 92. Livy, xxxix., 39. Val. Max., iii., 8, 3.
[5] Dion. Halic., iv., 84; v. 19; v., 72; v., 77; vi. 49.

and why, again, very often two men are declared elected when we know that the people detested them.[1] In the first case the reason was that either the president had not taken the auspices about those two names, or that, having been taken they had turned out unfavourable. Whilst in the other case two names only had been pronounced to be voted for; and there was no possibility of doing any more than vote yes, or no, for the names stated. Even when the people expressed its anger at such a nomination, by going away without voting, there remained a quorum to effect the election.

The power of the president, therefore, is evident, and the strength of the expression, "creat consules," is less astonishing. For it was he revealed the will of the gods, whose creation the consuls were. All that the people had power to do was to ratify the election and make choice amongst three or four names, if so many had met with favourable auspices.

Doubtless this manner of proceeding was favourable enough to the Roman aristocracy, but it would be a mistake to discern nothing in it but a trick contrived on purpose; for such a stratagem would have been inconceivable in the ages when this religion was believed. It was politically useless in the early times, since the aristocracy then always had a majority, and it might have turned against them by giving a single individual excessive power. The only explanation to be given of this practice, or rather of this ceremony of election, is that everybody sincerely thought the choice of magistrates belonged to the gods and not to the people, and that the divine voice ought to pronounce upon the man who was going to rule the religion and dispose of the fortune of the city.

The first rule for electing magistrates was that given by Cicero, that he should be chosen according to the proper rites. Whence it came to pass that, if, some months afterwards, information was given to the Senate of some ceremony having been omitted or badly performed, then the Senate bade the consuls abdicate, and they dared not disobey. Of this occurrence there are numerous examples, and if in two or three cases we can believe the Senate was glad to dismiss

---

[1] Livy, ii., 42; ii., 43.

an ill-disposed or inefficient consul, more frequently we cannot attribute to it any motive but a religious scruple.

The further examination into the merit of the newly-elected magistrate, whether consul or archon, shews very clearly what sort of officer he was considered to be. The Athenian Senate demanded of the newly-elected archon whether he had any bodily defect, whether he had a domestic deity, whether his family had always been faithful to its worship, and whether he himself had always fulfilled his duty towards the dead.[1] The reason of such questions is not difficult to find. A bodily defect would have proved the ill-will of the gods, and therefore a man's unfitness for priesthood and political office; a man who had no domestic worship could have no part in the national worship, nor sacrifice on behalf of the city; whilst if a family had not always adhered to its worship, then some of those acts had been committed which defile a sacred fire and make descendants hated of the gods; or if he himself had neglected the tomb of his forefathers, he was obnoxious to their anger, and pursued by unseen foes. Rash would have been the city that entrusted its fortunes to such a man.

It seems that the city asked no other questions, nor troubled itself about the magistrate's character or intelligence. The main thing was to see if he could fulfil his priestly duties, and that the city worship should not be compromised in his hands.

At Rome, a similar sort of examination was practised; its details are unknown to us, but its general character is evident from the fact that it was the pontiffs who conducted it.[2]

---

[1] Plato, *Laws*, vi. Xenophon, *Memor.*, ii. Pollux, viii., 85, 86, 95.
[2] Dion. Halic., ii., 73.

CHAPTER XXX.

THE LAW.

THE earliest laws of Italy and Greece, as well as of India, were mixed up with religion, and their books present at the same time a mass of prayers, directions for service, and legal enactments.

Laws about property and inheritance were scattered about in the midst of rules for burying the dead and offering sacrifice. The few remains of Roman law under the kings are as often relative to worship as to the affairs of civil life. One of these laws forbids a guilty woman to approach the altar; another forbids certain meats to be served in sacred repasts; a third lays down the religious ceremony to be celebrated by a victorious general on the occasion of his return. The code of the Twelve Tables, although more recent, still contained minute regulations about burial. Solon's law was three things at once, a code of laws, a constitution, and a book of ceremonial. The order of sacrifices and the price of victims was there laid down, as well as the rites of marriage and the way of worshipping the dead. The laws which Cicero recommends in his Treatise are rather repetitions of ancient laws in real existence than anything imaginary. The following are his first suggestions: "Let not man approach the gods but with pure hands;—Let the temples be kept up and the abodes of the Lares;—Let the priests make use of no meat at the sacred feasts but what is prescribed;—Let the Manes receive their due worship." It was not that the philosopher cared much for the old religion of the Lares and Manes, but, as he was tracing out a system like the old one, he felt obliged to put in laws about worship.

At Rome, a good pontiff must be a good lawyer, and vice versâ, for religion was so mixed up with common life that in many things the pontiffs were the sole judges. For instance, every dispute about marriage, divorce, and the civil and religious rights of children were brought before their tribunal. They judged incest as well as celibacy. Adoption too, being concerned with religion, could only be effected with the assent of the pontiff. Again, to make a will was to break through the order of succession established by religion, and therefore in early times a testament had to be authorized by the pontiff. Again, since the bounds between every two properties were marked out by religion, two neighbours at law must plead before the pontiff or the *fratres arvales*.

These facts explain why the same men were pontiffs and lawyers. In fact, law and religion were one thing.[1]

At Athens, the archon and the king had pretty much the same judicial functions to discharge as the pontiff of Rome.[2]

The genesis of ancient laws appears evident as we examine them, for they were the invention of no one man; but persons like Solon, Lycurgus, Minos, and Numa simply put in writing the existing laws of their cities. If legislator means a man who creates a code of laws by the power of his genius and imposes it upon other men, then such legislators did not exist amongst the ancients. No more did the votes of the people give rise to ancient laws, for the idea of legislation by voting does not appear to have been entertained until two great revolutions had transformed the character of ancient cities. Before then law presented itself to men's minds as something venerable and unchangeable. As old as the city, it had been delivered by the founder himself when he laid the walls of the city and kindled its sacred fire. It was instituted when the religion was instituted—not imagined by the founder himself—but brought into being spontaneously, in accordance with a belief that had entered into man's heart in pre-historic times. If we confront it with natural justice the two are found to be in contradiction but

---

[1] Cicero, *De Leg.*, ii., 9; ii., 19; *De Arusp. Resp.*, 7. Dion., ii., 73. Tacit., *Ann.*, i., 10; *Hist.*, i., 15. Dion. Cassius, xlviii., 44. Plin., *H. N.*, xviii., 2. Aulus-Gellius, v., 19; xv., 27.
[2] Pollux, viii., 90.

too often; that law was never sought for in the notion of absolute right or the sentiment of equity. But put it beside the worship of the dead and of the sacred fire, and compare it with the rules of this primitive religion, and the two will be found to be in perfect agreement.

For the invention of ancient jurisprudence man had not to consult his conscience and say, "Such and such a provision would be fair and right, and such another would be unjust." But man remembered that the care of the sacred fire was handed down from father to son by virtue of a religious law, and therefore the house and chattels were handed down along with it. As the son who buried his father believed that the spirit of the dead man took possession for ever of the field wherein he lay, it resulted that this field of burial and of sacrifice became the inalienable property of one family. Again, as religion said that the son alone could keep up a worship, and never a daughter; so the law re-echoed the ordinance, saying, the son alone can inherit land and never the daughter, and the nephew by the males and never the nephew by women.

Such was the origin of ancient law. It was the direct and necessary consequence of belief. It was religion itself applied to men's relations between one another. And in this sense were true those various old traditions which said that the laws of men had been given them by the gods. For the Cretans attributed their laws not to Minos but to Jupiter; the Lacedæmonians believed that their legislator was not Lycurgus but Apollo. The Etruscans had received their laws from the god Tages, and the Romans said that Numa had written down their own from the dictation of the goddess Egeria. There was this amount of truth in all those stories, that religious belief and not man's reason had originated them.

Even when it came to be admitted in after times that the will of man and the suffrages of a people could constitute a law, still religion was to be consulted and made a consenting party. The pontiffs had to approve the decision of the people, and the augurs must attest that the gods were favourable to the change proposed.[1] When one of the tribunes of

---

[1] Dion. Halic., xi., 41; ix., 49.

the plebs wished to have a law adopted by an assembly of the local tribes, a patrician demanded what right they had to make new laws or upset old ones, when they had no auspices, no power of accomplishing religious acts, nothing in fact belonging to them that was at all in common with religion, or with such a sacred thing as law.[1]

Laws, therefore, were long regarded as something holy and venerable, and it was no mere phrase when Plato said that to obey the laws was to obey the gods. Socrates giving up his life to obey the law was but the expression in act of the common Greek thought; and before the time of Socrates it had been written in no different spirit on the rock of Thermopylæ, "Traveller, go say at Sparta that we died here, to obey her laws." Law, therefore, was always sacred to the ancient mind; she was the queen of kings, when there were kings to reign, and in the days of republics she was the queen of peoples, whom to disobey was sacrilege.

Old laws, therefore, were never abrogated, even when new ones had been passed that contradicted them. Obsolete as they might be, they continued to exist alongside the other, and the stone on which they had been graven was considered inviolable, or, by the least scrupulous, only turned with its face the other way. So the code of Draco was not abolished by that of Solon,[2] nor the laws of the Roman kings by those of the Twelve Tables. Hence the great confusion to be noticed in ancient jurisprudence, laws of very different periods being found in juxtaposition, and all treated with respect. In a speech of Isæus, we are presented with two men disputing an inheritance, and each quoting a law in his own favour; but the two laws, though equally sacred, are absolutely contrary. And in the same way, the code of Manou, as we noticed before, whilst it retains the old law of primogeniture, writes down alongside of it a new law, which prescribes equal partition amongst brothers.

Ancient laws had no preamble and alleged no reasons, because their divine origin was their authority, and men must obey them on the principle of faith. Also, for many generations they were never committed to writing, but transmitted

---

[1] Dion., x., 4. Livy, iii., 31.
[2] Andocides, i., 82, 83. Demosth., *in Everg.*, 71.

from father to son, with the formulas of religion. And when they were committed to writing, they were consigned to the sacred books along with the same formulas. Thus, Varro quotes a law of Tusculum[1] which he had read in the sacred books of that city; and it appears from Dionysius of Halicarnassus, who had consulted the original documents, that before the time of the Decemvirs all the written laws of Rome were to be found in the [2]priests' books. Afterwards law was separated from ritual, but even then it was commonly laid up in a temple under the care of priests.

Whether written or not, these laws were always enunciated in the briefest sentences, like the slocas of the Book of Manou, or the verses of Leviticus. And it is most likely that the words were in rhythm,[3] for Aristotle says that before the times of writing laws were sung;[4] and they are called in Latin songs, *carmina*, and in Greek measures, νόμοι. Doubtless the rhythm helped to keep them unchanged, which was considered a great point; and the ancients were great slaves to the letter of the law, not troubling themselves so much about the spirit of it, but supposing its force lay in its correctness, as in a charm. Thus certain words must be made use of in all transactions, else they would not be binding. The lender of money must say to the borrower, "*dari spondes?*" "Dost thou pledge thyself that it has been given?" and the other must answer "*spondeo*," "I do," otherwise there could be no recovery of the debt. For conscience and justice were not so binding upon men as the sacred formulas; and without a formula there was no right. Gaius relates a story of a man whose neighbour had destroyed his vines, and against whom, after proving the fact, he proceeded, as he thought, according to law. But the legal form used the word trees, whereas he repeated vines; and so he lost his suit.

Moreover, every contract or law-suit being a sort of religious ceremony, the enunciation of the legal form must be accompanied by an outward and visible sign, as, for instance, in buying, the object bought must be touched with the hand, *mancipatio*, and if a property was disputed, there

---

[1] Varro, *Lingua Lat.*, vi., 16.
[2] Dion., x., 1.
[3] Plutarch, *Solon*, 25.
[4] Aristotle, *Prob.*, xix., 28.

must be *mannum consertio*, a fictitious combat, and, in fact, there was a whole pantomime of procedure.

Again, on account of their connexion with religion, the formulas of the law were kept secret from the stranger and the plebeian. It was not that the patricians thought they derived any great advantage by the exclusive possession of the law, but the law by its origin and nature seemed to be a mystery that no one could share in who had not first been initiated into the domestic or national worship.

It is further to be remarked that when the ancients made use of such expressions as *jus civile*, νόμοι πολιτικοί, they not only meant that each city had its own laws, as now-a-days each state has, but also that these laws were only binding between citizen and citizen. In order to profit by the laws of a city, it was not enough to reside there; a man must be a member of it, that is to say, a citizen initiated into its worship, and capable of offering sacrifices to its gods. A sojourner in the city or a stranger could not own land, nor inherit, nor make a will, nor effect any contract, nor make appearance in the ordinary law-courts, and all because there was no religious bond between him and the citizens.

CHAPTER XXXI.

THE CITIZEN AND THE STRANGER.

IF an exact definition of a citizen be required, we should say he is one[1] who shares the city religion, and therefore also all political and civil rights. And the stranger is one who has not access to the worship, who is not protected by the gods and has not the right to invoke them, to whom the entry of the temples is forbidden, and whose presence during sacrifice is a sacrilege. If a citizen renounced the city worship, he lost all political rights; for instance; at Sparta even unintentional absence from the public repast[2] deprived a man of citizenship, and at Athens[3] non-participation in the feast of the national gods entailed the same consequences. At Rome,[4] political rights would be taken away from the man who had not been present at the general purification, until the next lustre coming round enabled him to repair his neglect.

The dislike of the gods for all but citizens was manifested by the custom of the pontiff's wearing a veil, when he sacrificed out of doors, the reason being that the sight of strangers[5] would disturb the auspices. So any sacred object that had been handled by a stranger needed an expiatory

---

[1] Aristotle, *Pol.*, ii., 6, 21 (ii., 7).
[2] Bœckh., 3641, b.
[3] Velleius, ii., 15. Except soldiers in war, whose names were sen home.
[4] Demosth., *Nœr.*, 113, 114. συντιλεῖν—to join in sacrifice—to be a citizen—μιτεῖναι ἱερῶν καὶ ὁσίων.
[5] Virgil, *Æn.*, iii., 406. Festus, Verbo *Exesto*: Lictor in quibusdam sacris clamitabat, hostis exesto. Macrob., i, 17: hostis meant stranger, ὅστις; and in Virgil, *hostilis facies* means a strange face.

ceremony to remove the profanation; and after a city had been recovered from an enemy, the temples must be re-purified and every sacred fire extinguished and lit again, in order to efface the desecration wrought by the enemies' presence.

There seems to have been the greatest difficulty about granting the right of citizenship to strangers. Down to the time of Herodotus, Sparta had but accorded it to one person, a soothsayer, on whose behalf the honour had been demanded by an oracle from Delphi. By Athens the favour was granted more than once, but only after precautions which to our ideas seem excessive. Two assemblies of the whole people, with an interval of nine days between each were required, and no less than six thousand favourable votes must be recorded at each. Further, a vote of the Senate was required to confirm these two decisions; and then after all the decree was not safe from the opposition of any citizen who might choose to accuse it of being in contradiction with the old law. War might be declared or an entirely new law passed with far less difficulty than was found in thus conferring citizenship upon a stranger. The reason of this exclusiveness was not that the people were afraid of giving more votes to a party, but rather (as we gather from Demosthenes) that the sacrifices must be kept pure.[1] The exclusion of strangers seemed to be merely the exercise of proper vigilance over the sacred ceremonies. For it was admitting the stranger to participation in the city's religion, when the gods were known to be very jealous of the presence of any foreigner. Hence the fewness of the instances in which it had been granted, and the denial, even after admission to citizenship, of eligibility to the offices of archon or priest. And yet, generally speaking, a share in the worship conveyed all other rights, since the citizen who could be present at the sacrifice with which the assembly commenced could vote also in the assembly, and he who could sacrifice in the name of the city might be prytanis or archon. But it was death for a stranger to enter the sacred space marked out by the priest for the assembly; and a member of any other city was counted a stranger, seeing he could not belong

---

[1] Demosth., *Neara*, 89, 91, 92, 113, 114.

to two city religions at once, any more than he could to two family religions.[1]

For a long time the stranger had no recognized position in law, and if he had done wrong might be punished, like a slave, without any legal process; and when at length the need of justice for strangers was felt, an exceptional tribunal was established. At Rome, in order to become a judge of strangers, the prætor was obliged to make himself a stranger also (prætor peregrinus). At Athens, the polemarch, or magistrate charged with matters of war and all relations with the enemy, was the one who administered justice to the stranger.[2]

Neither at Athens nor Rome could a stranger own[3] land. If they married, the validity of the ceremony was not recognized, and the children counted as bastards;[4] nor was any contract[5] that they might make with the citizens binding. The right of trading[6] was originally forbidden, and the Roman law would allow no foreigner to inherit[7] from a citizen, and vice versâ. Indeed, the principle was pushed so far that if a stranger had obtained the right of citizenship, and his son, who had been born previously, did not obtain it at the same time, then the son became a foreigner to his father and could not inherit from him.[8] So that the distinction between citizen and stranger was stronger than the tie between father and son.

And although it may seem, at first sight, that a vexatious system had been purposely established against foreigners, yet really this was by no means the case, since both Athens and Rome welcomed and protected them for commercial and political reasons. But neither their benevolence nor their interest could abolish the old laws which religion had established. Religion did not allow the stranger to own land,

---

[1] Plutarch, *Solon*, 24. Cicero, *Pro Cæcinâ*, 34. Aristotle, *Pol.*, iii., 43. Plato, *Laws*, vi.
[2] Demosth., *Neær.*, 49. Lysias, *in Pancle*.
[3] Gaius, Fr. 234.
[4] Gaius, i., 67. Ulpian, v., 4; v., 9. Paul., ii., 9. Aristoph., *Birds*, 1652.
[5] Ulpian, xix., 4. Demosth., *Phorm*.
[6] Demosth., *Eubul*.
[7] Cicero, *Arch.*, 5. Gaius, ii., 110.
[8] Pausanias, viii., 43.

because the soil was sacred to the city's worship. It did not permit the stranger to inherit from a citizen nor a citizen from a stranger, because all transmission of goods entailed the transmission of worship also, and a citizen could not undertake the sacrifices of a stranger, nor a stranger those of a citizen.

Therefore a stranger might be welcomed, watched over, esteemed, but not admitted to a share of the religion and the laws. In some respects the slave was better treated, for the slave was linked to the city by means of his master, and under the protection of the gods. Whence, according to Roman religion, the slave's tomb was sacred, but not the stranger's.[1]

In fact, for a stranger to reckon for anything in the eye of the law, or to be able to trade, or to make contracts of any sort, or to enjoy his goods in peace under the protection of the law, it was necessary for him to make himself the client of some citizen and adopt a patron,[2] through whose instrumentality only he could obtain some share of civil rights and enjoy security.

---

[1] *Digest.*, lib. xi., tit. 7, 2 ; lib., xlvii., tit. 12, 4. Harpocration, προστάτης.

CHAPTER XXXII.

PATRIOTISM AND EXILE.

IT is probable that *patria* originally signified strictly the soil wherein a man's forefathers were buried, the little enclosure about the family tomb. But afterwards it was extended to mean the city with its prytaneum and its heroes, and the circuit of territory marked out by religion. State, city, and country was not then an abstraction as with us, but a visible local habitation of the gods where they were daily worshipped in all sincerity. Whatever was dearest to man was summed up in the word patria. There were his goods, his safety, his rights, his faith, and his gods. Away from the sacred walls of his native city and the land-marks of its fields, he could find neither the comforts of religion, nor any social bond. Out of his country he was out of all legality and all moral life, and within its bounds only were to be discovered a man's work, and duty, and dignity. And therefore an ancient took his country to heart, as a true husband takes his wife, for better for worse, loving her even when she turned against him, like Socrates in prison cheerfully preparing to die at her command. For above all an ancient was ready to give up his life at any moment and after any fashion for his country. Greeks and Romans did not die, as men have done since, for scruples of honour or out of devotion to any chief, but it was *pro aris et focis*, for the gods of their family and city. And so patriotism was not any mere *esprit de corps*, or attachment to a particular spot and regard for old associations (though all these feelings and interest besides were bound up in it), but it was the supreme virtue in which all other virtues were summed up, it was the piety of the ancients.

If a man's country had not been so dear to him, they would not have thought it the most severe of all punishments to deprive him of it; and yet exile was the commonest punishment of all great crimes.

Properly speaking, exile was the interdiction of the city's worship. According to a formula used both by Greeks and Romans, it was the prohibition of the use of fire and water;[1] the fire thus forbidden being the sacred fire of the hearth, and the water the holy water of religious ceremonies. "Let him be a fugitive," was his sentence, "nor ever approach the temples. Let no citizen receive or welcome him. Prayers and sacrifices be forbidden him, and let no one present him with holy water."[2] His presence defiled houses and persons, and those who had touched him or eaten with him were obliged to purify themselves. And it must be remembered that practically for men in those times God was not everywhere. If they had a vague idea of the deity of the universe, yet that was not the Providence they invoked. Each man's gods were really those of his house, his district, or his city; therefore when the exile left his country behind him, he left all that could console and protect him; he was literally without god in the world. When the right of worshipping in the city was taken away from him, his family worship also was denied him, and his sacred fire extinguished. As though he were dead, his land and chattels passed to his children, unless confiscated to the state. He ceased to be husband and father.[3] His sons were set free from his authority, and his wife might wed afresh. When Regulus was prisoner to the Carthaginians, by Roman law he was in a position equivalent to that of exile. Therefore he refused his advice to the Senate, because an exile is no more a Senator. The endearments of his family could not be accepted by one for whom wife and children have ceased to be—

---

[1] Hdtus., vii., 231. Cretinus, in Athenæus, xi., 3. Cicero, *Pro Domo*, 20. Livy, xxv., 4. Ulpian, x., 3.

[2] Soph., *Œdip. Rex*, 239. Plato, *Laws*, ix., 881. See Ovid, *Trist.*, i., 3, 43. Pindar., *Pyth.*, iv., 517. Plato, *Laws*, ix., 877. Diod., xiii., 49. Livy, iii., 58.

[3] See *Institutes*, i., 12. Gaius, i., 128. Dion., viii., 41. Horace, *Odes*, iii. Thuc., i., 138.

> Fertur pudicæ conjugis osculum
> Parvosque natos, ut capitis minor,
> A se removisse.

"For," as Xenophon says, "the exile loses fire, liberty, country, wife, children;" and, when dead, he cannot be buried in the tomb of his family.

We are not surprised, then, to find that ancient republics almost always allowed their guilty statesmen to escape death by exile, for exile was a capital punishment, and did not seem any milder than death.

CHAPTER XXXIII.

MUNICIPAL FEELING.

WHAT has been already said of ancient institutions, and more especially of their exclusiveness, will convey beforehand some idea of the profound gulf which always separated two ancient cities. The moral distance was infinitely greater than the physical, seeing they had separate gods, and worships which were mutually repulsive. For though afterwards modified in some degree, yet these beliefs had been in full vigour when the societies were formed, and the cities always retained the old impression.

Two circumstances are easily perceived, 1st, that each city had been constituted by its religion in a surprisingly strong and enduring manner, and, 2ndly, that no other form of society but the city was possible for many ages.

For, by the exigence of religion itself, absolute independence was requisite for each city. Each had its particular code of laws, its sovereign justice, its religious feasts and its calendar, to say nothing of particular coinage and separate weights and measures. The line of demarcation was so profound that all legislation was against intermarriage between citizens of different towns, and the children were counted as illegitimate, when such unions did occur, unless a special convention, *jus connubii*, ἐπιγαμία, had been entered into between the cities.

The most salient characteristic of Greek and Italian history, previous to the Roman conquest, is the minute partition of the land and the utter isolation of each city. Neither the Latin nor Etruscan towns, nor the tribes of Samnium ever succeeded in forming a compact body; and the same incurable division prevailed no less in Greece. Some have attributed this to the nature of the country and the many chains of mountains which seemed to establish natural lines of demarcation; but there were no mountains between Thebes and Plataeæ, or between Argos and Sparta, or Sybaris and Crotona; nor yet between the different cities of Latium or those of Etruria. Physical nature no doubt has some influence on the history of nations, but man's belief is much more powerful. The line of land-marks between the territories of two neighbouring states was more impassable than a range of mountains; and the exclusiveness of the several gods prevented the establishment of any organization larger than that of the city. For ages it did not enter into any one's head that two cities could live under a common government; for, whatever momentary alliance might be entered into, the union was never complete. And, indeed, as long as the beliefs and practices which we have considered, prevailed, it is hard to see how several cities could possibly form one single state; because no human association appeared intelligible or regular, unless it was founded upon religion and symbolized by a sacred repast eaten in common. And, though some thousands even of citizens might at the utmost gather round the same prytaneum, recite the same prayer and partake of the same food, yet how could it be possible with such practices to make one state out of all Greece? Where should they plant the prytaneum? or how assemble all the worshippers? What possibility was there of accomplishing the annual purification of every member? What would become of the land-marks already planted to separate distinct territories? and what of the heroes devoted to each district? For instance, Athens possesses the remains of Œdipus, the sworn foe of Thebes: how could Thebes and Athens join in the same worship and under one government? And then, again, before these superstitions began to fade and disappear, the lines of division had been cut too deep to be effaced, and the separation was fixed for ever by habit, by interest, by inveterate hatred, and the recollection of old struggles. The time had gone by when any state would be willing to sacrifice its autonomy, *i.e.*, its independent religion and policy; and each city thought it easier to subdue a neighbour than to unite with it; for the inhabitants of a conquered city might be turned into slaves, though they could not be accepted as fellow-citizens. There is but one late and tardy exception to the rule that in ancient times two cities never united into one state, nor the conquerors with the conquered, and of this we must speak by and bye; but when, for instance, Sparta conquered Messenia, it was not to make of the Spartans and Messenians a single people, but to drive away all the vanquished and to take their land. Athens did the same with respect to Salamis, Ægina, and Melos. She could not conceive of admitting the Æginetan to the same privileges as her citizens enjoyed. Would her old heroes Theseus and Cecrops accept the offerings or endure the presence of such foreigners at their altar? No; religion forbade that those who had a different religion should have the same magistrates and the same laws.

And here a suggestion occurs to the mind. Could not Athens at least have left a conquered city erect and sent a magistrate to govern in her name? Unfortunately, it was absolutely contrary to the principles of the ancients for a city to be governed by a man who was not a citizen, for in fact the magistrate's most important function was to sacrifice in the name of the city, and therefore a stranger who could not sacrifice could not be a magistrate. Sparta tried to establish harmosts in her conquered towns, but these men were not magistrates, did not administer justice, nor appear in the assemblies; and because they had no regular relation with the people of the cities, they were unable to maintain themselves there for any length of time. The unhappy result was that no conqueror had any alternative but either to destroy the city he had vanquished and take possession of its territory, or to leave it in all its independence. A city must be a sovereign state, or cease to exist. Its government grew out of the worship of its gods, and the worship once destroyed, the government perishes with it.

Cities could not help requiring absolute independence so long as the belief which had founded them continued to subsist. After religious opinion was altered, and several revolutions had passed over society, they needed no longer such rigorous separation, and the idea began to be conceived of establishing a larger State, ruled on other principles. But time was required to find these out, and society needed to be bound together with ties unknown to former periods.

NOTE ON AMPHICTYONIES.

The numerous amphictyonies or confederations of cities throughout Greece and Italy were as much religious as political associations. Every one of them had its common worship and sanctuary. That of the Bœotians served Athene Itonia, that of the Achæans Demeter Panachæa, that of the Ionians in Asia Poseidon Heliconius, whilst the Dorian Pontapolis adored Apollo Triopicus. The confederation of the Cyclades had a common sacrifice in the island of Delos, and the towns of Argolis had theirs at Calauria. The Amphictyony of Thermopylæ was an association of similar character. All their meetings took place in temples and were for the sake of offering sacrifice; certain citizens, called theori, and invested for the occasion with a priestly character, were sent to take part in these meetings. A victim, slain in honour of the god of the association, was cooked upon the altar, and shared among the representatives of the cities. This common meal with the songs or hymns, the prayers and games which accompanied it, constituted the bond of the confederation. Similar practices prevailed in Italy; for instance, the cities of Latium, at the feriæ Latinæ, partook of the flesh of a victim. The Etruscan cities did in like manner.

In these associations the rights of the separate cities were so very strong as to prevent their ever constituting a single state.

CHAPTER XXXIV.

RELATIONS BETWEEN DIFFERENT CITIES.

THE same authority, which religion exercised within each city, was also extended to all relations between separate states, as is very evident when we examine the way in which men in those times made war, concluded peace, and formed alliances.

A city being an association of gods and men within the same walls, when it made war against another similar association, the gods took part in the conflict as well as the men. Nor ought it to be supposed because we have descriptions in Homer and Virgil of such divine participations in human affairs, that this was merely a poetical invention. Every little army when it went to war had its accompanying statues, its altar, and its sacred emblems; and every warrior's mind was occupied with oracles, and the sayings of diviners and augurs. Every army pronounced an imprecation, like that which we find in Macrobius, on the hostile forces. "Ye gods, scatter terror and woe upon our enemies; let the inhabitants of their streets and fields be deprived by you of the light of the sun. May their lives and their persons, their towns and their fields, be devoted to destruction." Both sides usually fought in a spirit as ferocious as this prayer, for when religion is the abetter rather than the assuager of strife the most sanguinary slaughter may be expected; and in those days too generally the wounded were dispatched and captives butchered.

Even apart from the field of battle we find but little notion of duty towards an enemy; for, indeed, if the foreigner generally was considered to be out of the pale of all law, much less could he expect consideration from those at war with him. Justice towards the foe did not differ from injustice, as the admiration commonly felt for Mutius Scævola attests, who sought to assassinate the enemy of his country. In like manner, the consul Marcius publicly boasted of having deceived the king of Macedonia; and Paulus Æmilius sold into slavery one hundred thousand Epirotes who had voluntarily given themselves up into his hands.

When the Lacedæmonian Phœbidas, in the midst of a time of peace had seized upon the Theban citadel, Agesilaus was asked his opinion about the justice of the deed, and replied that provided it was advantageous to the city, it was well to do it. And his views seem to have been in accordance with those of Cleomenes, another Spartan king, who thought that all the harm one could do to one's foes was fair before man and gods.

So nothing need prevent a conqueror from using his victory as he pleased, nothing need arrest his vengeance or avarice. When Athens was decreeing the extermination of every Mitylenæan without distinction of sex or age, she did not seem to herself to be exceeding her right; and when next day she reduced the slaughter to that of a thousand citizens, she believed herself indulgent and humane. After the taking of Platææ, the men were massacred, and the women sold, yet no one accused the conquerors of having overstepped their rights.

It was not only against soldiers that war was made, but against the whole population, men, women, children, and slaves. Trees were felled, and houses burnt, as well as the crops, which had been previously devoted to the infernal gods. Sometimes the seeds were ruined that ought to bear fruit next harvest. In fact, a war might sweep away a whole race of people, obliterate their name and make their country a desert.[1] Hence the solitude that sprung around ancient Rome, fifty-three cities of Latium having totally disappeared, and the Pomptine marshes extending over the territory of twenty-three Volscian towns; whilst in Samnium for many years the places through which the Roman armies had passed could only be known by the traces of their camps, and the solitude which reigned around.

---

[1] Livy, iii., 8; vi., 31; vii., 22; x., 15. Pliny, xxxv., 12.

In place of exterminating the vanquished, the conqueror might suppress their city, that is, break up their religious and political association. Then the worships ceased and the gods were forgotten. The sacred fires went out, symbolizing in their extinction the destruction of law and civil right, of family institutions and property, and of all that was founded on religion.[1] Let us listen one moment to the words of the conquered man whose life has been spared, and who is made to pronounce the following words: "I give to the Roman people my person, my city, my land, my running water, my land-marks, my temples, my chattels, and all that belongs to the gods."[2] What the result of this was we shall shortly explain in speaking of the Roman empire.

When a war did not end by the extermination or subjection of one of two parties, a treaty of peace might be concluded. For this an agreement by word of mouth was insufficient, the addition of a religious act in the way of sacrifice being always required. Signing a treaty is quite a modern expression; the Latins said *icere fœdus* or *hædus*, *i.e.*, to strike a kid, where the name of the victim most commonly slain remains as a designation of the whole act; and the Greek expressed themselves in a similar manner, speaking of making a libation, σπένδεσθαι, instead of signing a treaty.

Without this sacred ceremony, which must be performed by priests (fetiales or σπενδοφόροι) and according to certain fixed forms, no treaty was binding. The history of the Caudine Forks is a case in point. There a whole Roman army by the instrumentality of its consuls, quæstors, tribunes, and centurions had made an agreement with the Samnites. But as no victim had been slain the Senate denied that the agreement had any value; nor did any pontiff or patrician suppose they were committing an act of bad faith.

No man was supposed by the ancients to have any obligation to another god than his own. So a Greek who worshipped the hero Alabandos said to another Greek who adored Hercules,[4] "Alabandos is a god, and Hercules is not a god." Therefore, in a treaty each party must be made to

---

[1] Cicero, *in Verr.*, ii., 3, 6. Sic. Flacc., passim. Thuc., iii., 50 et 68.
[2] Livy, i., 38. Plaut., *Amphit.*, 100—5.
[3] See Festus, V°· fœdum et fædus.
[4] Cicero, *De Nat. Deor.*, iii., 19.

swear by its own deities, as the Platæans say to the Spartans in Thucydides, "We and you have made a treaty, you calling to witness the gods of your fathers, and we the gods that occupy our land."[1] Sometimes they might find deities common to both cities to invoke, or they might swear by those gods whom all could see, the sun who enlightens all, and earth, who is the universal mother; but the protecting gods and demi-gods of each came much nearer home to men's hearts, and these must be attested, if religion was really to bind them.

It was considered necessary in a treaty to bind the gods also, for they were believed to have been engaged as well as men in the previous conflicts; and in order to prove that the gods were allied, sometimes two people would be allowed to appear at each other's festivals; or, they opened their temples to one another and effected an exchange of sacred rites.[2] Rome once stipulated that the god of Lanuvium[3] should henceforth protect the Romans, who might enter his temple and pray there. Often, also, one of the two contracting parties engaged to worship the other's deities. So the 'Eleans by treaty with the Ætolians used to offer victims to the heroes of the latter. And medals are found of divinities holding one another by the hand, as the Milesian Apollo and the Genius of Smyrna, the Pallas of the Sideans and the Artemis of Perga, the Apollo of Hierapolis and the Artemis of Ephesus. Virgil, in speaking of an alliance between Thrace and Troy, says that their Penates were allied.

If there was reason to suppose that the deities of two cities had any motive for being friends, that was enough to bind the peoples also. The first city with which Rome contracted friendship was Cære in Etruria, because in the Gaulish invasion the Roman gods had found refuge at Cære, and had received worship there; whence a sacred bond of hospitality was formed between the Roman gods and the Etruscan city; and henceforth religion forbade enmity between the two peoples.

---

[1] Thuc., ii; v., 18.
[2] Thuc., v., 23. Plutarch, *Thes.*, 25, 33.
[3] Livy, viii., 14.
[4] Pausan., v., 15.
[5] Livy, v., 50. Aulus Gellius, xvi., 13.

CHAPTER XXXV.

THE ROMAN; THE ATHENIAN.

THE religion which had founded society and governed it so long also formed the character of man, and by its doctrines and practices gave the Greeks and Romans a certain way of thinking and acting, from which they were long in freeing themselves. The great love of God being yet unknown to them, they were mostly devoid of all religious comfort, and in continual terror at the irritable malevolence of their own idols. Livy's extracts from the priestly annals shew that the Romans were in such constant fear of offending the gods that there was no cessation to their acts of expiation.

But let us consider the place that religion occupied in the private life of a Roman. His house was to him what a church is to us; for there was his worship and his gods. Not only his fire is a god and the land-marks round his field; but the walls, the doors, and the threshold are the same.[1] The tomb is an altar, and his ancestors are divine beings.

Every one of his daily actions is a rite; and all the day long he is engaged upon religion. At morning and evening he invokes the sacred fire and the shades of his ancestors; when he goes out of the house and when he comes in, he addresses a prayer to them. Every meal, being shared with the domestic deities, is a sacred act. Outside his door he can scarcely take a step without meeting some sacred object, a temple, a shrine, a spot smitten with thunder, or a tomb. Sometimes he must retire within himself and utter a prayer; sometimes he must turn away his eyes, and cover his face to avoid seeing an object of evil augury. He must go back if he sees certain birds, if a serpent crosses his path. Not only

---

S. Augustin, *Civ. Dei.*, vi., 7. Tertullian, *Ad. Nat.*, ii., 15.

do the great events of his life constitute solemn acts of worship, as birth, initiation, assumption of the toga, and marriage, with their several anniversaries, but he must sacrifice daily in his house, monthly in his curia, several times in the year in his gens or tribe. And besides all these gods, he still owes adoration to those of the city, and it was said that at Rome there were more gods than citizens.

Many sacrifices were offered by way of thanksgiving, but more to appease the anger of the gods. One day the citizen has to take part in a procession, dancing to the sound of the sacred flute; another day he drives the cars that bear the recumbent statues of the deities. On another occasion it is a *lectisternium* he must attend; when a table is laid in the streets, and the statues of the gods are placed around on couches, whilst every Roman bows as he passes by, having a garland on his head, with a laurel-branch[1] in his hand. There are, besides, feasts for sowing, for reaping, for pruning. Before the corn is in the ear no less than ten sacrifices must be made, and as many as ten separate deities invoked for the success of the harvest.

At every moment he consults the gods to know their will, and can only act after inspection of entrails, or observation of birds flying, or the sound of thunder. He is in constant terror of bad omens, and there are words that he must never pronounce in his life. He hears that it has rained blood, and that an ox has spoken, and he trembles for fear. He only goes out of his house right foot first, and will not have his hair cut unless the moon is at the full. His walls are covered with charms against fire, and he knows forms of words which keep off sickness, and others to cure diseases; only one must repeat these twenty-seven times and spit in a certain way each time.[2]

He will not deliberate in the Senate if the victims have not presented favourable signs, and he will quit that assembly at the cry of a mouse. His best-arranged plans must be renounced at a bad omen or the sound of an unlucky word. In battle he is brave enough, but only on condition that the auspices promise him the victory.

---

[1] Livy, xxxiv., 55; xl., 37.
[2] Cato, *De re Rust.*, 160. Varro, *De re Rust.*, i., 2; i., 37. Plin., *Nat. His.*, xvii., 28; xxvii., 12; xxviii., 2.

Nor is this a picture of the ignorant and low-born Roman, whose weak intellect is rendered more superstitious by ignorance and misery. We are speaking of the rich and powerful patrician. He is by turns warrior, magistrate, agriculturer, merchant; but more than all he is priest, and occupied with sacred things; for, however strong in his soul may be the sentiments of patriotism, ambition, and avarice, yet the fear of the gods surpasses all; and it would be impossible better to sum up the Roman's opinion of his own concern with religion than in those words of Horace:

> Dis te minorem quod geris, imperas.

It has been said that this religion was the mere invention of policy; and we are asked to believe that a body of three thousand patricians with a senate of three hundred was unanimously agreed for several centuries to deceive the people! nay, that amidst all the struggles of rivalry and personal hatred not one single voice was ever raised to say this is a lie. Surely some ambitious patrician, seeing how impatiently the plebeians endured the yoke of this religion, by cleverly revealing the deception of these auspices and priestly functions, could have acquired sufficient credit to make himself master of the state. If all the patricians were unbelievers, the temptation would have been strong enough to induce one of them at least to let out the secret. And is it not an error to suppose that human nature is capable of thus establishing a religion by convention and maintaining it by imposture? Let it only be counted how many times in Livy this religion was the greatest embarassment to the patricians themselves, and how often the Senate was shackled by it in its action, and then let it be asserted if possible that this religion was invented for state reasons by politicians. It was only quite late in Roman history, in the days of the great Scipios, that religion began to be thought useful for the purpose of governing, but then religion was dead in the belief of all.

Let us take as an example a Roman of the better times, a warrior who was five times dictator and who conquered in more than ten battles, the great Camillus. And to give a true description of him he must be represented as being as much of a priest as of a warrior. He belongs to the Furian gens, and bears a surname which points to a priestly function. As a child he is made to wear the purple stripe which marks his caste, and the golden bulla which averts bad luck. During the time of his boyhood he has daily been present at the services of his religion; and he has passed his youth in learning its rites. It is true that on the outbreak of war the young priest has turned soldier; and has been observed in a cavalry fight to tear the weapon from his wounded thigh and continue the combat. After many campaigns he is raised to office, and as consular tribune has offered sacrifice, has judged, and commanded an army. At length the day arrives when he is thought of for the dictatorship. On the previous night the magistrate in office has watched the sky by starlight and whispered the name of Camillus. None but favourable signs having appeared, he is named dictator.

And now he is the head of the state; behold him leaving the city at the head of the army, charged with the duty of terminating the ten years' war against Veii. But he does not enter upon the campaign without having first consulted the auspices and immolated many victims, nor unaccompanied with priests, a pontiff, augurs, soothsayers, feeders of sacred chickens, slaughterers of victims, and a bearer of the sacred fire.

Veii being an Etruscan and therefore a sacred city, necessitates a struggle of piety as well as of courage. The duration of the siege is caused by the superior skill of the Etruscans in pronouncing charms and performing rites which please the gods. Rome on her side has had recourse to the Sibylline books, and has demanded of them what might be the divine will. It seems that some flaw had vitiated the celebration of the Latin festival, and that the sacrifice must be renewed. Nevertheless, the Etruscans have still the superiority; and only one resource remains, to lay hold of an Etruscan priest and discover from him the secret of the gods. A Veientine priest, having been taken and brought before the Senate, confesses that "Rome might be victorious, if the level of the Alban lake were lowered without letting the water fall into the sea." In consequence, a number of canals and ducts are dug, so that the water may be absorbed in the fields.

It was at this juncture that Camillus was made dictator.

He is certain of success, because all the oracles have been declared and all the orders of the gods obeyed; and moreover, when he left Rome he promised feasts and sacrifices to the gods; yet he neglects no human means of obtaining the victory. He increases the army, renews the discipline, and hollows out a subterranean way into the citadel. On the day appointed for the attack, Camillus quits his tent to offer sacrifice and examine the victims. The priests and augurs gather round. Clothed in his *paludamentum*, he invokes the gods: "Under thy guidance, O Apollo, and inspired with thy good will, I march to take and to destroy the city of Veii; to thee I promise and vow one tenth part of the booty." And as it is not enough to have some gods on his side whilst others are opposed to him, Camillus thus evokes the powerful deity who protects the Veientines: "Queen Juno, who now inhabitest Veii, I beseech thee to come with us conquerors; follow us to our city; let our city become thine." Then, when all the sacrifices have been accomplished, all the prayers said, and all the forms recited, when the Romans are sure that the gods are for them, and that none protect the foe, then the attack is made and the city taken.

Such a man was Camillus; and generally the Roman leaders were men who could make themselves obeyed and fight admirably, but who believed firmly in auguries, who daily performed religious acts, and who were convinced that the most important thing was neither courage nor discipline, but the correct enunciation of certain forms of words which charm the gods and win from them the victory. The highest possible reward for such a general is the Senate's permission to perform the triumphal sacrifice. Then he mounts the sacred car, drawn by four white horses; he is clothed with the sacred robes which the gods wear on festivals; upon his head is a crown, in his right hand a branch of laurel, and in his left a sceptre of ivory, in exact imitation of the statue of Jupiter. In such almost divine grandeur he is manifested to his fellow-citizens, and proceeds to render homage to the mightiest of Roman gods. He climbs the slope of the Capitol, and offers the victims before the temple of Jupiter.[1]

---

[1] Livy, x., 7; xxx., 15. Dion., v., 8. Appian., *Punic War*, 59. Juv., x., 43. Plin., xxxiii., 7.

The Greeks also, no less than the Romans, having been brought up in the lap of religion, long shewed very evident signs of their education. We have mentioned the scruples of the Spartans who would not enter upon an expedition except when the moon was at the full, and the number of victims that had to be slain before they would begin the battle of Plataeæ. The Athenians were no less timid about commencing an expedition before the seventh day of the month; and when the fleet was to be launched once more the statue of Pallas did not fail to appear in a fresh coat of gilt.

According to Xenophon,[1] there were more feasts at Athens than in any other city of Greece; and Aristophanes'[2] exclaims, "What victims! what statues! what processions! One is always seeing religious festivals and animals in garlands." The city of Athens itself, and its territory as well, were covered with temples and shrines, some for the city itself, some for the tribes, some for the demes, and some for families. Indeed, every house is a temple, and every field has a holy tomb.

Whatever may be said of the fickleness of the Athenians and their way of free-thinking, yet they had a singular respect for old traditions and old practices. When we see their devotion to the ancestral religion, and mark such laws as that forbidding a word to be uttered that might offend the heroes, St. Paul seems to have been very near the truth when he said that they were more than usually given to fearing the gods. It has been said that a priest who deviated from an old rite was punished with death; and some of these rites were singular enough. At the sacrifice in honour of Aradne,[3] who died in child-birth, they imitated the cries and throes of a woman in travail. The Oschopheria were a perfect pantomime of Theseus' return to Attica, and the costumes of the period were worn, the herald's wand being garlanded like that of the original herald, and a certain shout uttered like that to which he had given vent. On another day, no Athenian fails to boil some vegetables in a particular sort of pot, for what reason nobody knows, still the practice is devoutly repeated every year.

---

[1] *Gov. Ath.*, iii., 2.
[2] *Nubes.*
[3] Plutarch, *Thes.*, 20, 22, 23.

There were days at Athens, as at Rome, when justice was not administered,[1] when nobody could marry, or begin an undertaking, or attend the public assembly. The eighteenth and nineteenth[2] of every month were devoted to purifications. The most unlucky day of all was the day of the Plynteria, when the statue of Athene was veiled, whereas on the day of the Panathenœa the veil of the goddess was escorted in procession by all citizens, without distinction of age or rank.

Athens preserved a collection of old oracles, and boarded soothsayers[3] in the Prytaneum, whilst the streets were full of diviners, priests, and interpreters of dreams: for public belief in omens was strong, and a sacrifice would have to be recommenced if spoilt by a word of bad news; as also public assemblies would separate at an unfavourable sign in the sky. And in private life, before going on board ship the auspices must be taken, before being married the flight of birds observed, and any undertaking might be stopped by a fit of sneezing or a ringing in the ears.[4]

The word good-luck, or, as we may say, the name of the goddess Fortune, was continually on the Athenian tongue, and appeared even at the head of all decrees.[5] "So the goddess orders," would an orator repeat throughout his speech; which he had also commenced with an invocation of the heroes who inhabit the soil.

The history of Nicias[6] will afford an excellent instance of religious feeling in an Athenian. He belonged to an important family, and whilst still young had conducted a θεωρία to Delos, that is to say, victims to be sacrificed and a chorus to sing the praises of the god. On his return to Athens he devoted part of his fortune to the gods, dedicating a statue to Athene, and a shrine to Dionysius. He is alternately giver of public feasts and provider of choruses for sacred days. No day passes without his offering some sacrifice, and the diviner who is attached to his family is at hand every

---

[1] Plato, *Laws*, vii., 800.
[2] Philoch., Fr. Collect. Didot, i., 414.
[3] Aristoph., *Pax*, 1084.
[4] Schol. Aristoph., *Birds*, 721.
[5] Lycurgus, i., 1. Aristoph., *Knights*, 903, 909, 1171, 1179.
[6] Plutarch, *Nicias*.

instant to be consulted on public or private matters. Having led an expedition against Corinth, he perceives, as he is returning, that two of his dead soldiers had remained unburied on the hostile soil. The fleet is stopped, and a herald sent to demand permission of the Corinthians to bury the two corpses.

Some time afterwards, the Athenian people were debating on the expedition to Syracuse. Nicias declares from the tribune that, according to his diviner and soothsayers, the omens are against the expedition. As the diviners of Acibiades declare the contrary, the people are in a state of indecision, when more information arrives from Egypt, whence the god Ammon sends word that the Athenians will take all the Syracusans.

The war was decided upon and Nicias sent as general, in spite of all he could say. Before starting, of course he sacrifices. Of course, also, he takes with him a troop of diviners, soothsayers, sacrificers, and heralds. The fleet has its sacred fire, and every vessel bears the emblem of some god. But Nicias has no hope, because so many signs of misfortune occur. Pallas's statue has been injured by some crows; a man has mutilated himself on an altar; and the departure of the fleet is fixed for the unlucky day of the Plynteria! Therefore he is sure this expedition will be fatal to his country and himself; and we find him timid and cautious beyond measure during the whole course of it, and, though known for a brave soldier and skilful general, ever loath to give the signal for the battle.

When Syracuse was clearly not to be taken, and great loss had been sustained, it was determined to return to Athens. The fleet is prepared and the sea is still free to them ; but an eclipse occurs, and Nicias consults his diviner, who says the omens are unfavourable and he must wait thrice nine days. During all this time Nicias does nothing but offer many sacrifices to appease the anger of the gods, and the enemy take advantage of this inaction to close the port and destroy his fleet. Nothing remains but to attempt a retreat by land. This, however, is found to be impossible, and neither Nicias nor any of his soldiers escape the Syracusans.

It is worth while remarking how the Athenians received news of the disaster. They knew the personal courage of

Nicias and admired his fortitude; and did not dream of blaming him for following the indications of religion. Only one reproach could be uttered against him; he had taken out an ignorant diviner. For the man had been guilty of a great blunder respecting the eclipse of the moon; and should have known that for an army which wishes to retreat, a moon that gives no light is a favourable sign.

CHAPTER XXXVI.

WANT OF INDIVIDUAL LIBERTY.

THE strength of the ancient city lay in its being founded on religion and constituted as a church, and the State so brought its double power to bear upon each citizen that he had no individual liberty left. The tax on blood and the tax on property were practically unlimited. Military service was due at Rome from the citizen until he was fifty years old, at Athens until he was sixty, and at Sparta always. The state could at any time order women to give up their jewels, creditors to abandon their debts, and owners of olive-trees to cede their oil for nothing ;[1] so that we may safely say a man's fortune was always at the disposition of the state.

Private life was never free from state interference, and power. The Athenian law forbade a man remaining a bachelor,[2] whilst at Sparta he was punished for marrying late. At Athens it was ordered that a man should work ; at Sparta that he should remain idle. Tyranny was exercised in the smallest things : pure wine might not be drunk by men at Locris, by women at Rome, Miletus, Marseilles.[3] The dress of both sexes was generally prescribed by the state, and Sparta interfered with the hair-dressing of her women. The Athenian ladies might not carry more than three dresses[4] with them when they travelled ; and the men of Rhodes and Byzantium were forbidden to shave.[5]

---

[1] Aristotle, *Æcon.*, ii.
[2] Pollux, viii., 40. Plutarch, *Lysander*, 30.
[3] Athenæus, x., 33. Ælian., *H. V.* Iliad, 37.
[4] Fragm. Hist. Græc. Didot, ii., 129, 211. Plutarch, *Solon*, 21.
[5] Athenæus, xiii. Plutarch, *Cleomenes*, 9. See particularly Plutarch, *Cato Senior*, 23.

Deformed children were to be destroyed by the old laws of Rome and Sparta ; and Aristotle and Plato inscribed a similar provision in their ideal codes. When many Spartans had perished in the disastrous battle of Leuctra, the parents of the dead shewed signs of joy, whilst those whose sons had returned from the combat lamented and wept ; so much more important was the interest of the state considered than that of any private person. And Plutarch says plainly that the Romans thought no one ought to have free choice about marrying, about having children, about choosing his calling, about keeping holiday, or in short following out any of his desires and tastes, unless examination had been made and judgment passed in favour of the course proposed.

The state would not let a man be indifferent to the public interests. So the philosopher or man of letters could not live apart, but was obliged to vote and take his turn of office. In factious times the Athenian law even compelled a man to choose his side, and fight for one or other under pain of confiscation of his property.

Education was so far from being free in Greece that the state entirely took its own way in the matter. At Sparta, the father had no say at all about the bringing-up of his child, and if at Athens rather more liberty was allowed, yet all the boys must be brought up together under masters appointed by the state. And we get a fine picture in Aristophanes[1] of the boys marching together, in order, according to their districts, in dense ranks, whether in rain, or snow, or burning heat, as though they already understood they were fulfilling a public duty. Plato[2] says, "Parents ought not to be free to send or not to send their children to the masters whom the city has chosen : for children belong less to their parents than they do to the state." The city had gymnastics taught for military purposes, and the recital of sacred hymns as well as the practice of religious dances, for the sake of the public worship.[3]

The story of Socrates proves how little toleration there was for all who did not uphold the city religion. A man

---

[1] Aristoph., *Nubes*, 960, 965.
[2] Plato, *Laws*, vii.
[3] At Athens, the state did not allow of competition with state education. Xenophon, *Memor*, i., 2. Diog. Laert., *Theoph*.

might scorn the deities of a neighbouring town, or disbelieve in general deities like Jupiter, Uranus, Cybele, or Juno. But any doubt at Athens about Athene or Cecrops was a deadly sin, and to refrain[1] from religious celebration of the state festivals was instantly punished with severity.

The ancients knew no liberty either in their private life, or in education, or in religion; and the person of man counted for nothing against the omnipotent power of the state. It mattered not whether a man was guilty or not when the city's interest was involved; he might be removed from the country like Aristides, for being too good, by way of precaution. And Ostracism was not peculiar to Athens, but is found at Argos, Megara, Syracuse: perhaps it existed in all Greek cities.[2] At Athens, a man might be put on his trial and condemned for want of affection to his country; and before the dangerous maxim that the safety of the state is the supreme[3] law, justice and morality and all gave way. A man who had the intention of making himself king[4] might be killed by Roman law, for a man's life was nothing compared with the interest of the state.

It is a great error, then, to believe that in the cities of old mankind enjoyed true liberty; for mankind did not even conceive the idea of it. They knew not what it was to maintain their rights against the city and the gods. Moreover, the state's omnipotence survived all changes in the form of government. Individual liberty, which is the only true liberty, was enjoyed neither under monarchies, aristocracies, nor democracies. What the ancients called liberty was to possess political rights, power of voting and naming magistrates, power of holding office; but with all these powers a man was a slave to his state. The rights and importance of society were exaggerated by all the ancients, but especially by the Greeks, no doubt for the reason that society had originally been invested with a sacred and religious character.

---

[1] Pollux, viii., 46. Ulpian., *Schol. in Demosth. Midias.*
[2] Aristotle, *Polit.*, viii., 2, 5. Scholiast, *Aristoph. Knights*, 851.
[3] Cicero, *De Leg.*, iii., 3.
[4] Plutarch, *Publicola*, 12.

CHAPTER XXXVII.

THE REVOLUTIONS.

IN these times the family seemed to be an institution most strongly constituted, and independent enough to last for ever, containing within itself, as it did, gods, worship, priest, and magistrate. And the ancient city possessed a power much greater than that of modern states, because it wielded the authority of church as well; nevertheless, a series of revolutions befell this state of society, and in the end completely modified it.

No exact period can be fixed for the beginning of these changes, which, indeed, in different cities commenced at different times. But it is certain that in the seventh century before our æra, mankind became discontented with this organization and attacked it on all sides. After that period nothing but a skilful mixture of resistance and concession sustained it in being. After a struggle of several centuries, society was at length transformed.

Two principal causes may be assigned for this decline and fall. One is the change of opinion brought about by the natural development of the human intellect, which undermined all old beliefs, and brought down along with them the social edifice that themselves had chiefly erected and sustained. The other is the existence of a class of men who saw themselves left outside of this organization, and who, keenly feeling their exclusion, unceasingly struggled to overcome it.

No city escaped this law of transformation. Sparta fell under its influence as well as Athens, Rome as well as Greece. The sequel will shew that as Greece and Italy had originally the same beliefs, and the same institutions arising from those beliefs, so eventually the same revolutions passed over all, sweeping men away to an end they knew not, in fact, by the merciful law which evokes life from death, to greater good and a higher form of life.

CHAPTER XXXVIII.

PATRICIANS AND CLIENTS.

OF the inferior classes of society we have not yet spoken, as it was not our business to do; because these classes did not properly enter into the organization of the city, at least for long ages, whence it seemed wiser to wait until we had arrived at the period of revolutions before studying the position of clients and plebeians.

Distinctions of ranks existed in all ancient towns from the very first, such as that between the Eupatridæ and Thetes at Athens, between the Equals and the Inferiors at Sparta, and that between the Knights and Commoners in Eubœa. Roman history is full of the struggle between the patricians and plebeians; and the like took place also in the Sabine, Etruscan, and Latin cities.

It is to be remarked that the further back we push our research into Italian and Grecian history, the more marked is the distinction of ranks. And this seems to prove that the difference did not arise merely with lapse of time, but existed originally, and was contemporaneous with the birth of the cities. If we can get to understand on what principles the division of classes was formed, the demands and wants of the lower orders in the ensuing struggle, as well as the grounds of defence occupied by their superiors, will be rendered clearer to our minds.

And we shall find that before ever the city was formed, the families which were its constituent parts contained within themselves this difference of order. The family always had its head or *pater*, who was master, magistrate, and priest; and the eldest son always succeeded his father from generation to generation, inheriting both the authority and the property. After their father's death, his brothers occupied the same position with respect to him as they had done to their father, and formed in the course of time a number of younger branches, which remained in a condition of inferiority to the elder branch, and obeyed its authority.

There were, besides, a number of servants who did not leave it at will, being attached hereditarily to it, and who bore different names in different places, but at Rome, clients, and at Athens, Thetes. The client was in a lower position than any member of the younger branches of the family, chiefly because the latter, in going back up the line of his ancestors, would come, sooner or later, to a *pater*, or head of the family, one of those divine beings invoked by the family in its prayers, whilst the client could point to no ancestor higher than a slave or other client. It was because of their descent from a *pater* that the Romans termed the younger sons, and the sons of younger sons, *patricii*.

Again, the superiority of the one and the inferiority of the other is manifest in what concerned their material interests. The member of the younger branch had at all events a reversionary interest in the family property, whereas the client could never become an owner of land. That which he cultivated was merely entrusted to him, and in case of his death reverted to the *patronus*. Even the client's money was not his own, but might be taken possession of by the patron at any moment of need. In virtue of this ancient rule the Roman law compelled the client to contribute to the dowry of his patron's daughter, to pay his fines, to provide him with money for ransom, and share in the expense of his magistracy.

The distinction is manifest again in religion. None but a descendant of some *pater* could perform the ceremonies of the family worship. The client was always incapable of fulfilling the priestly office, and must have an intermediary between himself and the domestic deity. If the family became extinct, the clients could not continue the worship, but must disperse; for the worship to them was but a borrowed thing, something of which they had the enjoyment but not the ownership.

The right to have a god and to pray was hereditary in those times and in that race; and the sacred rites and forms which influenced the gods were only transmitted by blood. So that before ever society issued from the patriarchal state, a distinction of classes was established; in each family religion had caused a difference of ranks. When afterwards the city was formed, no change took place in the internal organization of the family. For, as we have shewn, the city was not originally an association of individuals, but a confederation of tribes, curiæ, and families; and each of these bodies remained entirely as it had been before. The chiefs of these groups united amongst themselves, but each remained absolute master of the little society which called him chief. This is the reason why Roman law so long left the *pater* absolute authority over the family, and jurisdiction over the clients: it was because the distinction of classes that had originated in the family was continued in the city.

None but heads of houses were originally citizens, as we see by the example of Sparta, where the younger sons had no political rights, and by an old law of Athens which forbade any one to be a citizen who had not a domestic deity.[1] Aristotle[2] also remarks that it was anciently the rule in many cities that the son should not be a citizen during the life-time of his father, and that only when the father was dead the eldest son enjoyed political rights. As, then, younger branches produced no citizens, and the clients still less, the true citizens, as Aristotle further remarks, were very few.

No one will believe now-a-days with Cicero that Romulus called the senators fathers or *patres*, to mark the fatherly affection they ought to have for the people. The Senators naturally had the title because they were all of them heads of gentes. The union of these men made up the city, but each of them at home was a petty king.

Besides the Senate, there was another more numerous assembly at Rome, called the assembly of the curiæ; but the difference between the two was not great. The *patres* were the principal persons in both meetings, only, at the latter, each shewed himself surrounded with his relations and clients, to mark his power. There was but one vote for each family; and though the head of it might consult his dependents, clearly he was the only one who voted. The client, not belonging to the city at all but by virtue of his relation to his patron, and without him being unable to appear in its assembly or to benefit by its laws, could not publicly

---

[1] Harpocration, Ζεὺς ἑρκεῖος. [2] Aristotle, *Polit.*, viii., 5, 2, 3.

hold or express an adverse opinion. Indeed, such behaviour was forbidden by law.[1]

And we must beware of imagining the cities of this period to have been a random collection of men within certain walls. They were scarcely so much aggregations of dwellings in those ages as places of meeting and sanctuaries of the gods. Perhaps they were fortresses where the king resided and the priests, and where justice was administered. For many generations men would come in from the country from the different spots where their lands lay. Then, when there was a council to be held about war or peace, or when a feast was to be kept and a sacrifice performed, each chief arrived with his servants and relations at his back (sua manus), and they grouped themselves by curiæ, or phratriæ, and constituted, in case of need, the king's army.

---

[1] Aulus-Gellius, xv. 27.

CHAPTER XXXIX.

THE PLEBEIANS.

THERE was a broad distinction of ranks in the primitive ages. First of all came the heads of families, called in official language at Rome *patres*, but whom their clients called *reges*, as in the Odyssey they are termed βασιλεῖς or ἄνακτες. Below them came the younger sons and sons of younger sons; below them again, clients; and very much lower again, came the plebs.

It was religion which had given rise to this classification. When the forefathers of the Hindoos, Greeks, and Romans were living together in Central Asia, it had been the invariable rule that the eldest son should say the prayers, and inherit the priesthood, and from this sprung the superiority of the elder branch in all things. Still religion held also the younger branches of much account, for it might devolve on them, if the elder failed, to maintain the worship. And the client and the slave were also good for something; for they had been initiated, and had their place in the service. But the plebeian, who had no part in the worship, counted for absolutely nothing.

And this was the essential character of the plebs, that it was alien to the religious organization of the city and even of the family. By this we distinguish the plebeian from the client. The latter belongs to the gens, from which the former was excluded. And so we find that the historians of early Rome do not at all confound the two. For instance, Livy tells us in one passage that the consuls were elected by the patricians and their clients, as the plebeians would take no part in the ceremony; and in another that it was a subject of complaint with the plebeians that the votes of the clients gave the patricians too much weight in the comitia. And Dionysius of Halicarnassus says, in like manner, that the "plebs went out of Rome and retired to Mons Sacer, whilst the patricians remained alone in the town with their clients," as also elsewhere "that the patricians with their clients took up arms and carried on the war, because the plebs from discontent refused to enlist." Again, the words of an old prayer, still repeated in the times of the Punic wars, asked the favour of the gods upon the people and the plebs;" whence it is evident that the plebs was once not comprehended in the populus.

Nor is it hard to explain, from what we have said above of the religious and social state of primitive times, what must have been the origin of this class. As the religion of no family was capable of propagation beyond its own limits, so those families which had not the genius to contrive a worship for themselves, with hymns and prayers and method of sacrifice, must remain in a state of inferiority to the others, and be excluded from the phratriæ and from the city. It happened also that some who once had a worship lost it through negligence and forgetfulness, or in consequence of crime that prevented a man approaching his own holy fire. Again, clients who had gone away on account of ill-treatment, or been sent away for bad behaviour, and sons of women who had not been initiated,[1] who were like bastards, had no part in any family worship. All these men fell into the class of persons destitute of sacred fire, and constituted what at Rome was called the plebs.

And a class corresponding to the Roman plebs was to be found attached to every ancient city, Greek or Italian. At a very early period the cities of the Greeks seem to have been double, so to speak; the city, properly so called, πόλιν, which had been religiously founded, and which contained the shrines of the national gods, being generally placed on the summit of some eminence, whilst at the foot of the hill was an agglomeration of houses, run up without any religious formality and destitute of sacred enclosure. This last was the domicile of the plebs, who were accounted unworthy to inhabit the sacred precincts of the city.

---

[1] The κουρίδιοι ἄλοχοι alone, probably, produced sons who could continue the worship.

At Rome, the patricians and their clients had been established by Romulus on the flat summit of the Palatine.[1] But the habitation of the plebs was in the asylum, a sort of enclosure on the slope of the Capitoline, where Romulus gave refuge to the fireless, homeless outcasts who were inadmissible to his sacred city. And afterwards, as new plebeians flocked to Rome, they were established outside the pomœrium on the Aventine.

The Plebeians had no sacred fire, nor domestic hearth; they had no ancestors to worship, and no family to which they could boast of belonging. Natural family there might be, but nothing that religion had constituted or could respect. Even their marriages were not hallowed; and the expressions commonly employed about them by the patricians of Rome were, *gentem non habent; connubia promiscua more ferarum.*

As his family was not religiously constituted, so neither had the plebeian father the usual absolute authority. And because there was no sacred fire, no tombs, no termini, so there could be no right of property for the plebeian, "Except by the right of the Quirites," said the law, "no man can be a land-owner;" and it was long before the plebeian was counted amongst the Quirites. The *ager Romanus* was originally divided among the tribes, curiæ and gentes, and as the plebeian could claim to belong to none of these, he must certainly have been left out in the partition. It is an historical fact that only after three centuries of struggles they obtained possession, as owners, of the Aventine hill on which were situated their homes.

Again, the plebeian had no share in the benefit to be derived from equal laws and fairly-administered justice. The client had superior advantages in this respect, through the medium of his patron, who was bound to defend him in the courts of justice. Dionysius of Halicarnassus says that the sixth king of Rome was the first who made any laws applicable to the plebeians, though the patricians had long possessed theirs. And even this tardy concession was afterwards taken away; for when tribunes of the plebs were appointed, a special law ordained that no one should strike or

---

[1] The patricians of Sabine origin were domiciled on the Capitol and Quirinal. Probably the asylum, from its Greek name, was of Pelasgian origin, and anterior to Romulus.

kill a tribune as he would do a plebeian; which shews at least that the plebs was without the pale of the law, and might be injured without risk of penalty.

Neither had the plebeians political rights, since they were not citizens at first and could not be magistrates. For two centuries the only public assembly was the comitia curiata, which did not include plebeians; and, indeed, so long as the army was distributed into curiæ, no plebeian could belong to it.

But the worst badge of inferiority attaching to the plebeian was his exclusion from the city religion, and his incapacity for fulfilling any sacred office. Perhaps at first he could not be admitted to join in the prayers or know what were the sacred ceremonies. Perhaps he was looked upon as the *Soudra* in India, "who ought always to be kept in ignorance of the sacred rites." If not unclean like the leper, he was scorned and abject, deprived of all religion and law, destitute of proper family, and no true member of society. But this injustice brought on its own remedy. Too many men felt it their interest to destroy a social organization which humiliated instead of benefitting them, for it to remain as it was.

CHAPTER XL.

THE FIRST REVOLUTION.

The kingly authority is taken away, and the aristocracy govern; the kings retaining religious authority.

AT first the king, having been invested with sacerdotal authority, and being grand-priest of the public hearth, joined also to these functions the offices of president of the assembly, judge, and general. In fact, at one time all the power of the state was collected into the hands of the king.

But the *patres*, or heads of great families, and still more the chiefs of tribes and phratriæ, formed a very powerful aristocracy alongside of royalty. Indeed, the king might be said not to be alone in his dignity; each *pater* being quite as powerful in his own gens, and even having at Rome the name of king; whilst at Athens each phratria and tribe had its chief, the latter of whom were called in Greek φυλοβασιλεῖς. There was, in fact, a hierarchy of chiefs having all similar powers and duties, only in wider or narrower spheres. The king of the city could not interfere with the interior of families, and resembled somewhat those feudal kings whose subjects were great vassals, severally their equals in strength, and with *united* forces much more powerful. At an early period it became evident that a great difference of opinion prevailed between king and subjects as to the amount of obedience to be rendered, and in spite of the respect paid to the king as head of the worship and guardian of the sacred fire, he was unable to enforce submission. In every city a struggle commenced between the king and the aristocracy, and in every case the king was vanquished.

However, as the king was a religious person, who by means of prayers and sacrifices drew down the favour of the gods, his existence and office could not altogether be dispensed with. Therefore in all the cities whose history can be discovered the king's priestly authority was not at first interfered with, but only his political power taken away. For this latter was but a sort of appendage to the priesthood, and not in the same way inviolable. Religion did not seem to be endangered by its removal.

So royalty was preserved as a priesthood without other power. Aristotle says that "in very ancient times the kings had absolute power both in peace and war, but eventually some resigned it of their own accord, and others had it taken away from them; till all that remained to them was the care of the sacrifices." Plutarch, in like manner, writes: "Since the kings shewed pride and hardness in their rule, most of the Greeks took it away from them and only left them the care of religion." And Herodotus, in speaking of Cyrene, says: "They left to Battus, the descendant of the kings, the care of the worship and the possession of the sacred lands, taking away, however, the enjoyment of that power which his fathers had possessed."

The royalty, thus reduced to its priestly functions, continued generally to be hereditary in the sacred family which had kindled the fire and begun the national worship; and seven or eight centuries after this revolution (when Rome had emperors) Ephesus, Marseilles, and Thespiæ could shew families still invested with the titles and insignia of ancient royalty, and whose chiefs still presided at religious ceremonies. Elsewhere, sacred families having become extinct, the kingdoms were made elective and mostly annual.

§ 2. *History of this revolution at Sparta.*

It would seem that the first Dorian kings were absolute monarchs, and that the differences began in the third generation after the invasion of the Peloponnese. After that time for a space of two centuries the struggle between the kings and the aristocracy made of Sparta the most unquiet city in Greece, until the father of Lycurgus perished in a civil war.

"Concerning Lycurgus," according to his biographer, "nothing can be said which is not controverted." But it is clear that he appeared when the greatest agitation prevailed, and that his reform gave royalty a blow which it never recovered. Aristotle says that "aristocracy took the place of royalty, when Charilaos was king." Now the reign of Charilaos corresponds with the reform of Lycurgus; and it appears further from Plutarch that Lycurgus was charged with his commission in consequence of an insurrection, in which king Charilaos was obliged to seek refuge in a temple.

Lycurgus might have suppressed royalty altogether, but doubtless he considered that royalty was a necessary thing and inviolable. He contented himself with subjecting the kings to the Senate, of which they continued to be for some time presidents and executive officers. But a century afterwards even this executive power was taken away and conferred upon certain annual magistrates called ephors.

What functions were left to the kings we can discern from those conferred upon the ephors. These latter judged civil cases, as the Senate did in criminal matters. The ephors declared war at the will of the Senate, and arranged terms of peace. They also settled the plans of the campaign and directed its operations. The Spartans usually said that the king commanded, because one of the two kings performed the daily sacrifice, consulted the omens, marched at the head of the troops, and gave the sign for battle. When a Spartan king[1] really had supreme command it was by an exceptional vote of the Senate, as in the case of Agesilaus. But it was perfectly understood by Greek historians that the functions of the Spartan kings were religious. Herodotus writes: "If the city sacrifices, the kings take the first place at the banquet, are served first, and receive a double portion. They also are first to pour the libation, and they receive the skins of the victims. Moreover, each of the two is presented twice a month with a victim to offer to Apollo." Xenophon also says: "The kings perform the public sacrifices and have the best part of the victims."

In fact, royalty at Sparta was but a hereditary priesthood. Kingship, as we understand the word, was suppressed at Sparta as elsewhere. The real power belonged to the Senate

---

[1] Dr. Arnold (in the Appendix on the Spartan Constitution, in his edition of Thucydides) believes the Spartan kings really commanded. And so do other historians.

as a directing body, and to the ephors as the executive; and the kings obeyed the ephors wherever it was not a question of religion. Therefore Herodotus and Aristotle are both right when the one says that Sparta knew not monarchy, and the other that Sparta was aristocratic.

§ 3. *The same revolution at Athens.*

In primitive times the population of Attica consisted of a number of independent families under hereditary chiefs. Their junction constituted the Athenian city. This work of union is attributed by tradition to Theseus, but he had very great opposition to overcome. And the important point in the history of this period is to understand who it was that opposed him. Now the clients and the poor rather gained than lost by having a chief placed over their immediate leaders. But these leaders, $\phi\upsilon\lambda o\beta\alpha\sigma\iota\lambda\epsilon\hat{\iota}s$ or $\beta\alpha\sigma\iota\lambda\epsilon\hat{\iota}s$, who had had supreme power in their $\gamma\epsilon\nu os$ or tribe, defended their power as long as they could, and, when they had lost it, sought to regain it.

Theseus was unable to destroy an authority which religion had established and rendered inviolable. An examination of the traditions concerning this period shews that the Eupatridæ could only have consented to join in forming a city on condition that 'the government should be really federal, and every one have his say in the management of it. Though there was a supreme king, yet nothing important could be done without the chiefs being convoked to vote on the matter.

Succeeding generations said that Theseus had changed the government of Athens from monarchial to democratic or republican. Thus write Aristotle, Isocrates, Demosthenes, Plutarch; and though this may seem erroneous, it has a foundation of truth; for Theseus certainly did give up the power into the people's hands. Only the people in those days, $\delta\hat{\eta}\mu os$, was not so extensive as in Demosthenes' time. It was nothing else but the heads of families or $\gamma\epsilon\nu\eta$; in fact, an aristocracy. Theseus was no longer king merely of the little rock where Cecrops had dwelt and ruled. The formation of one state for all Attica necessitated an entire change in the conditions of government, and one which Theseus was obliged to accept. The Eupatridæ, each of whom was still lord in his own clan, would not unite in one association, without having stipulated for much respect towards their existing rights. So that if the king of Athens was now king of Attica, his power in the latter was anything but as absolute as it had been in the former.

A trial of strength necessarily arose between the aristocracy and the monarch, and the pretext, true or false, which the warrior-priests set up was that Theseus tried to destroy the prytanea of the little towns, and was lowering the credit of the local worships. What struggles he had to sustain and what insurrections to repress it is impossible now to know; but it is certain he was conquered at last, driven from Athens, and died in exile.

The Eupatrids then carried the day; not utterly suppressing royalty, but making a king of their own choice, namely, Menestheus. However, the family of Theseus regained the chief power after Menestheus, and held it for three generations. Another family, called Melanthidæ, then followed; and civil wars prevailed, of which no accurate record has been kept.

The final victory of the Eupatridæ coincides with the death of Codrus. Still they did not yet suppress royalty, for religion's sake, but they separated political power from it. The traveller Pausanias, who lived long after these events, but who was very careful in consulting tradition, says that royalty then lost many of its attributes, and became dependent, which doubtless means it was made subject to the Senate of the Eupatridæ. This period of history is now generally called the time of the archons, and most modern writers add that royalty was abolished; which, however, is only partly true, as the descendants of Codrus being indifferently called kings[1] or archons, exercised religious functions for thirteen generations, though without political power—just like the kings of Sparta. At the end of three centuries of such kingship, the Eupatridæ modified it once more, and only allowed the same man to hold the priestly dignity for ten years. But the royal family was the only one from whom archons were eligible. About forty years passed in this way; when one day the royal family stained itself

---

[1] See the marbles of Paros.

with a great crime; and it was declared no longer capable of fulfilling the priestly duties. It was then determined that the archons should be chosen elsewhere, and all the Eupatrids considered eligible. After another forty years, either to lower the dignity still more, or to render it accessible to more persons, it was made annual, and its functions were divided. Hitherto the archon had been king, but now the two titles were made distinct. The archon henceforth watched over the perpetuity of families, authorized or forbade adoption, admitted wills, and gave judgment in matters respecting landed property. The king was judge in cases of impiety, and performed the solemn sacrifices. To these two great officers were added a war minister, and six law officers called thesmothetæ. The whole nine were loosely called archons.

At Argos, a similar revolution left the descendants of Temenos nothing but the name of kings without any power. But the title remained for generations. At Corinth, the family of the Bacchidæ retained the royal dignity for a century after the political power had been taken away, and yet the office was only held for a year by each priest-king. At Cyrene, Battus's descendants at first had both priesthood and political power, but after four generations the latter of these functions was taken from them.

§ 4. *The same revolution at Rome.*

The royalty of Rome at first resembled what we have seen in Greece, the king being, in ordinary times, grand-priest of the city and supreme judge; and, in time of war, commander of the citizens under arms. Alongside him in authority were the patres who formed a Senate, that he was obliged to consult on all important matters.

And if we find mention of an assembly of the people as the main political body in the time of the first kings, we are not to suppose that this assembly was any more than the gathering of the aristocracy in force. The populus did not include the plebs, nay, was even used as a distinctive term to mark the patricians from those who were not yet admitted to be citizens. For according to all evidence the populus met by curies, when each of the gentes that composed the curia had but one vote, which was given by its head. The younger branches of the gens and the clients might stand behind their chief, and even be consulted by him, but they could not express any opinion that differed from his.

The circumstances, then, of Rome were not different from those of the other cities in which the king had to face a very powerful aristocratic body, which derived its power from religious belief. And we shall find the history of the seven kings to be the account of a long struggle between the two powers.

The first of the seven sought to free himself from the authority of the Senate, and to increase his own power by paying court to the lower orders. But the Patres opposed him resolutely, and he was finally assassinated at a meeting of the Senate.

The aristocracy then tried to abolish the office of king, and themselves in turn performed the royal functions. The lower classes, however, refused to be governed by the heads of the gentes, and demanded a king as before. The patres console themselves for having to yield by making the king elective, and that in a way to suit their purposes. For the Senate was to choose him, the patrician assembly of the curies to confirm this choice, and finally, the patrician augurs to declare whether the newly-elected monarch was pleasing to the gods.

It was after these rules that they elected Numa; and he, accordingly, shewed himself very religious, more of a priest than a warrior, a very scrupulous observer of all rites, and much attached to the ancient constitution of the families and the city. He was a king after the hearts of the patricians, and died peaceably in his bed.

It would seem that under Numa royalty was reduced to its priestly functions, as had happened in the Greek cities. At all events, a clear distinction was drawn between the religious and the political authority, and a king might now have the first without the second. The proof of this is that there was a double election, and a king must have passed both to have the *imperium*, or political functions, as well as the sacerdotal. Cicero's description of the ancient constitution makes this evident.

The third king united both powers in his person, and was even more of a warrior than a priest. Having been invested with the generalship as well as the priesthood, he despised the latter and sought to lessen the influence which rendered the aristocracy so powerful. He welcomed a great number of strangers to Rome against the spirit of the national religion, which would have excluded them; nay, he even lived in the midst of them on the Cœlian, and distributed amongst the plebeians lands which were designed to provide for the sacrifices. The patricians accused him of having not only neglected, but (which was worse) of having modified and depreciated them. And, therefore, he died like Romulus, smitten along with his sons by thunder from the gods of the patricians.

This violent stroke of policy regained the authority for the Senate, and permitted them to name a king of their own sort, who made war as little as possible, passed his life in the temples, and died in his bed, beloved of the patricians.

However, Tarquin, the fifth king, obtained the throne by aid of the lower classes and in spite of the Senate. He was so incredulous on religious subjects that a miracle was required to convince him there was any truth in the science of augury. As he interfered with the old constitution of the city by making new patricians, and as he thwarted the old ones as much as possible, he perished by assassination.

Servius Tullius made himself king by sudden violence, and was never recognized as legitimate by the Senate. He courted the lower orders, and gave them land without regard to the principle of religion on which the right of property reposed. They were even allowed political rights. Servius was murdered on the steps of the Senate-house.

The quarrel between the kings and the aristocracy was now assuming the character of a social struggle. For the latter were in danger not merely of having to bow before a king, but of having to yield to the despised plebeians and to their own clients. By the latter the religion of the family, and by the former the religion of the state would be outraged. In the kings, then, who helped them and set them on, the aristocracy began to see their own worst foes. And this feeling was increased by one more experiment which failed. The second Tarquin was one of those kings who deceive the expectations of those who appoint them. He would be master and lord, and not merely a priest. Whatever harm he could do to the patriciate, by *lowering their tallest heads*, by ruling in disregard of their advice, by making war or peace as he pleased, he did. The patricians seemed to have been conquered, when an opportunity presented itself in the absence from Rome of Tarquin himself and the army which sustained him. The chief power both in civil and military matters was for the moment in the hands of patricians. For such were both Lucretius, prefect of the city, and Junius,[1] the master of the horse. In conjunction with other patricians, a Valerius and a Tarquinius Collatinus, they prepared the insurrection, having as their place of meeting not Rome, but Collatia, which belonged to the last of the conspirators. There they shewed the people the dead body of a woman who was said to have killed herself after being dishonoured by the king's son. The people of Collatia rise and march to Rome, where the same scene is renewed. Men's minds were perplexed, and the king's partisans discouraged, especially as all legal power was then in the hands of Junius and Lucretius.

The conspirators carefully avoid assembling the people, but present themselves before the Senate, who pronounce Tarquin dethroned and royalty abolished. It was necessary that the decree of the Senate should be confirmed by the city, but Lucretius, the prefect of the city, alone had the right to summon the assembly. When the curiæ met, they agreed with the conspirators, deposed Tarquin, and created two consuls.

It remained to nominate the consuls in the comitia centuriata. And here, if it be asked why did not the centuries oppose what the Senate and the patrician curiæ had done, the answer is that they could not, according to their forms of procedure. For all that the centuries could do was to vote yes or no, without any speaking, on a subject proposed by the president. In this case the president appointed by the Senate was Lucretius, one of the conspirators, and the only subject which he proposed to them to vote upon was whether two men should be consuls. The names presented

---

[1] Dionysius Halic., iv., 68, says that the Junian family was patrician. The family of Brutus who killed Cæsar was plebeian, and he only took the name of Brutus because the Junius who conspired against Tarquin was so named. With regard to this explanation of the conspiracy against Tarquin, we may remark that it is very possible Tarquin had disgusted plebs as well as patricians. The history of Lucretia does not read as if a fabrication.

to the suffrages of the centuries were those of Junius and Tarquinius Collatinus, and of necessity these were elected. Then the Senate ratified the election, and, finally, the augurs confirmed it in the name of the gods.

Nevertheless, many plebeians were discontented with this alteration, and, joining the king in exile, attached themselves to his fortunes. On the other hand, a rich Sabine patrician, at the head of a numerous *gens*, by name Attus Clausus, considered the new government so much to his mind, that he came and settled in Rome.

But it was only the political royalty that was suppressed. Religious royalty was too holy to be dispensed with. Accordingly, they named forthwith a king for the purpose of sacrificing, *lex sacrorum*, having taken every imaginable precaution that he should never abuse his prestige to the extent of seizing on supreme power.

CHAPTER XLI.

THE ARISTOCRACY RULES IN THE CITIES.

A period of aristocratic rule followed, of varied duration in different cities. It was longer generally in Greece than at Rome, where, however, we shall see that its final overthrow was less complete. As a whole, the period may be characterized as dull and uneventful, national life being in a certain measure suspended. Men lived separately in the country, and had fewer interests in common. The patrician families both of Rome and of Attica[1] were to be found on their estates, surrounded with very many servants and dependents, and practising the family religion under the direction of the Eupatrid or pater. They came to town for feasts only, and assemblies. Historians mark with surprise that after so many details of the kingly period at Athens, four centuries should succeed with so little said about them. But during that period doubtless the horizon of human life was bounded by the little burgh or village where each man lived, in his capacity of Eupatrid or servant.

The Odyssey presents us with more than one faithful picture of this state of society in the western part of Greece. Certain powerful families own all the land, which is either cultivated by their labourers or pastured by their flocks, but the way of living is so simple that masters and servants sit down at the same table. Although these chiefs are numerous, they are all termed kings, as were the heads of clans at Rome by their clients, and the chiefs of the γένη at Athens. To shew that their dignity was founded on religion, the poet terms them divine. They have indeed a supreme king, but

---

[1] Thuc., ii., 15, 16.

he has not much power, seeming to preside merely at the council of the chiefs. Indeed, there are certain signs of his being elective, for Telemachus will evidently never become king unless the other chiefs choose him to be such. And when Ulysses returns, he seems to have no other subjects but his own servants, for the poet finds no fault with the servants of the chiefs slain by Ulysses for continuing the struggle against him. In Phæacia, Alcinous has supreme authority, but we find him attending a meeting of the chiefs; and it is noticeable that it is not the king who has summoned the council, but the council that has sent for the king. Then the assembly of the city as described by the poet is far from being an assembly of the multitude; none but the chiefs alone, convoked separately by a herald, as at the *comitia calata* of Rome, gather together. They all seat themselves on thrones of stone; the king beginning the discourse, and addressing his auditors as sceptre-bearing kings.

In the city of Hesiod, the stony Ascra, we find a class of men whom the poet calls kings, βασιλεῖς, who administer justice to the people. And no one can read an ode of Pindar without perceiving that the aristocratic feeling had lasted down to the time of the Persian wars in very great strength. It is easy to divine how powerful these families had been a few generations earlier. Birth is still the greatest boast; and every city has several families. In Ægina alone, Pindar names the Midylidæ, the Theandridæ, the Euxonidæ, Blepsidæ, the Chariadæ, the Balychidæ. At Syracuse, he extols the priestly family of the Jamidæ, at Agrigentum that of the Emmenidæ, at Thebes those sprung from the dragon's teeth, and so on for all the towns of which he had occasion to speak.

At Epidaurus, for a great length of time the whole body of citizens only consisted of one hundred and eighty members. The rest were without the city.[1] At Heraclea, the true citizens were still fewer, and even in the best families the younger sons had no political rights.[2] Nor was the case different at Cnidus, Istros, and Marseilles. At Thera, all the power was in the hands of certain families deemed sacred. At Apollonia,[3] the case was the same. At Erythræ, there

---

[1] Plutarch, *Quæst. Græc.*, i. [3] Aristotle, *Pol.*, iii., 9, 8; vi., 3, 8.
[2] Aristotle, *Pol.*, viii., 5, 2.

was an aristocratic class named the Basilidæ. The superior classes in the towns of Eubœa were termed knights,[1] it being a privilege then, as in the Middle Ages, to fight on horseback.

When Corinth sent out a colony to found Syracuse, monarchy existed no longer in the mother city. And therefore the new town also was destitute of royalty, and governed from the commencement by an aristocracy. These were called the landowners, γεώμοροι, because it was they who from the day of the city's foundation had shared the territory with religious rites. They remained for some generations masters of the government, and retained their exclusive possession of the soil. A similar aristocracy long reigned at Miletus and Samos.[2]

At Athens, from the death of Codrus to the time of Solon the Eupatrids retained all the power of the state. They only were priests and archons; and none else administered justice or even knew the laws, which were not written, but handed down by memory from father to son.

And, in like manner, at Rome none but the sacred caste could furnish flamens, augurs, Salians, pontiffs, Vestals. They alone could be consuls or compose the Senate. And if the assembly by centuries was not suppressed, so as to exclude entirely the plebeians, yet the comitia curiata were looked upon as the only sacred and legitimate meeting. Although the former assembly seemed to have the power of electing consuls, yet we have seen that all they were capable of doing was to vote upon the names presented to them by the patricians, whilst afterwards their decision had to be submitted to the triple approval of Senate, curiæ, and augurs. And finally, as in Greece, none but patricians could administer justice, or knew the forms of the law.

---

[1] Aristotle, viii., 5, 10.
[2] Diodor., viii., 5. Thucy., viii., 21. Hdtus., vii., 155.

CHAPTER XLII.

SECOND REVOLUTION.

CHANGES IN THE CONSTITUTION OF THE FAMILY; THE RIGHT OF PRIMOGENITURE DISAPPEARS; THE GENS IS DISMEMBERED; AND CLIENTS BECOME FREE.

THE revolution which we have just been considering had been effected by the upper classes against the royal ally of the lower, in order to preserve the constitution of the family. In fact, a political revolution had delayed a social one; and, though it may seem paradoxical to say so, the revolution had been conservative.

But the danger existed none the less, and even increased with lapse of time; for old institutions were now tottering, and important changes about to be effected in the construction of the primitive family. Residence in cities was found to be inconsistent with the régime of the *gens*, and the force of society began to set itself against the undivided existence of those great families, which, it was felt, might be maintained in a state of isolation, but could not remain alongside the new elements of the commonwealth. By his very residence in a town the power of the great chief was lessened, since he was obliged to accommodate himself to the interests of others. Then, numbers count for much in the most aristocratically constituted society. Even the consequence which a chief acquired from a large following, taught his retainers their value. Also rival leaders sought to weaken each other's power, and to make themselves popular in the city for the sake of office. And then local sovereignties were neglected or forgotten, and a relaxation in the constitution of the gens ensued, which made its friends less firm and its enemies more aggressive.

As for the disappearance of the right of primogeniture, no exact date can possibly be assigned to it, for it must have taken place in different years in different families, as fathers died whose property and power was to be inherited. The change took place first in one family and then in another, till the rule was general; and the revolution was so gradual as to be unperceived. For families did not pass at one leap from indivisibility of patrimony to equal division amongst several brothers. There was most likely a transition from one state of things to the other; as in India, where the Law, after having prescribed that estates should be undivided, next ordains a double portion only for the elder, and finally recommends an equal share to be given to every son.

But all that we can say for certain is, that the right of primogeniture once existed and afterwards is found to have disappeared. Cities differed as to the length of time that they maintained the right. It was still in vigour at Thebes and Corinth in the eighth century before Christ. The laws of Solon at Athens still manifest a certain preference for the elder son; and at Sparta the rights of the eldest lasted unimpaired until democracy triumphed. In some towns only insurrections removed it, as at Heraclea, Cnidos, Istros, and Marseilles, where the younger sons took up arms to destroy at one blow paternal authority and the right of primogeniture.[1]

Such movements, of course, were followed by a great increase in the number of privileged citizens; some Greek towns, for instance, where there had been but one hundred, now counting five or six. All these were now eligible to the Senate, and to the great city offices.

We cannot specify a date for the disappearance of the privileges of the elder son at Rome, any more than for Greece. Perhaps the kings in the course of their struggles against the aristocracy did something to disorganise the gentes in this way. At the commencement of the republic we find one hundred new members in the Senate. Livy thinks that these were plebeians; but this would certainly have been too great a concession for the patricians yet to make The new members were not called patres like the old, but

---

[1] Aristotle, *Polit.*, viii., 5, 2.
[2] Festus, Vº· *Conscripti, Allecti.* Plutarch, *Quest. Rom.*, 58.

conscripti, which Festus[2] explains to mean chosen in addition ; whence we may perhaps conclude that the younger branches of the aristocracy only joined Brutus's conspiracy on condition of receiving civil and political rights ; thus acquiring in a moment of need what the same class had won by arms at Heraclea, Cnidos, and Marseilles.

And now, as the Roman lawyers expressed it, *singuli singulas familias incipiunt habere.* Each younger brother could have his own sacred fire, kindled doubtless from the common hearth of the race. He was enabled to leave the parent-stock and found a house of his own ; indeed, the Romans said *familiam ducere*, to lead out a family, as they said, *coloniam ducere*, to lead out a colony. Then the elder branch, and the gens itself, had no more to do with the new family than to maintain a sort of priority and supremacy of worship, to re-unite them on certain occasions and make them remember that they had the same name and the same origin. There remained a chief-priesthood which descended from eldest son to eldest son, but all the younger branches were virtually independent.

And so the constitution of the primitive sacred family became relaxed ; and more changes were to follow from this beginning.

CHAPTER XLIII.

THE CLIENTS FREE THEMSELVES.

§ 1. *What clientship was at first.*

THE emancipation of the clients was another of those silent revolutions, to which no positive date can be assigned, and which are only perceptible by comparing men's condition at two different periods. Ancient writers say nothing on the subject, for there was no great struggle, no battle to engage their attention. The people themselves scarcely perceived the change that was taking place, so gradual was it. It was like that great change which took place in the condition of the rustic population of Europe during the middle ages. Whilst it is taking place no one speaks of it, but those who compare the end with the beginning say that a great revolution has been brought about.

The institution of clients is represented sometimes as worthy of the golden age. What can be more humane than the patron's protection of his client before the court of justice, his maintenance of him in poverty, and his education of his children? And what could be more touching than for the client to maintain in his turn the patron in adversity, to pay his debts, and to help to provide his ransom? But this amount of sympathy and disinterestedness is hardly found at the bottom of great political institutions. It should be remembered that the client could not leave his patron at will and choose another, and that his servitude was hereditary. That alone would be enough to make his lot hard. Again, the client could not own land at all in his own right. He could but toil for the profit of one who had a domestic worship and fellowship in the city. Even the client's money might be withdrawn to pay the debts of the chief or to ransom him from captivity. The patron was bound to maintain him, it is true, as well as his children; and he could not exactly be called a slave; but still he had a master whose will must be obeyed in all respects, and he was a client for life, and his sons after him.

If we only remember that the principle on which the serfdom of the middle ages was founded was quite different from that which was at the bottom of clientship (for religion bound the client to the patron, whilst the serf went as a piece of property with the soil), there was much similarity in the condition of the two. From generation to generation neither was his own master; and it would appear from a passage of Livy that the client could no more marry out of the gens than the serf out of his village. At all events, the client could not marry without the patron's permission. And then the patron might resume possession of the soil which the client cultivated, as well as of the money which he had gained, just as the lord could do to the serf. And when the client died, all that he had the use of reverted to the patron, as the serf's inheritance fell to his lord.

It must be added that the patron was also judge as well as master, and could inflict death as a punishment. Nor was this all, for he was also the religious chief, thus embracing every sort of authority at once, and capable of oppressing soul as well as body. It is true that the patron had his duties to perform towards his client, but of these he was the judge himself, and there was no penalty for the non-observance of them. The client had no protector against his lord, being incapable of appearing before the city tribunals except in the person of his patron, and having no knowledge of the sacred forms of the law. Indeed, had he been able to make these his study, he would have found that the first law for him was never to speak against his patron; that without the patron he could have no justice, and against him no remedy.

Their relations to one another being of this sort, it is easy to believe that hatred soon sprung up between the patron and client. On one side was complete power, on the other no assured rights. Unreserved and hopeless obedience was exacted by unrestrainable might. The best of masters might have his fits of passion and his whims, and the most resigned of servants his grudges and his discontent. Homer would put Ulysses before us as an example of a good master, by the paternal affection which he shows to Eumæus and Philætius. But he puts to death a servant who has insulted him without knowing who he was, and the females who have fallen into temptation through his absence. He is responsible to the city for the death of the suitors, but for the death of his servants no one brings him to account.

The institution of clientship existed in the Hellenic race, as well as at Rome. In the Dorian cities, it is true, no traces remain, because the Dorians had so early got rid of the γένος, and bound their vanquished subjects to the estates which they cultivated, and not to the family of the lord. But the thetes and pelatæ of the Ionians and Æolians were identical with the clients of the Romans, only that the former are generally found in the country, and the latter in town. These thetes and pelatæ could never leave the γένος in which they had been born, and were just as much subject to the Eupatrid or other lord as the client was to the patron. Nor were the Romans the only people of Italy who had clients; persons in a similar position were to be found in the suite of the great Etruscan and Sabine chiefs.

So long as the credit of the old religion continued, and the great families remained in the country, the client had but little temptation to seek for freedom. The family to which he was attached constituted his furthest horizon, and he looked up to the head of it as to a superior being. If he had a master, he had also a protector, who gave him a worship and the comforts of religion. And where else could he lead a quiet life and be sure of a maintenance? He felt quite sure that if he left the family he would be out of the pale of human society, and become an outcast.

But when the city was once founded, the clients of the different families could see and talk to one another; they could now compare masters and ventilate complaints. Each man saw something beyond the family to which he had been attached. The idea occurred that even to be out of the family would not be an irremediable one. The master's authority begun to be questioned, and an ardent desire to be free took possession of men's minds. But still we find no record in the annals of any city of a general insurrection of this class. If any struggles took place, they were confined to the family in which they occurred. But an invincible necessity compelled the masters to abate somewhat of their omnipotence. After subjects have ceased to believe a certain authority to be just, it takes time to convince the masters also; but that comes also at last; and then the defence is feebler, and finally command is given up altogether. In this case, it was perhaps needful for the patron's interests to pay some regard to the client's wishes, and make concessions from time to time. For the client, by his toil, made the wealth of his patron, and, in the struggles and rivalries of families and cities, was useful in bearing arms and swelling the following of a chief.

And so, by degrees, his condition was ameliorated; from living in the house of his master, he had a plot of land assigned to cultivate for the patron's benefit. Habit made him love it, even if it were not his own; and when several generations had been living on the same plot, a strong tie had been formed between the labourer and that portion of soil, not a tie like that with which religion bound the same soil to the master, but one whose strength still made itself felt.

The next step taken was when the client no longer cultivated for the master, but for himself. On condition of paying every year at first a variable portion and then a fixed one, he was allowed to have the harvest to himself. Thus the sweat of his brow began to be not all in vain, and independence and liberty dawned upon his soul. Festus[1] says that ancient masters of families used to give plots of land to their inferiors, as they would to their own children. And in the Odyssey we find Eumæus saying, "A kind master gives his servants land and a house," to which he adds, "a beloved spouse," because the client as yet could not marry without the master's permission, or any other than a woman chosen by him.

One thing still remained to complete the happiness and the freedom of the client. The land he toiled upon was not completely his property. The god Terminus planted in the soil by one who had qualifications beyond his own, prevented his perfect possession. For each land-mark was, so to speak,

---

[1] Verbo *Patres*.

a sort of off-shoot of the patron's central hearth, and the standing guardian of another's interests. The *villicus* felt he was a stranger in the house and fields where he dwelt, because the sacred fire of another was always burning there, the *Lar familiaris* of his patron; and therefore he was eager for complete ownership of the fields which he occupied.

How he at last succeeded in removing the sacred landmark we cannot clearly explain, but it is evident enough in Greece that the right of toil prevailed at length over the religious right, pretty much as in Europe the slaves of the middle ages first became serfs taxable at will, then serfs at a fixed payment, and finally (except in the British isles) have become peasant proprietors.

§ 2. *Clients disappear at Athens: Solon's work.*

When royalty had been overthrown at Athens, the system of the *gens* revived, and the Eupatrids, uncontrolled, swayed each his large body of dependents. The population of Attica retained an unpleasant recollection of those times, and by comparison extolled the preceding period, when kings had ruled them, into an age of gold. The belief arose that inequality only commenced when kings no longer were. And it is probably a common illusion for tradition to place the beginning of misery at the point where it begins to be felt. The Eupatrids of the seventh century before Christ were but upholding previously-existing rights. Where they erred was in maintaining rules which now weighed too heavily upon their people. So, though the new generations were really less hard than their forefathers had been, they were actually more detested.

But notwithstanding the supremacy of this aristocracy, a great step was taken about this time in ameliorating the clients' position. Possession of land was obtained on the sole condition of paying a sixth part of the harvest. In fact, the clients became almost free. Away from the master's superintendence and with a home of their own, they could breathe at ease and work for themselves.

Such, however, is the nature of man, that in proportion as the condition of these dependents improved, so did their dissatisfaction increase at what remained of inequality. They did not yet feel the need of being citizens and sharing in the government, but they were hurt at not owning the land on which they had been born and on which they had spent their strength. And it must be confessed that if their present situation presented any advantages, these were entirely destitute of stability. No actual law assured them possession of the soil or the independence which results from that. We gather from Plutarch that, not merely if the former servant failed in paying his dues could the patron reduce him again to slavery, but also this might be done for slighter causes.

Therefore, important causes were agitated in Attica for four or five generations. It could scarcely be expected that men would willingly remain in that uncertain and irregular position to which a slow and gradual progress had led them; and then one of two things must happen; they must either fall back into the bondage of their former hard servitude, or by a fresh progress get advanced to the position of owners of the soil and free men.

The struggles that necessarily ensued seem to have had a different result according to the geographical position of the families or clans in which they took place. On the plain where the Eupatrid himself resided continually, his authority remained intact over the little group of servants who could not quit his eye. But those who were further removed from his influence on the sides of the mountains, being more independent and courageous, risked more for freedom, and shewed a greater dislike of the sacred landmark. They could not bear to see their land enslaved.[1] As for the inhabitants of the districts that bordered the sea, or paralians, they, of course, were less covetous of actual soil, because the sea was open to them, and had actually enriched some of them by means of commerce. Wealth had almost freed them. Without, therefore, having the bitter spirit of the mountaineers, they were not so resigned as dwellers on the plain, and desired more stability in their good fortune, and a better assurance of their rights.

The true work of Solon would seem to have been to give whatever satisfaction was possible at the time to these different aspirations. There is much uncertainty in what the ancients tell us about one part of his doings, but this at least

---

[1] Solon, edit. Bach., pp. 104, 105.

seems certain, that, whereas before his time most of the inhabitants of Attica had but a precarious hold on the soil and might fall back into slavery, after him this numerous class is to be found no more, the right to the soil is possible for anyone, no Athenian can be a slave any more, and the lower classes are emancipated from the Eupatrids.

We do not know who could have effected this great change if it was not Solon. Certainly, if we interpreted strictly the words of Plutarch, the effect of Solon's legislation would have been merely to mitigate the law affecting debtors, and to prevent the creditor enslaving him. But in the first place we must remember how long Plutarch lived after the time when these events took place. Then it is difficult to believe there was commerce or money enough to occasion as much lending and borrowing as he would suppose. Those were very early and very simple times, when credits and loans were almost unknown. And whatever money was lent, was naturally not entrusted to the poorer classes, who had nothing to offer as security. It has been suggested that the borrowers pledged their land : to which the answer is that, first, the modern system of mortgaging was unknown then ; and, secondly, that it was inconsistent with the principle on which the right of property reposed. It seems much more reasonable to suppose that what debts there were, were the yearly payments to the great landlords of part of the harvest in return for lands assigned. The debtors were the ancient thetes or clients, and the slavery into which they fell was the relapse into the condition of client in case of non-payment. Solon either abolished the payment, or, more likely, reduced it to a moderate amount, at the same time forbidding for the future all relapse of insolvents into slavery. Nor was this all. Whereas in time past the old clients, however long they had occupied the soil could never become the owners of it, on account of the insuperable obstacle presented by the patron's land-mark, yet even this seemingly " hopeless task " (to use his own words) "was accomplished by the aid of the gods." " I call to witness," he writes, " the goddess mother, black earth, whose land-marks in many a place I have pulled up, that the soil which was enslaved is now free." And if this be so, it was certainly a great revolution that Solon effected. Land was taken away from religion to be given up to labour.

Along with the Eupatrid's power over the soil was taken away at the same time his authority over man, and Solon might truly say in his poem, "Those who on this earth were undergoing cruel slavery and trembling before their masters, did I make free."

And therefore there is little doubt that this enthralment of man to man was the burden which Solon's contemporaries understood him to have thrown off, when they attributed to him the σεισαχθεία or shaking of burdens. But succeeding generations, whether from pride or ignorance, fell into error. Having become accustomed to liberty, they could not conceive the servitude of their forefathers, and being more conversant with money-matters, they explained the strange word as marking only the abolition of debts. But there is something in the tone of Solon's words that indicates a greater revolution; and our opinion is confirmed by the plain statement of Aristotle, who, without entering into any account of Solon's doings, says simply, "He put a stop to the slavery of the people."[1]

§ 3. *Transformation of the clientship at Rome.*

The differences between clients and patrons at Rome could have been no less profound than at Athens, and must have occupied as long a period of history. We find nothing on the subject in Livy, because this was not the sort of thing he noticed, and the priests' books, on which his authorities were based, gave no accounts of domestic struggles.

But one thing is undeniable. When Rome began to be, there were clients in it, and there is clear evidence of the state of dependence in which their patrons kept them. And yet, when, some centuries later we look for them again, they are gone. The name remains without the fact. For there is the greatest difference between the clients of the primitive times and those plebeians of Cicero's age who called themselves a rich man's clients for the sake of the dole. The *freed man* more resembles the ancient client; for as the slave in early days, on issuing from his slavery did not immediately become a free citizen, but remained subject to his master, so at a later period the freed man remained attached to the

---

[1] Aristotle, *Govt. Athens.* Fragm. Coll. Didot, vol. ii., p. 107.

family and (as in the former case) bore its name. He was not merely expected to be grateful, but also to render such services as might be required of him. The freed man was under the master's jurisdiction like the client, and in case of ingratitude might even be reduced once more to slavery.[1] In fact, there was but one difference between the two. The condition of client was hereditary; whereas that of freedman ceased at the second, or, at all events, the third generation. Although, therefore, the first set of clients had ceased to be such, the same condition held good for a new set of persons, with the sole difference that it was no longer hereditary. But we can assign no special date for the operation of this considerable change.

The following are the gradual ameliorations effected in the condition of clients. At first he is assigned a plot of land to cultivate, and practically holds it for life so long as he shall contribute to the expenses which befall his old master. He must have had enjoyment for life of the soil, when he was saddled with the ransom and the fine of his patron, and the dowry of his daughter. At a later period, the client may leave by will his occupation to his son. If he has no son, it reverts to the patron. It was a further step gained when, without having a son, a client could make a testament; though here there was some variation in custom, the patron sometimes resuming half the property, sometimes nothing, so that in the worst case the will is not without value,[2] and if the client was not absolute owner, he had the completest enjoyment possible of the property.

It is hard to say when the freedom was quite complete, and the clients entirely emancipated from patrician control. Perhaps they were full citizens at the commencement of the republic.[3] Perhaps they had already been so in Servius's time. We could not absolutely say for certain that they had not voted in the comitia curiata, though even this would not prove their affranchisement complete, because the patricians might have found it useful to give political before civil rights,

---

[1] *Digest.*, xxv., 2, 5; l., 16, 195. Val. Max., v., 1, 4. Suet., *Claud.*, 25. Dion. Cassius, lv. The law of Athens was similar. See Harpocration, Vº. ἀποστάσιον. Demosth., *Aristog.* Suid., Vº. ἀναγκαῖον.
[2] *Institutes*, iii., 7.
[3] Livy, ii., 16.

and a power to vote on their own side before the clients could be owners of land.

It would seem that the emancipation of the clients at Rome was not brought about suddenly at all, as had been the case at Athens, but in a slow and imperceptible manner, without any formal law to sanction it.

The arrangements of Servius Tullius were of the greatest advantage to the clients. For now the army was no longer divided after the patrician manner into tribes, curiæ, and gentes; but as according to the principle of riches, into centuries. The client now marched with his fellows, and had another leader in battle than his patron.

And as this division into centuries held good also for purposes of voting as well as for fighting, here was another most important occasion when the client could act independently of his patron. The result was that the clients sought to detach themselves from the gens and become members of the plebs. And this design was furthered to the utmost of their power by the kings (whilst there were kings), because their chief aim was to weaken the gentes; and by the plebs and its tribunes in time of the republic.

A law-suit of the Claudii against the Marcelli, in later times, illustrates the disappearance of the condition of clients as it was understood in early times. The Marcelli seems to have been a branch detached from the Claudian *gens*, for they were Claudii but not patricians. Having been freed at an early period, and enriched we know not how, they raised themselves first to the dignities of the plebs, and then to those of the city. For many centuries the Claudian race forgot its rights over them; but one day in the time of Cicero,[1] it suddenly laid claim to them again. A freedman or client of the Marcelli had died and left an inheritance which ought to revert to the patron. The patrician Claudii asserted that the Marcelli, being only clients themselves, could not have other clients, and that their freedmen, inheritance and all, belonged to the patrician family, which alone could exercise the rights of patrons. This suit very much astonished the public and puzzled the lawyers; and

---

[1] Cicero, *De Oratore*, i., 39.

Cicero considered the question very obscure. There seems little doubt that four centuries earlier the matter would have seemed simple enough, and the Claudian cause been triumphant. But in Cicero's time, the rights upon which the claim was founded seem so old, that the court were enabled to decide in favour of the Marcelli. In fact, the institution became obsolete.

CHAPTER XLIV.

THIRD REVOLUTION.

THE PLEBS ADMITTED TO THE CITY.—LAWS RESPECTING PROPERTY ARE MODIFIED.—GOVERNMENT BEING CONDUCTED ON THE NEW PRINCIPLE OF THE PUBLIC INTEREST, MEN DEBATE AND VOTE.

§ 1. *General history of the plebeian progress.*

THE changes which had at last been brought about in the constitution of the family, eventually altered also the constitution of the city. By the abolition of the right of primogeniture[1] and by the gradual enfranchisement of the clients, the unity and power of the gens perished. Now the lower orders, instead of being distributed among the gentes, maintained an existence apart, and formed a body to themselves. Consequently, the city assumed a totally different aspect, and in place of being a union of distinct clans, weakly bound together, became the seat of two hostile peoples, of which the patricians formed one and the men of the lower orders the other. The struggle was no longer obscurely maintained in the retirement of separate families; there was open war in every city. The aristocratic party wished to maintain the old religious system, and to keep the government in the hands of the sacred families. But the other wished to break up the old barriers which held them away from law, religion, and political society.

In the former part of the struggle, the birth-aristocracy had the advantage; because, though robbed of its former subjects, it still retained the prestige conferred by religion, its regular organization, its habit of command, and its

---

[1] That is, the custom of the sole inheritance of the eldest son.

hereditary pride. They thought sincerely that they were defending religion and law. On the other hand, the people had nothing but numbers on their side; they were destitute of leaders and discipline, and were held back by habits of respect, of which it is not easy to get rid. No other principle of association having yet been found by this race beside the hereditary family religion, and no other idea of authority but that which springs from worship, it is easy to understand that a long period was required for the plebs (who had always been excluded from the rites of religion) to form anything but an ill-constituted and disorganized mass.

The inferior classes saw no other means of combating the aristocracy, but to oppose to them the monarchy. Therefore, if in any town the new classes had attained sufficient discipline whilst the kings still reigned, they encouraged the sovereign to augment his power to the utmost. At Rome, they enforced the re-establishment of royalty after Romulus, caused Hostilius to be appointed, made Tarquinius Priscus king, loved Servius, and regretted Tarquin the proud. And when the aristocracy had overcome the kings, the people aspired to restore the vanquished monarchy under another form. During the sixth century, in Greece, they succeeded generally in procuring leaders, whom they could not call kings, because that word implied the idea of religious functions, but for whom was found or invented the new appellation of tyrants.[1]

This word, whatever its original meaning, had nothing to do with religion, and could not be applied in prayer to the gods as "king" and "father" were. In fact, it indicated something quite new in the Aryan race, an authority not founded on religion, and the hitherto unknown principle of obedience of man to man. Up to this time all had been done in the name of the gods,[2] but now they rejected the gods, that they should not reign over them. For the idea had not yet been conceived of man raising his fellow to such complete power over him.

But so it was in almost every ancient city at a certain period. At Corinth, Cypselus perceived that the people

---

[1] Hdtus., v., 92. When a popular chief happened to be of one of the religious families, he might retain the name of king.
[2] 1st Sam., viii., 7.

could not tolerate the domination of the Bacchidæ, and offered himself as leader against them. The Bacchidæ were driven out, and he became tyrant. At Miletus the tyrant was Thrasybulus; at Mitylene, Pittacus; at Samos, Polycrates. There were tyrants in the sixth century before Christ at Argos, Epidaurus, and Megara; and Sicyon had them without interruption for one hundred and thirty years. Among the cities of Magna Græcia, we find tyrants at Cumæ, Crotona, Sybaris, and elsewhere. In 485 the lower classes of Syracuse made themselves masters of the town, and drove out the aristocracy. But as they were unable to govern themselves or maintain their ascendancy, they gave themselves a tyrant after a year of republicanism.

The same policy was pursued everywhere by these tyrants, with more or less of violence. What this policy was, is indicated in the symbolical advice given by the tyrant of Miletus to the tyrant of Corinth, when he knocked off the heads of the tallest stalks of corn.

At Rome, the plebs kept plotting to restore Tarquin, and afterwards would have made tyrants of Publicola, Spurius Cassius, and Manlius. For the accusations of the patricians against members of their own body were not all calumnies, and the wishes of the plebs are indicated by the fears of the nobles.

However, it must be remarked that if the people of Greece and Rome sought to restore monarchy, it was not that they loved the tyrants, so much as that they detested the aristocracy; but the tyrant had no root in the people's heart, and when the cruelty of the aristocracy was forgotten the tyrants fell. This method of government was but a resource till a better way presented itself.

About 600 B.C., agriculture ceased to be the only source of riches in Italy and Greece. Industry and commerce caused the appearance of money, and personal property was no longer unknown. Money caused a great revolution, being what the Roman lawyers call *res nec mancipi*. It could pass from hand to hand without any formality, and, unlike the soil on which religion had stamped its peculiar mark, could pass without difficulty into possession of the plebeian.

---

[1] Nicol. of Damas., Fragm. Aristotle, *Pol.*, v., 9. Thuc., i., 126. Diodor., iv., 5.

We now find artizans, sailors, merchants, and manufacturers; and some of them rich, whilst the luxury that enriched the plebeian seemed in many cases to have impoverished the noble. Especially it was remarked, at Athens, that many Eupatrids had fallen into difficulty. Now when wealth is thus changing hands, an alteration of rank is imminent.

Amongst the lower classes themselves, in consequence of the different degrees of wealth, distinctions of rank arose, as will be the case in every human society. But this was not an evil, because the people thus became less of a disorganized mass, and could find leaders of their own sort. The plebeian aristocracy had the good qualities which usually accompany riches acquired by toil, the feeling of personal worth, the love of tranquility as well as of liberty, and the sense to wish for amelioration of condition without risking present advantages. For the sake of such men, the people renounced tyrants, seeing that it possessed in its own bosom the elements of a better government; and, in fact, as we shall see by and bye, riches became for a time a principle of social organization.

And there was another change which very much aided the lower classes in their struggle to rise, namely, that which had taken place in military matters. In former times the cavalry had formed the strength of armies, whether fighting from a chariot or from the horse's back; and the foot-soldier was little accounted of. Accordingly, the aristocracy had reserved to itself the right of using horses in battle; obtaining in some towns the title of knights. Romulus's *celeres* and the Roman knights at first were all patricians. However, the infantry gradually gained importance, as better arms, better training, and more self-confidence enabled them to withstand cavalry. Afterwards, the greater facility with which infantry are manœuvred obtained the legionaries and the hoplites the first place. And these were plebeians. Add to this, and especially in Greece, that maritime warfare often placed the fortunes of a city in the hands of the rowers, who were men of the same rank. Now a class of men which is strong and clever enough to defend a society, is also strong enough to conquer its own rights, and win a high position in the social scale.

In the next place, the lower classes succeeded in inventing or adopting a religion of their own; for having the common feelings of humanity as to the spiritual world, and seeing the necessity of prayer and sacrifice, they contrived in various ways to get rid of that superiority in religious matters which birth had bestowed on the patricians. Sometimes the plebeian who had no family worship would have recourse to the city gods; as, for instance, at Rome many plebeians offered an annual sacrifice to the god Quirinus. Others built a temple for themselves, as that of Diana on the Aventine;[1] and there was also the temple to Plebeian Modesty. Again, just as in India Buddhism was gladly received as an opposition to caste, so many Oriental worships were welcomed at Rome and in Greece by the lower orders. Again, very often the plebeians would make to themselves gods like those of the patrician curiæ and tribes. So king Servius raised altars in every quarter of the city for the multitude to sacrifice; and the Pisistratidæ planted Hermæ in the streets and open spaces of Athens, to be the gods of the democracy. And by this possibility of praying and sacrificing, the lower orders added much to their dignity in a state of society where religion was so highly considered.

When, then, the lower orders could boast of rich men, and soldiers and priests, the aristocracy could not help counting them for something in the state, and their rights were evidently to be no more denied. The history of Greece and Italy from 700 to 500 B.C. is occupied chiefly with the entry of the lower orders into the city. They won the victory everywhere; though not everywhere in the same manner or by the same means. In some places as soon as they found their strength, they rose in insurrection, and forced the gates of the sacred city in which they had not been allowed to dwell, and either drove out the nobles and occupied their houses, or contented themselves with obtaining equal rights. So it happened at Syracuse, Miletus, and Erythræ. In others, less violent measures were employed, and moral pressure alone compelled the great families to make concessions. Then, as at Athens, a legislator was appointed and the constitution changed. Elsewhere, as at Cumæ, a still

---

[1] Varro, *L. L.*, v., 13.

more gradual progress raised the lower classes to equality with the higher. There, the number of citizens had originally been very small; next, those who could keep a horse were added. Afterwards the number of the citizens was made a thousand, and by slow degrees they arrived at democracy.

There were towns, like Rome, where kings at first admitted the plebeians to citizenship. Popular tyrants did the same at Corinth, Sicyon, and Argos. And then if the aristocracy got the upper hand again, the title was wisely allowed to remain. At Samos, the aristocracy could not get rid of tyrants (though they struggled long), without also perfectly emancipating the lowest classes. Everywhere the result was the same: the lower orders penetrated the city and made part of the body politic.

The effects of the same revolution at Megara may be gathered with instruction from the writings of the aristocratic exile, Theognis. He had striven his best against the overthrow of ancient institutions, but all in vain. Stripped of his possessions, and dwelling in a foreign land, he was forced to accept his defeat. Still he retained a strong feeling of having been wronged, and protested vigorously in his verses. He laments over the conquest of the *good* men, or aristocratic party, by the *bad* or democrats, who had neither courts of justice nor laws (*i.e.*, who had not the right of citizenship), and who lived without the gates like savage beasts. In former times these κακοί could not be present at religious meals, nor marry into the families of the ἀγαθοί. But now all is changed. Justice is disturbed, old laws abolished, riches the only object, marriage mingles races. The gods have quitted the earth; the race of the godly has disappeared; nor do men think any more about the immortals.

§ 2. *History of the third revolution at Athens.*

Four dull centuries of aristocratic rule in Attica at length wearied the people, and determined them to make every effort to get rid of the Eupatrids. In 598, Cylon, who was an Eupatrid himself, made an abortive attempt at overthrowing the rule of his caste and establishing himself as popular tyrant. The archons foiled his endeavour, but the agitation continued afterwards, and was allayed by none of the religious devices to which the upper order had recourse. Their announcement that spectres had been seen and that the gods were angry, their elevation of altars to Violence and Insolence, their purification of every part of the city, were all in vain. A mysterious person named Epimenides, son of a goddess, was sent for from Crete, and performed more expiatory ceremonies; but religious feeling could not be revived, nor the aristocracy fortified. The people would have reform. After sixteen additional years of opposition, more patiently conducted by the sea-faring population, and more violently by the mountaineers, it was agreed to have recourse to Solon for the termination of the complaints and the prevention of more serious evils. Solon was an Eupatrid by birth, but had been engaged when young in commerce, and is proved by his poetry to have been free from caste prejudices, whilst his conciliating manners and his turn for pleasure proved him to belong rather to young Athens than to the old religious party.

We have already explained his emancipation of the clients; but this was not all he effected. The lower classes would have had no assurance of freedom without political rights, and, as Solon says himself, they needed a buckler to defend their new liberty. Though Solon's constitution is not known in its entirety, it seems at least clear that all Athenians henceforth could take part in the public assembly, and that the Senate was open to other than Eupatrids. Even archons now need not be of the sacerdotal caste; to such an extent were old rules annulled. A distinction of classes indeed remained, but what marked one man from another was now riches alone. The poor noble had come to be of no account, and the people applauded in the theatre when the comic poet made one of his characters answer the question, "The birth of this man is...?" "Oh, rich, for that is what noble comes to now."[1]

But Solon's new system had scarcely been established when it was found to have two powerful enemies, first, the Eupatrids, who regretted their lost privileges; and, secondly, the poorest classes, who were dissatisfied that any possibility of reigning was left to their old foes, and who also liked the

---

[1] Eurip., *Phœniss.* *Alexis*, in Athenæus, iv., 49.

new sway of the wealthy as little as they had done that of the noble. The revolution seemed incomplete whilst any Eupatrid could be archon or senator; and this might easily be the case under the republican forms of government which Solon left. Wherefore, after the example of many other Greek cities, they desired a tyrant.

The Eupatrid Pisistratus, animated by a merely personal ambition, attached the lower orders to his interests by promises of land; and one day, pretending to be wounded, demanded a body-guard. Then, though some Eupatrids sought to expose the falsehood, the lower orders shewed a strong determination to uphold him, and put to flight the parties both of the well-born and of the wealthy. And so the Athenians disgraced their new-found liberty by giving their country a master by one of their earliest independent acts.

Still the reign of Pisistratus seems in no way to have prevented the development of Athenian destiny. Indeed, its great effect may be said to have been to secure the previous revolution against all re-action; for the Eupatrids never rallied again.

So long as Pisistratus lived we find no eagerness on the part of the people to recover their liberty. The party of the nobles twice coalesced with that of the rich to turn him out, but twice he recovered his power; and his sons ruled Athens after him. A Spartan army was required to overthrow their power.

The downfall of the Pisistratidæ seemed to the old aristocracy a good opportunity for attempting to recover their power; but so far from succeeding when they attempted it, they received a severer blow than they had yet experienced. Cleisthenes, who came of a noble family which they had disgraced, found means of utterly extinguishing whatever strength they had left. For he swept away all the old religious organization that Solon had allowed to remain in being. During the rule of Pisistratus the population had been divided into two or three hundred γένη, twelve phratriæ, and four tribes; and as in earlier times each of these groups had its hereditary worship, and a priest-chieftain who was an Eupatrid. By means of these relics of a slowly waning past, old traditions, old customs, and old ways of thinking still survived. As religion had called into being this frame-work of society, so now in turn it was supporting religion and the power of old families. By mere force of habit, so long as it subsisted, it retained some minds under the religious authority of the Eupatrid. The laws of Solon declared in vain that every man was free and might vote in the assembly, so long as it was still esteemed a mark of inferiority to belong to no gens, or phratria, or tribe. Therefore, after Solon's political reform, there remained a religious one to be taken in hand. And this was the work that Cleisthenes performed, when he suppressed the four religious tribes and replaced them with six local tribes, divided into demes.

These new tribes and demes were made as much as possible to look like the old tribes and γένη. For they all had a worship, a priest, and a judge, and sacred ceremonies, and assemblies to discuss common interests. But in spite of the seeming likeness, there was a very important difference; and this was that the new divisions being local, and not on the principle of birth, no Athenian citizen was excluded from the privileges and comforts of religion. Birth had no more value. Buried Eupatrids were no longer worshipped by the tribe or deme; but the tribe chose some new hero, Eponymus, in whom all could feel an interest, whilst the guardian deity of the deme was invariably Zeus Herkeius (Jove of the precinct), or the paternal Apollo. Now, too, the priestly dignity was but annual, tenable by anybody or every body in turn.

Thus an entire transformation took place in Athenian society. Caste was abolished, and the aristocracy of the Eupatrids overthrown. The same change took place in many more Greek cities, as Cyrene, Sicyon, Elis, and Sparta, but Aristotle instances the arrangements of Cleisthenes as most complete for founding democracy. For this purpose, he says, one must establish new tribes and new phratriæ; one must replace hereditary sacrifices of families with others that are open to all, confounding men's relations as much as possible, and breaking up all previous associations.

§ 3. *History of the third revolution at Rome.*

There are several reasons why the plebs soon became strong at Rome. The peculiar position of the city in the midst of Latins, Sabines, and Etruscans, gave rise to endless wars; for the carrying on of which a large population was needful. Wherefore the kings welcomed all strangers alike, and when they had conquered a city transferred its population bodily to Rome. Then, though the families that had been noble elsewhere were made noble also at Rome, these were much out-numbered by those who became clients and plebeians.

Commerce also attracted many strangers to a place which was conveniently central, whilst political discontent brought in many from the neighbouring countries. All these were plebeians. The same great class received also clients who were deserting their gens, degraded patricians, and bastards. Its importance was increased by the struggles between the aristocracy and the monarchs, and by the firm alliance which the latter formed with it. Servius, for instance, not content with giving them the lands of conquered people, published laws for their benefit, chiefly relating to their contracts with patricians. Again, he had recourse to a measure resembling that of Cleisthenes, mixing up the plebeians with the patricians in twenty-one local tribes, and leaving out no man on the score of birth. It is true the ancient division according to birth was not done away with, but the floating multitude of plebeians who hitherto had had so little real connexion with the city were now made a fixed part of it, and had a regular organization of their own. They now really seemed to belong to the city, having for each tribe a sacred fire and a sacrifice, with Lares at every crossing and in each rural district. So those who had no gods to worship by right of birth were now not left out of religion, and might celebrate the religious feasts of their quarter (compitalia, paganalia), in much the same way as the patrician celebrated the sacrinces of his gens and curia.

At the same time a great change was effected in the sacred ceremony of lustration (census). For now the people were no longer arrayed in curiæ, to the exclusion of those who did not belong to this aristocratic division. Every free dweller in Rome had his place at the sacred act, as being a member of some one of the new local tribes. After the king had marched round this mixed assembly with the priests singing the sacred hymns and the victims that were to be sacrificed, every person in it had become as much of a citizen as the oldest patrician.

Again, whereas before Servius's time there were but two great classes of men, the sacerdotal caste of patricians with its clients, and the plebeians, classes marked off from each other by the hereditary religion, now Servius divided them afresh on the principle of riches, making, first of all, the two natural orders of those who had something and those who had nothing, and then again dividing the first and more important of these into five[1] classes, according to the amount of their fortunes. So that now wealth was substituted for religion as the great distinction between man and man.

The same division was applied also by Servius to military service, and the plebeians having been made owners of property and citizens, were now also admitted to serve in the legions. Members of curiæ had hitherto alone composed the army; but now every person who possessed anything might enter, and the proletarii alone were excluded. And the soldier was no longer armed according to his birth as patrician or client. The army was arrayed according to riches, like the population. The first three lines of the legion were formed by the first class (who were completely armed), together with the second and third (who had at least shield, sword, and helmet). The fourth and fifth classes acted as skirmishers and slingers, and consequently were but lightly armed. Each class was divided into companies called centuries, and of these there were in the first class eighty, in each of the others twenty or thirty apiece. The cavalry was now reckoned apart, according to a new system; for whereas hitherto the young patricians alone had made up the centuries of knights, Servius allowed a certain number of the richest plebeians to fight on horseback, and made of them twelve new centuries.

1st class,	heavy-armed	80	companies.
2nd ,,	armed with shield, sword, and helmet { ....20 to 30		,,
3rd ,,	{ ....20 to 30		,,
4th ,,	light-armed { ....20 to 30		,,
5th ,,	{ ....20 to 30		,,
Cavalry,	plebeian	12	,,
,,	patrician	6	,,

[1] See Cicero, *De Repub.*, ii., 22. Aulus-Gellius, x., 28. Some writers erroneously count six. But the knights and the proletarii were not classed.

But the army could not be modified without an accompanying alteration of the political constitution; and Servius rendered the military organization useful also for public assemblies and for voting. The citizens were convoked to the Campus Martius, where each one found his century, his centurion, and his flag. An old law forbade any army to enter the city, but the centuries could meet outside, hear the king's speech, and vote. The six centuries of patrician knights and the twelve of plebeian voted first, and then the centuries of infantry each in the order of its class. Such were the *comitia centuriata*, an assembly, where every soldier had the right to vote, and where scarce any distinction remained between patrician and plebeian.

Servius's constitution was a great advantage won for the plebeians, in the struggle that had even then begun. It did not yet mix them up with the patricians, who still formed a compact body, and had their Senate, their curiæ, and their hereditary worships; but it enabled the plebeians to stand up independently on *their* side, proud of their new wealth, arms, and worships.

NOTE ON THE COMITIA CENTURIATA.

We adduce the following proofs of the identity of this assembly with the Roman army:—

1. Latin writers call this assembly the army, Varro, vi., 93, *urbanus exercitus*. Livy, xxxix., 15, *miles ad suffragia vocatur et comitia centuriata dicuntur*. Ampelius, 48.

2. The way in which the comitia were convoked exactly resembled the way in which the army entered on a campaign. Varro, v., 91. The trumpet sounded, a red flag was hoisted for the infantry, and a green one for the cavalry.

3. These comitia were always held in the Campus Martius, because the law forbade the army assembling in the town. Aulus-Gellius, xv., 27.

4. Every voter went with his arms. Dion. Cassius, xxxvii.

5. They were arranged by centuries or companies, the infantry on one side, and the cavalry on the other.

6. Every century had its centurion at its head and its ensign, 'ὥσπερ ἐν πολέμῳ. Dion. Halic., vii., 59.

7. Men beyond sixty, discharged from the army, could no longer vote. Macrob., i., 5. Festus, Vº. *Depontani*. And it may further be remarked that the word classis used to signify a troop.

At first, the proletarii had no part in the assembly, but eventually, as they furnished a century for manual labour, they were also allowed to form a century in the comitia.

It is true, the patricians afterwards had their turn. They murdered Servius, and exiled Tarquin, took away from the plebeians the land that had been given them, for no other reason than that they *were* plebeians, thus re-affirming the ancient principle that the right to property went with the possession of a hereditary worship.

For the same reason, the laws which Servius had made for the plebs were taken away from them, and it was established that the hereditary religion alone was to govern men. The patricians doubtless had not coolly determined to crush the plebs by oppression; but they understood no other system of society than that whose rules had been traced by the old religion. The new worships of the plebeians seemed a new and a false assumption, which they could not tolerate.

Yet it was never forgotten that Servius had not merely given hopes of liberty and dignity to the plebeian, but had actually established a better state of things. Much that Servius had done could never be undone; the patricians dared not refuse the title of citizens to their inferiors, nor prevent them figuring in the census; because the continual wars in which Rome was engaged forbade the disorganization of the army. Yet, though willing to use the services of the plebeians, the patricians had no satisfactory policy to substitute for that of the king's which they had set aside. Their own religious system in time past had had its value, nay, had founded society, but was inapplicable to present circumstances, when thousands of families, living amongst them without laws or magistrates, were practically putting the question what was to be done with them. The system of religious exclusion seemed to be making all laws and government impossible for the plebeians.

And nothing but the old system seems to have occurred to the patricians as possible. If they had a policy it was to reduce the plebs to the condition of clients, and bring them within the frame-work of the *gens*. And a notable attempt of this sort seems to have been made. The question of debts which fills up the history of these times is inexplicable, unless it runs also into the matter of clientship and serfdom. It must be remembered that the revolution had deprived the plebeians of their lands, and prevented them from any longer gaining a livelihood by agriculture. They were obliged to have recourse to the money-lenders who acted for the patricians, and who lent in the fashion of those times, *per æs et libram*, that is, by a sacred form which conveyed a man over, as if sold to his creditor, in case of non-payment. Till the money was due, the plebeian had stipulated for freedom and had it; but if he could not pay he was reduced to servitude, and became a client.

Had this policy succeeded, society would have reverted to the old condition of things which subsisted before the time of the kings, ere Servius and the others had tried to elevate the condition of the common herd. But the plebs abhorred the idea of clientship, and strove their best against their patrician creditors. We hear of debtors who had been seized, appealing to their fellow plebeians, declaring they were free men, shewing the scars they had received in battle, and calling the patrician's house no better than a prison for hard labour. The whole mass of the plebeians struggled hard to get out of the precarious position in which the fall of royalty had placed them. Not that it yet entered their heads to claim equal rights and the same laws as the patricians. The only means that presented itself for ameliorating their condition was to effect a complete separation and leave Rome for good. "Since the patricians will have the city to themselves," are the words put into their mouth by the historian, "let them enjoy it at their leisure; we are but quitting a foreign town; no hereditary worship attaches us to this place. For us all lands are the same, and the place where we find liberty shall be our country."[1] So they established themselves on Mount Sacer, beyond the limits of the Roman territory.

On the subject of this secession, the opinions of the Senate were divided. Some thought they were well rid of the plebeians, and were willing to sacrifice the future greatness of their country for the sake of class supremacy. Others felt the want of them for military purposes, and wished to bring them back. The plebeians, in the meantime, on Mount Sacer, after some months, began to feel their need of organization and laws. The Secession differed very much from the foundation of an ancient colony, and though they

---

[1] Dion. Halic., vi., 45; vi., 79.

might supply their own material wants they began to feel that they were deficient in more important though less tangible matters. In fact, having no sacred fire, no properly constituted magistrates, no laws, they did not seem to form a regular society on Mount Sacer any more than they had done at Rome. Accordingly, a treaty of alliance was concluded (much in the same forms that were wont to terminate a war between two different peoples), by which the plebeians did not obtain a share in the religion and laws of Rome, but only a sort of organization under chiefs of their own.

This was the origin of the tribunes of the plebs, a sort of officers differing entirely from anything hitherto known, and not at all like the ordinary magistrates. For the tribunes had no religious ceremony to perform, were selected without auspices, and needed not the assent of the gods for their appointment.[1] They had neither curule chair, nor purple robe, nor crown of leaves, nor any of those tokens which in ancients' cities were wont to point out the priest-magistrates to the veneration of their fellows. And so the tribunes were never counted among the number of the Roman magistrates. Not but what a religious ceremony took place on the occasion of their creation, but it was of a distinct and peculiar character.[2] The rites are unknown, but the effect of them was to make the tribunes *sacro-sancti*, that is to say, their persons were henceforth classed among those objects which religion forbade to be touched ; and whosoever laid hands upon them was thereby rendered unclean.[3] Whence any religious person who met a tribune on the way, did not fail to purify himself, when he reached home.[4] This peculiar character belonged to the tribune as long as he was in office, and was also transmitted by him to his successor, just as the consul passed on the auspices and right of performing sacrifice. After an interruption of two years, which once occurred, the ceremony that had originally taken place on Mount Sacer had to be

---

[1] Dion., x. Plutarch, *Quæst. Rom.*, 84.
[2] Livy, iii., 55.
[3] This is the proper meaning of the word *sacer*. Plaut. Bach., iv., 6, 13. Catull., xiv., 12. Festus, V° *Sacer*. Macrob., iii., 7. According to Livy, it was not the tribune who were called *sacro-sancti*, but the man who injured his person.
[4] Plutarch, *Quæst. Rom.*, 81.

renewed. We are not able to say for certain whether this character of sacro-sanctity rendered the person of the tribune honourable in patrician eyes, or an object of malediction and horror. The second alternative seems the more probable. However, the tribune was inviolable, since no patrician could touch him without the gravest impiety. And not only would any one who might strike a tribune be rendered impure, but his goods would be confiscated to the temple of Ceres, and one might kill him with impunity. The vagueness of the concluding formula was of great help to the tribunes in later times when they sought to increase their power. "No magistrate," it said, "or private person shall have the right to do anything against a tribune." Further, all the citizens took an oath to observe this strange law, invoking on themselves the anger of the gods in case of violation.[1]

The means whereby the tribune acted for the protection of the plebs was by the intervention of his person (intercessio). For instance, if any plebeian was being ill-treated by a consul and condemned to prison, or if any patrician laid hands with violence on a plebeian, the tribune could stop it at once. But the tribune must be there. Out of his sight, or beyond the reach of his voice and hand, no one felt his power. Still, experience proved that though the patricians had granted no rights, the inviolable character of the tribunes procured enough security for all. They were like living and moving altars where everyone could take refuge. They had no right of judging or even of summoning any one before them at first; but they won the right gradually; or perhaps we may say it was a development of their power of intervention; for they could lay hands on a man, and whosoever was touched obeyed, even if a patrician or consul. For the audacity of the tribunes led them to make many encroachments. Nothing authorized them to call together either the curiæ or the centuries, and, seeing they had nothing to do with the patrician city or populus, it was doubtful whether they could appear in the Senate, much less speak there. However, we find them by and bye assembling the people

---

[1] Dion. Halic., vi., 98; x., 32; x., 42.

[2] Tribuni antiquitus creati, non juri dicundo nec causis querelisque de absentibus noscendis, sed intercessionibus faciendis quibus præsentes fuissent, ut injuria quæ coram fieret arceretur. Aulus-Gellius, xiii., 12.

and then sitting in the Senate, first at the door, afterwards in the interior. Indeed, so powerful were the solemn rites by which the tribunes were rendered inviolate, that at last there seemed to be no means of resisting a tribune but by winning over another tribune, and inciting him against his fellow.

But now that the plebeians had leaders of their own, deliberative assemblies were not long in being accorded also, though they were of a different character from the patrician meetings. For the latter were religious, commencing with a sacrifice, and being liable to dismissal at the word of a pontiff or augur who might think the gods unfavourable. Whereas the plebeian assembly paid no regard to the gods, and was composed of men who voted neither by the rules of religion nor by riches, but according to the locality of their dwellings. And this assembly was not convoked to consider the general interests of the city, to nominate magistrates, or carry laws; it only made plebeian officers and carried *plebiscita*. For Rome beheld for a long space of time a double series of decrees, *senatūs-consulta* for the patricians and *plebis-scita* for the plebs; the latter decrees gaining no obedience from the patricians, nor the former from the plebs. In fact, two peoples existed within the same walls, having but little in common. A plebeian could not be consul of the city, nor a patrician tribune of the plebs. The plebeian could not enter the comitia curiata, nor the patrician the meeting of the tribes.[1]

The ideas of these two peoples were essentially different. If the patrician spoke in the name of religion and law, the plebeian knew not the hereditary religion nor the laws resulting from it. If the patrician cited a sacred custom, the answer of the plebeian was in the name of nature's rights. Each accused the other of injustice, being just himself according to a different principle. To the plebeian the meeting of the patres in their comitia curiata seemed the exercise of an odious privilege; whilst the patrician regarded the meeting of the tribes as a reprehensible and irreligious gathering. The consuls were to the plebeians arbitrary and

---

[1] Livy, ii., 60. Dion., vii., 16. Festus, V°. *Scita plebis*. This is true only of early times. The patricians were enrolled in the local tribes, but took no part in assemblies which met without auspices and without religious ceremonial.

tyrannical authorities; and the tribunes were in patrician eyes something impious and abnormal. By it the order of the city seemed disturbed; and it was like a heresy in their eyes, so that a patrician once said: "The gods will be against us, as long as we cherish this consuming ulcer that spreads corruption through the whole body of the state." And indeed, for a century Roman history is occupied with this game at cross purposes, the patricians persisting in excluding their inferiors from the city, and the latter continuing to establish institutions of their own.

The chief bond of union was war, for which purpose the plebeians had been allowed to retain the title of citizens, which Servius had given them; since otherwise they would not have been liable to serve in the legions. And it had been stipulated that the inviolability of the tribunes should not extend beyond the walls, in order to preserve military discipline, and that at least before the foe Rome might be one.

The comitia centuriata, also, or meeting of the army for political purposes, was a neutral ground on which both sides met for common purposes; and this institution came more and more into use, being finally called the great comitia.

Lastly, the richer plebeians, whether they had won their wealth in Rome itself, or had been transported from some conquered city, constituted an intermediary body, the classes not having been yet abolished, and some plebeians always voting in the first class with the patricians. These persons belonged to the discontented party, and yet wealth tended to make them conservative, since they had so much to lose if Rome fell.

We do not find that the plebeians had that rage for equality which is so noticeable in some countries in modern days. For it does not appear that their five-fold classification was at all objected to, since thirty-six years after the institution of tribunes their number was raised to ten, in order that each class might have two. And the lowest order does not even make a claim to have a tribune chosen from amongst its members.

The patricians, likewise, seemed to have been undisturbed by the increasing importance of riches, for they themselves also were wealthy, having neglected neither agriculture, commerce, nor manufacture; and deriving great gains from conquest; for the nobles of Rome were not like the Eupatrids of Athens, of whom so many fell into obscurity when wealth began to be the distinction between man and man. At Rome, therefore, the wealthy plebeians, who could not be despised by the nobles, and who had many relations with them, ended by winning them over to see the justice of abating somewhat of their prerogatives. Ambition and interest led these persons rather to wish for a share in patrician dignities than to remain at the head of a separate order, framing laws by plebiscita that affected only part of the city. And after their example the plebeians generally began to aim at an union of the two orders on conditions of equality.

The first demand was for a code of laws no longer applicable to the patricians alone, not sacred and secret, but written and published, and giving a right of property to the plebeian as well as to the others.

The tribunes at first desired that the legislators should be all plebeians, but the patricians maintained the demand to be monstrous, and declared it could only have arisen from their ignorance, seeing that laws were sacred things only to be promulgated by those who were conversant with religious matters, and who could take the pleasure of the gods. Fearful prodigies that occurred about that time seemed to prove the patricians right, for the heaven was seen on fire, spectres flitted in the air, and it rained blood. For eight years nothing was agreed to, each order remaining in astonishment at the obstinacy of the other. Then the tribunes proposed that the legislators should be of both orders, thinking they were making a great concession. But the religious principles of the patricians made little account of this, and would have no legislator who was not of a priestly family. At last it was settled that all the law-makers should be of the superior order, but that their code, before being sanctioned and used, should be submitted to the approval of the public.

The laws of the Decemvirs, after exposure in the forum, and plenty of free discussion, were accepted by the comitia centuriata, or meeting of both orders. Henceforth the same law applied to all, and in all the code not one single word is found about inequality between patrician and plebeian, either as regards right to property, or about contracts and obligations, or in the forms of litigation. Henceforth the plebeian met the patrician on equal terms, and Rome saw a radical change in the manners and feelings of man to man. The principles of law, the dignity of persons, and men's behaviour to one another were altered.

Ideas advanced so rapidly that within a year, since some laws still remained to be made, amongst the new decemvirs were three plebeians; and generally manners tended towards equality. For instance, since religion and custom no longer sufficed to prevent marriage between the two orders, a law was passed forbidding it; but no sooner was the law made than it fell into universal disrepute, and was withdrawn. Not to speak of the Licinii, very soon members of the Fabian, Cornelian, and Manlian *gentes* had plebeian wives, and plebeian blood henceforth continued to be mingled with the patrician.

When equality in private life had been won, the hardest matter seemed to be accomplished, and it seemed natural that in politics also men should be on a like footing. The plebeians asked why the consulate should be withheld from them, and could understand nothing of the patrician scruples about the priestly functions of the office, which they said required, besides courage and intelligence, a sacred character and a peculiar birth to make the sacrifices acceptable to the gods. When arguments failed, the patricians used address to keep the plebeians out of the magistracies, and, as soon as the consulate seemed in danger, separated the censorial functions from it, in order to preserve what was most holy from the plebeian grasp. At another time, when it was becoming beyond their power to resist the plebeian ambition, military tribunes were substituted for consuls; and seventy-five years were brought to end before the ambitious wish was realised.

The generality of the plebeians were by no means as eager for these great offices to be held by members of their order as were these leaders themselves. Licinius and Sextius (who wished for the consulships), in order to pass a law that one consul must be plebeian, were obliged to tack on two other rogations to this, viz., first, a diminution of debts owed, and, secondly, a grant of lands to the people. And when the common herd were willing to take these two enactments without the other, the tribunes were obliged to declare them inseparable. Even then for ten years the Senate refused to hold the great comitia to pass them, and, though Livy glides lightly over the matter, blood was shed before the patricians yielded. A decree of the Senate approved beforehand all measures that the people might vote that year; and after the tribunes had passed their bills, every succeeding year saw one plebeian consul in purple robe with fasces before him, administering justice and commanding the legions.

The other offices followed the consulate, but the priesthood seemed harder to win, for the knowledge of ceremonies and the possession of gods was hereditary. The city worship was supposed to belong exclusively to those families which had formed the primitive city. If the priestly offices had been separated from political functions, the plebeians perhaps would not have been so eager to obtain them; but everything was originally mixed up. The priest was a magistrate, the pontiff was a judge, and the augur could dissolve assemblies. It was clear that equality did not really exist so long as these functions were denied the plebeians. The old arguments about offending the gods were brought forward once more, but this time again in vain, and it was settled at last that half the augurs and half the pontiffs should thenceforth be selected from amongst the plebeians.

Nothing more remained to be won. The patricians had lost even their precedence in religion, and now retained but a nominal superiority. Of the old religion which had so long classified and governed men there remained but the outward formalities. That which had been for four hundred years of royalty and republic the plebeians' greatest foe, was now fallen, and the principles which had lain at the foundation of Rome and all other ancient cities, were superseded.

CHAPTER XLV.

CHANGES IN THE LAWS ABOUT PRIVATE PROPERTY; THE TWELVE TABLES; SOLON'S LEGISLATION.

SOCIETY as it developes itself and is changed in manners and belief, so also is obliged to modify its rules. Wherefore law, like all other works of man, is anything but absolute and unalterable. When the patriarchal system gave way before that which arose from the association of men in cities, then the gens, which was its expression, broke up; the elder brother no longer retaining his authority over the younger, nor the patron over the client, whilst the inferior order, which did not properly belong to the association, attained equality with the true citizens. These were the changes in social life which necessarily entailed changes also in law. For the lower orders detested the old domestic religion, which had been the source of their long humiliation and oppression, as much as the patricians and Eupatridæ loved it; and naturally strove with all their might to abolish laws which seemed unjust, if they were not incomprehensible.

We find a very great difference between the laws of primitive society and those of the period when the lower orders had become citizens. In the first place, they are no longer concealed as something sacred and mysterious, handed down by word of mouth from age to age with pious respect, or written out by priests and committed to memory by men of sacred families. On the contrary, they are now open to all, read and discussed by everybody. Now legislation is altered in its source, having become an emanation of the people's will, and being enunciated in their interest. Its principle is now the public good; and not the will of the gods.

It no longer reveals the divine pleasure, but simply the wishes of the majority. With these ideas the Decemvirs at Rome, as well as Solon at Athens, published their laws; and, as the Twelve Tables expressed it, "The law is what the votes of the people finally ordain." Sacred custom, *mos*, was giving way before *lex*, mere text; or in other words, formulas which it was sacrilege to discuss were replaced by the expressions of man's varying will, to which we may apply the words of the English poet,

> "A breath may make them as a breath has made."

Another consequence was that the Law belonged to everybody, instead of being the patrimony of certain sacred families, and now the plebeian could plead in the law-courts. It is true that at first the Roman patricians (who were more tenacious or more clever than the Eupatrids of Athens) tried to hide from the vulgar the forms of procedure, but this could not last long, and soon the law was the property of any and every citizen.

Still, the law is not a thing which can be altered at a stroke. Athenian and Roman history both prove that laws about private property change even more slowly than political institutions. The laws of the Twelve Tables, made by patricians at the request of plebeians for the use of both, is a transition between the primitive law and the succeeding or prætorian law.

The following points remain unaltered from ancient times:

1. The power of a father over his son, by which he could judge and condemn him to death; and by which also he could sell him. The son did not attain his majority so long as the father lived.

2. The laws of succession remained unaltered, the inheritance passing to *agnates*, and in default of agnates to *gentiles*. Cognates, or relations through women, are not yet recognized; for neither does the son inherit from the mother, nor the mother from the son.

3. Emancipation and adoption retain their old character and effects. The emancipated son has no longer any share in the worship of the family, nor consequently any right to inherit its property.

We next adduce the points on which the legislation of the Twelve Tables differs from the primitive law.

1. It is formally allowed that a patrimony may be divided amongst brothers (actio familiæ erciscundæ).

2. A father could only dispose of his son's person three times, after which he would be free. This is the first interference of Roman law with paternal authority.

3. A more important alteration was that which gave all men the power of making wills. Hitherto the eldest son had necessarily inherited from his father, or if there were no son, the nearest agnate, and if there were no agnate the property reverted to the *gens*, in memory of the time when the gens, being as yet undivided, was sole proprietor of the estate that was afterwards divided. The Twelve Tables set aside these ancient principles, which had become obsolete, considering the property to belong no more to the gens but the individual, and recognizing consequently the individual's right of disposing of it as he would by will.

Not that testaments had been unknown in times past; for men had been able to choose legatees who were not members of their gens, on condition of the choice being approved by the comitia curiata. But this rule also was now dispensed with, and, by pretending to sell his possessions to his chosen heir, a man really made a will that did not compel him to come before the public assembly.

One great advantage of this form of testament was that it was permissible to the plebeian also, who in old times had not been able to make a will, because he had no connexion with the comitia curiata. And generally it may be laid down that legal processes were now invented that were applicable to the plebeians, whereas the former rules and formalities only suited families that had a domestic worship.

Plebeian marriages had hitherto been without religious ceremony, and only reposed for fixity on the mutual consent of the married parties, whence the patrician laws recognized no value at all in them; and the plebeian husband and father had not that great authority which was wielded by the patrician. But now a formality was invented for plebeian use, which in civil matters would produce the same effects as the sacred marriage. They had recourse, as for the testament, to a fictitious sale; and the wife was bought by the husband, after which she was recognized as rightfully belonging to the husband and making part of his property (familia); then she was in his *manus*, and was unto him as a daughter, *in filiæ loco*, just as though the religious ceremony had been performed.[1]

It is possible that this procedure had been in existence when the Twelve Tables were written out, but if so, the new legislature adopted it, and thus gave the plebeian a right of property analogous in effect to that of the patrician, though founded on different principles.

The husband had another way of acquiring conjugal and paternal power,[2] besides this mode of buying his wife. Use was considered equally valid with sale (usus, coemptio), after that a plebeian had married in the usual plebeian manner (by *mutuus consensus* and *affectio maritalis*). Then a year's co-habitation had the same legal effect as a religious ceremony or the proceeding by way of sale.

Still the conjugal power of primitive times had consequences, which at the period of history at which we have arrived, began to seem excessive. We have seen that the wife was subjected without reserve to her husband, who could even alienate and sell her. Doubtless, in Gaius's time (i., 117, 118), this power was fictitious, but at first it may have been real. And most likely the utter separation of the wife from her father's family seemed undesirable to the plebeians. The object of this separation had been to prevent any person belonging to two *gentes*, or sacrificing at two fires, or inheriting of two houses. This was no longer necessary. Accordingly, the law of the Twelve Tables, whilst giving the husband his full power by means of a year's co-habitation, was obliged to allow married people also a possibility of evading such a rigorous bond. And therefore, if the wife interrupted her co-habitation each year by an absence of only three nights, it was enough to prevent the establishment of the greater marital power. By this means,

---

[1] Gaius, i., 114.

[2] Gaius, i., 114. Quæ anno continuo *nupta* perseverabat. Co-emptio was so far from being solely a way of marrying that a woman might contract it with another besides her husband, as for instance, with a guardian. And so *usus* was not a way of marrying, but of acquiring power.

the wife retained her connexion with her own family, and could inherit from it.

It will be evident without entering into longer details that the code of the Twelve Tables was a great alteration on the primitive law, and that Roman legislation was about to be modified along with the improvement of the government and the progress of society. And it may be seen, as generation follows generation, that some fresh change takes place. First, marriage is allowed between patricians and plebeians. Then, the Papinian law forbids the debtor's pledging his person to the creditor. Next, the abolition of legal formulæ simplified procedure, to the great advantage of the plebeians. Then the prætors, continuing to advance in the path traced in the Twelve Tables, marked out an entirely new system of laws, not dictated by religion, and nearer to the suggestions of nature.

ATHENS.

A similar revolution shews itself in Athenian law. Draco and Solon, it is well known, drew up two codes of laws at a distance of thirty years. The first was promulgated when the two classes were most violently opposed, and before the Eupatrids were yet overcome: whereas Solon's code did not see the light until the inferior orders had won the victory. The differences, therefore, are great between the two systems.

Draco, as an Eupatrid, learned in religious law, testified to the feelings of his caste by putting down unchanged every old custom. He begins with the following: "Let men honour the gods and the heroes of the country, and offer them the yearly sacrifices without deviating from the ancient rites." By him murderers were excluded from temples and forbidden to touch lustral water or the sacred vessels. Succeeding generations said that his laws were cruel; and indeed, they were the produce of an implacable religion, which supposed the deity might be offended by every error, and that he could not forgive. Thus, theft was punished with death. Another law (which allowed no one but relations of a murdered man, or those who were of the same γένος, to prosecute) is interesting as shewing the power which the institution of the γένος still retained; for the city was not allowed to interfere in its affairs, even to avenge it. The γένος then had a stronger hold on man than the city. What remains of Draco's legislation seems to prove it was but a reproduction of the primitive laws, that were transmitted by oral tradition. It has all their harshness and stiffness. It makes a broad distinction between classes; for the lower class always detested it, and after thirty years procured its abolition.

Solon's code is easily seen to correspond with a great social revolution. The first thing noticeable in his laws is that they are the same for all, making no distinction between Eupatrid, free man, or thete. Solon boasted that he had made the same law for great and small, and indeed, not one of those distinctive appellations presents itself in any of the clauses which have come down to us.

Like the Twelve Tables, Solon's code differs much on some points from primitive law, whilst on others it remains the same. Of course the Decemvirs did not copy the laws of Athens; but the two separate legislations, being the work of the same period and the result of the same social revolution, could not help resembling one another. And further, the resemblance is but in the spirit of the laws; since, when we descend to details, we find considerable divergence. On some points, Solon keeps nearer to primitive law than the Twelve Tables, and on some he wanders further away.

Whereas the primitive law gave the inheritance to the elder son alone, Solon says formally that the patrimony must be divided between brothers. But it is to be remarked that he agrees still with the old law in giving nothing to the sister.

Nay, even an only daughter could not inherit; since Solon agreed with the old law in bestowing the patrimony on the nearest agnate. Still he did something for the daughter, by forcing the heir to marry her.

By the old law, relationship through women was unknown. By the new law it was recognized, but considered inferior to relationship through men. Solon says: "If a father have but one daughter, the nearest agnate inherits and marries her. If he leave no child, the brother inherits, and not the sister; and the brother by the same father, not the brother by the same mother only.

If there be no brothers or sons of brothers, the sister succeeds to the property. If there be neither brothers nor sisters, nor nephews, then the cousins, and cousins once removed on the father's side inherit. And if there be no cousins on the father's side, that is, amongst the agnates, then the succession devolves upon the collaterals of maternal branch, that is to say, upon the cognates." Thus we find the females beginning to have a right to succeed, though a right inferior to that of the males; and, in fact, the principle is thus formally stated by the law: "Males and descendants by males exclude women and descendants by women." But, at all events, this sort of relationship is recognized to such an extent as to prove that natural feelings are beginning to speak as loudly as the old religion.

Again, Solon introduced into Athenian legislation what was a new thing, in the testament or will. Before him, property had passed necessarily to the nearest agnate or gentile (γεννητής), since the γένος, and not the individual, was thought to be the real owner. But now the γένος was breaking up, and each estate was made the property of an individual. Therefore the law allowed a man to dispose of his fortune and choose an heir as he would. But at the same time whilst the rights of the γένος were abolished, it was otherwise with those of the natural family. The son and no other, if there was one, succeeded the father; whilst, if there were but a daughter, no one, who was not willing to marry her, could be arbitrarily chosen as heir. But a man who had no children might follow his own whims in making a will. And this last rule is noticeable as being absolutely new in Athenian law. It shews how entirely changed men's ideas had become upon the subject of family.

By the legislation of Solon, the paternal power was very much modified at Athens, no longer extending as it had done over the liberty of a daughter or the life of a son, and probably also forbidding the sale of the son. For the paternal power passed away more rapidly at Athens than at Rome, which was always more conservative. The Twelve Tables laid it down that after the third sale the son should be free, but at Athens he became independent at a certain age; and if the son had not acquired a power of possessing property, we should not find the law as we do, which enjoins him to maintain his father when infirm or old, a law that would have been unnecessary at Rome, where the son did not own property, and was not free from the paternal power.

As for women, the law of Solon still conformed to the primitive law. They could not make wills, because women were never real owners of property, and had but enjoyment for life. But the old law was so far altered that now a woman could recover her dowry.

Another change was that, contrary to Draco's law, any citizen could now prosecute for murder, and not only the γένος of the murdered man. This was another rule of the old patriarchal system that disappeared.

So at Athens, as well as at Rome, law was generally being altered. A new state of society required it. As manners, belief, and institutions were modified, laws that had once been just and good ceased to appear so, and by slow degrees were abolished.

CHAPTER XLVI.

A NEW PRINCIPLE OF GOVERNMENT; THE PUBLIC INTEREST; VOTING.

THE revolution which we are considering did not merely raise the inferior order to a level with the priestly class; old principles also were set aside, and new rules began to govern society. Old names, indeed, of offices and the ancient formalities survived. There were archons at Athens and consuls at Rome as before; and religious ceremonies were unchanged; but at bottom in this new period, neither belief nor manners, nor law, was the same. The new principle that was substituted for religion as the governing idea of society was public interest.

It has been seen that what bound society together in ancient times was the necessity for accomplishing certain rites. From this religious want had been derived for some men the right of commanding, for others the obligation to obey; hence the rules of proceeding in law, in public assemblies, in war. The question had never been put in any city whether certain institutions were expedient; they existed for religious reasons. Interest and convenience had not contributed to their establishment, nor had the priestly class defended them on those grounds. The holy name of religious tradition sufficed for their maintenance.

But in the period upon which we are about to enter, the ruling principle that gives force to every institution, and the only one to dominate individual will, is the interest of the many. That which the Greeks called τὸ κοινόν, and the Latins *res publica*, is what is about to be substituted for the old religion. Henceforth, in the deliberations of Senates and of public assemblies, whether it be a question of law or of constitution, about a political institution or about property, the prescriptions of religion are no more considered, but only the demands of public interest.

A question which was put to Solon, with the answer which he gave to it, shews what a change had come over society. "Did he think he had given his country the best constitution possible?" he was asked, and answered "No; only that which suited it best." Infallibility and immutability were certain signs of the old system, and religion settled constitutions without thinking of accommodating herself to the wants and manners of rising generations. But now absolute truth was given up as an impossibility, and it was thought that the rules of government should be flexible and variable. All that Solon hoped for his laws was an observance of one hundred years.

Now, it is nearly always possible to debate and discuss what it is that the public interest requires. In old times, the auspices had borne the chief weight of deliberation, and the opinion of the priest, king, or sacred magistrate was omnipotent. The voting had been of importance merely as a matter of form, and was scarcely intended to make known anybody's opinion. But henceforth votes were taken on all subjects, and every one's opinion was asked. The suffrage became the great means of government, the source of institutions, and the rule of right. What was expedient and what was just even, was settled in this way, nor could magistrates or laws be continued except by favour of this new sovereign of states.

Of course the nature of government changed at the same time, its function being no longer to perform rightly the ceremonies of religion, but rather now to maintain order and peace at home, and dignity and influence abroad. Secondary objects became primary, politics taking precedence of religion, and city-government being looked upon as a human thing. Consequently, it came to pass that either new magistracies were created, or at least that the old ones assumed a new character.

ATHENS.

At Athens, the office of archon was not suppressed, but new officers were appointed, called generals, στρατηγοί, who answered better to the wants of the period. Their functions were not purely military, but concerned also finance and police-matters. In fact, it may be said that the archons had in their hands religion and religious affairs, whilst the generals possessed the political power. The latter scarcely even concerned themselves with the ceremonies which were indispensable in case of war, but by degrees they got into their hands all real authority. They might be chosen from other classes than the Eupatrids, and their qualifications were no longer religious as of old, or such as were demanded of the archons. For of the archons it was required that they should be of a pure family, that had domestic gods; but for a man to be a "general" nothing was needful beyond the possession of some property in Attica, and that he should have hitherto faithfully discharged the duties of a citizen. The archons had been designated by lot, *i.e.*, by the voice of the gods; but it was not so with the generals. More than piety seemed necessary in the increasing difficulty and complication of government, and men desired themselves to be assured that their generals possessed ability, prudence, courage, and the habit of commanding. So, whilst the Athenians left it to the gods to designate in the old way their own priests, that is, the archons, they determined themselves to elect the officers who should manage the city's material interests.

ROME.

A close examination of the institutions of Rome will shew that similar changes were taking place there also. In the first place, the tribunes of the plebs resembled the strategi, at least negatively, in having no priestly character, and also positively in that they gradually got into their power all the internal affairs of the public. Then a good deal of the priestly character was taken away from the consulate, for as soon as plebeians could be consuls, the ceremonies that were still performed, out of respect for tradition, became mere empty forms. The change was slow and unperceived at the time, but it was not less true that the consulate became less and less of a priesthood and more and more of a command. Most likely the institution of military tribunes, in 443 B.C., marks the transition from one sort of consulship to the other; and any one can perceive that the consulship, as held by Publicola, was a very different office from that held in the times of the Scipios.

At the same time, a change in the way of naming the consuls becomes evident. In fact, at first, the vote of the centuries in the election of magistrates was, as we have seen, a mere formality. Practically and truly the consul of each year was created by the consul of the year preceding, who took the will of the gods and transmitted the auspices. The centuries could but vote about the two or three candidates presented by the consul in office, and no discussion was permitted. Even if the people detested a candidate, they must vote for him. But at the period of history at which we are now arrived, with the same outward forms the election is quite different. There still remains a religious ceremony and a vote, but now it is the ceremony which is a mere form, and the vote is really efficient. Candidates are not less presented by the presiding consul; but the consul is forced by custom, if not by law, to present all candidates and to allow that the auspices are as favourable to one as another. And so the election belonged no more to the gods, but was in the hands of the people, the centuries naming whom they liked, and gods and auspices being compelled to accept everybody.

CHAPTER XLVII.

FOURTH REVOLUTION.

AN ARISTOCRACY OF RICHES TRIES TO ESTABLISH ITSELF; BUT IN VAIN: DEMOCRACY SUCCEEDS; AND TYRANTS ARE POPULAR.

DEMOCRACY did not immediately follow the religious aristocracy. It is true that in some towns the lower orders made insurrection, but they could found nothing durable, and the long disorders into which Syracuse, Miletus, and Samos fell, shew that in order to establish anything solid there was need of a class distinguished at least by wealth and the qualities which accompany wealth.

Solon did not expect to be able to obliterate the old distinction founded on hereditary religion, except by setting up new divisions on the principle of riches. He distributed the people into four classes, who had unequal rights, the richest only being able to arrive at the highest office, whilst the lowest of all could not take any place in the Senate or courts of justice.[1]

In the same way at Rome, Servius could not destroy the power of the patricians but by setting up a rival aristocracy. His twelve centuries of knights, chosen from amongst the richest plebeians, laid the foundation of the equestrian order which was ever after distinguished for its wealth. The plebeians who were not rich enough to be knights were divided into five classes, according to their possessions, and the proletarii belonged to no class at all, being practically destitute of political rights, since, though they might appear at the comitia centuriata, they did not vote there.[2] These

---

[1] Plutarch, *Solon*, 18; *Aristides*, 13. Aristotle quoted by Harpocration at the words ἱππεῖς θῆτες. Pollux, viii., 129.

[2] Livy, i., 43.

distinctions, though made by a king, sufficed for the republic, and the plebs did not shew itself very desirous of making its members equal.

The increased power of wealth is seen also in other cities. For instance, at Cumæ, political rights were only given at first to those who, being rich enough to own horses, could form an equestrian order; afterwards, the same rights were bestowed upon those whose fortune approached that of the knights, and even this measure only raised the number of citizens to a thousand. At Rhegium, the government was long in the hands of the thousand richest people of the city. At Thurii, a very large fortune was required for a man to be a member of the body politic. Theognis of Megara shows us very clearly in his poems that, after the fall of the nobility, it was the wealthy who ruled. At Thebes, to be citizen and to have all the privileges of the position, a man must be neither artizan nor tradesman.

Thus the political rights which in the preceding period had been attached to birth, now for a time clung to wealth; and an aristocracy of riches formed itself in every city, not on any deliberate plan or through anybody's contrivance, but because the minds of men after a long period of patriarchal and aristocratic rule felt the want of some sort of leader.

And it must be understood that riches stood for something else also; for instance, the possessors of it aimed always at being the military class at the same time, charging themselves with the defence of the cities which they governed, bearing the heaviest arms and braving the greatest danger in battle, and wishing generally to imitate the class of nobles whose place they were taking. In every city the richest constituted the cavalry, and those who were well-to-do the heavy-armed infantry. The poor were either excluded from the army, or at most employed as skirmishers and light-armed troops, or in the navy as rowers. The organization of the army corresponded exactly with the political organization of the city, and dangers were proportioned to privileges, material force being in the same hands as wealth. Thus we have seen that the comitia centuriata at Rome were nothing else than the army convoked for political purposes, which is proved by the fact that men who had passed the age of serving as soldiers could not vote. And though for Athens historians do not mention any similar rule, yet we find a singular correspondence between the number of soldiers and the number of citizens; thus at the beginning of the Peloponnesian war, Thucydides[1] tells us Athens had 13,000 hoplites. If we add the knights, whom Aristophanes reckons, in the Wasps, at a thousand, that makes 14,000 soldiers; and we gather from Plutarch that 14,000 was also the number of the citizens at this period, 430 B.C.

Thus, in almost all cities whose history is known to us, there was a period during which the wealthy, or at all events the well-to-do, were in possession of power. Like most political arrangements, this system was not without its merits, and, if the patriarchal nobility had founded society and helped it to live for centuries in peace and happiness, this new aristocracy of wealth gave a great push to intelligence and civilization. Every clever, hard-working, energetic man found his value; and the times were not only favourable to commerce and industry, but also to education, and Rome as well as Greece made great strides in every sort of progress.

But the wealthy could not retain their hold upon power nearly so long as the old nobility had done, because their title to consideration was not so worthy. They had no hold on man's conscience, nor any thought sufficiently elevated to make men revere them. Their wealth inspired envy instead of respect, and only led the poorer and less privileged citizens to repine at existing distinctions.

Besides, a general feeling of instability is generated when more than one revolution has occurred; and old traditions and ancient rules are not swept away without much harm being done. A time comes to some nations when no constitution can last; and so in those ancient times the new aristocracy was attacked as violently as the preceding had been, the poor desiring to be citizens and struggling to enter the body politic.

It would be impossible to enter into the details of this fresh struggle. The history of cities, as it gets further from their origin, becomes more diversified. They pass through the same revolutions, but these revolutions present themselves under varied forms. One thing is noticeable, at all events,

---

[1] Thuc., ii., 31 and 13.

that where the riches of the highest class consisted in land this class was longer-lived and more powerful ; whilst cities like Athens, where fortunes had been made in commerce, or by manufacture, bred a more envious lower order, which attacked the plutocracy more violently and earlier.

It is astonishing with what feebleness the wealthy Greeks held out. They could not appeal, it is true, to religious tradition ; but even their military superiority failed them. They would have lasted longer had peace been possible, but war pressed on the rich. Having been posted in the front rank of a great battle, very often the rich class came back decimated and weakened, and henceforth incapable of holding out against their antagonists. Thus at Tarentum, when the highest class had nearly all perished in war against the Japygians, democracy was instantly established in the city. Argos had gone through the same experience thirty years before, when, in a disastrous war against Sparta, so many citizens had perished that the rights of citizenship had to be extended to a great number of periœci.[1] In dread of a similar need, Sparta was excessively sparing of her citizens' blood. And a great deal of the history of the revolutions at Rome is only to be explained by her continual wars. First of all the patrician caste was destroyed by war, scarcely a third of the original three hundred families remaining after the conquest of Samnium. And, in like manner, afterwards the rich and brave plebeians who constituted the five classes and formed the legions, were violently mown down.

So arms were necessarily entrusted to the lower orders. At Athens, the need of rowers for their navy bestowed an importance on the lowest class which constitutions had refused. When the thetes had served some time as rowers, as sailors, and even as soldiers, they began to feel their value, and were emboldened. And this, in fact, was the origin of Athenian democracy. Sparta was afraid of war ; Thucydides shews us how loath they were to enter upon a campaign. Almost in spite of herself she was dragged into the Peloponnesian war, and after she had begun how many efforts she made to get free ! That was because she was compelled to arm her inferior classes, the ὑπομείωνες, the neodamodes, the mothakes, the Laconians, and even the

---

[1] Aristotle, *Polit.*, viii., 2, 8 (v., 2).

helots; and she knew the danger of arming the oppressed, and the strong measures that alone could keep them down. And at Rome, the Senate was calumniated when the plebeians accused it of ever seeking to be at war. The Senate, which after the kings had renounced a very extensive dominion in Italy for class supremacy at Rome, knew well how much war cost it in blood; and how many concessions and checks in the forum would follow each enlistment. But the wars could not be avoided.

So war slowly filled up the gulf between the noble and the rich, and privileges seemed too invidious. Add to which that a principle of government had been adopted, in that of public interest, which could not long authorize such marked distinctions. It slowly led the people to democracy, and sooner or later every man, it was evident, must have political rights. As soon as the plebs at Rome demanded a meeting to itself, the proletarii must be admitted and the old distinction of five classes ignored. Nearly every city beheld within itself the formation of truly popular assemblies and the establishment of universal suffrage.

And it must be remembered that then the suffrage was incomparably more valuable than in the countries where everyone now can vote. For then the lowest citizen had a hand in every piece of business, whether legislation, administration of justice, decision as to peace or war, or the making of treaties. It was a true democracy then that was established by this extension to all of the right of voting.

Possibly if the cities could have founded what Thucydides calls ὀλιγαρχία ἰσόνομος, and given the government to a few and liberty to all, the arrival of democracy might have been prevented. But the Greeks had no clear ideas about liberty, individuals always wanting security in their cities. Thucydides was not too zealous for democracy, and yet he says democracy was required, to be a refuge for the poor and a restraint upon the rich. The Greeks never knew how to give civil equality and political inequality. It seemed needful to them for the protection of the poor man that he must have a hand in the administration of justice and be a potential magistrate. The state was so omnipotent that no individual could resist it for a moment; true liberty was impossible; therefore men sought to possess what was next best, to be members of this sovereign autocratic body, and to possess political rights.

CHAPTER XLVIII.

RULES OF DEMOCRATIC GOVERNMENT: ATHENS.

AS the series of revolutions continued its course, and states got further away from the patriarchal system, government became more difficult and more complicated.

At Athens we find, in the first place, a great number of magistrates, a great many new ones having been added to the old ones, whose office was still maintained, though with less political power. Of the first sort were the archon, who gave his name to the year and watched over domestic worships; the king, who performed sacrifices; the polemarch, who appeared at the head of armies and administered justice to foreigners; the six thesmothetæ, who appeared to be ministers of justice, but who really only presided over the juries. There were besides the ten ἱερόποιοι, who consulted oracles and performed some sacrifices; the παράσιτοι, who accompanied the king and the archon in sacred ceremonies; the ten athlothetæ, who remained four years in office to prepare the festival of Bacchus; and finally, the prytanes, of whom there were fifty, and who constituted a permanent body, charged with tending the public fire and the continuance of the sacred repasts. This list will shew that Athens remained faithful to the traditions of antiquity; and that all her revolutions had not made her less regardful of the gods.

Afterwards came the magistrates specially created for the democracy, who were not priests, and who watched over the material interests of the city. First amongst these came the generals or strategi, who were concerned with war and foreign affairs; then the ten astynomi, who were police-officers; the ten agoranomes, or inspectors of markets; the fifteen sitophylakes, who superintended the sale of corn; then ten superintendents of weights and measures, ten guardians of the city treasure, ten receivers of accounts, and the eleven who were charged with the execution of sentences. And add that the greater part of these offices were repeated in each tribe and in each deme, so that the smallest group of population in Attica had its archon, its priest, its secretary, its receiver, its military leader. Probably no one took a step in the town or country without meeting a magistrate. The functions of these magistrates were annual; whence there was not a man who could not hope to be one in time. The first sort of magistrates were elected by lot, because they were priests and it was the gods who were to be pleased. The other sort were chosen by the people themselves.

There were, however, precautions taken against a wild choice on the part of either the gods by their lots, or the people by their vote; for every newly-elected person was subjected to an examination, either before the Senate or the outgoing magistrate, or lastly the Areopagus, not to test his capacity or talent, but to make sure of his own and his family's respectability. It was required also that every magistrate should have landed property.

Nor were these magistrates (though elected by their equals for a year only, and responsible, nay, removable) without respect and authority. Even the Athenians readily obeyed them, not having yet unlearnt the habits of subordination which had been so well taught them by the long domination of the priestly class.

The magistrates had but executive power, having over them both the Senate and the Public Assembly. The former did but deliberate, and had no sovereign power. Its members were chosen by lot, as being prytanes, or priests of the public fires, but there was besides an examination as to respectability. The Senate renewed every year, and consisted of the fifty prytanes of each of the ten tribes, who exercised their sacred functions in turn, and considered what measures might be proposed to the Assembly.

It was the Public Assembly which was really the sovereign body; and yet as in well-constituted monarchies the king is surrounded with precautions against his own whims and errors, so also Athenian democracy subjected itself to certain invariable rules.

The Assembly was convoked by the prytanes or strategi, and was held in a sacred enclosure, called the Pnyx, which the priest had marched around that morning sacrificing victims and invoking the protection of the gods. The people were seated on benches of stone, and the prytanes on a raised platform with the proedri who presided, sitting in front, as their name implies. There was an altar near the tribune, and the tribune itself was considered to be a sort of altar. When everyone was seated, a herald (who had a more religious character than the heralds of the middle ages) bade everyone maintain a religious silence, and pray to certain deities, which he named, that everything done in the assembly might be for the greater advantage of Athens and the prosperity of its citizens. Then answer was made on the part of the people, "We invoke the gods who protect the city; and may the best advice prevail. Cursed be he who would counsel ill, who would change decrees and laws, or who would reveal our secrets to the foe."[1]

Then the herald, at the command of the presidents informed the assembly as to the subject which would occupy its attention; which must always be something already studied and discussed by the Senate; for the people had not what is called the initiative. The Senate brought forward the bill, and the people might accept or reject it; but nothing else could be discussed.

After the herald had read the bill, the debate commenced, the orators mounting the tribune in order of age. Every man might speak on the following conditions:—that he had not been deprived of his political rights, that he owed nothing to the state, that he was of pure life and legitimately married, that he owned land in Attica, that he had fulfilled his duties to his parents, that he had served in every expedition on which he had been sent, and never thrown away his shield in battle.

When these precautions had been taken, the people gave themselves up to the guidance of their orators, not thinking

---

[1] Æsch., i., 23; iii., 4. Dinarch, ii., 14. Demosth., *in Aristocr.*, 97. Aristoph., *Ach.*, 43, 44; and Schol., *Thesmoph.*, 295—310.

that words injured action, to use the expression of Thucydides, but, on the contrary, knowing that they needed to be enlightened, and that it was wise to have clever men to think for them and to make clear to their minds the arguments for and against each course of action. Whether it be true or not that, as some think,[1] the orators were paid for each speech, at all events the people were very attentive to what they said; so much so that the comic poet represents the people as listening with their mouths open, sitting motionless on their seats of stone.[2] And in all the descriptions of these public assemblies, we find none of those interruptions which are the bane of discussion. Whether the people were reproached or flattered, whether Pericles or Cleon spoke, Æschines or Demosthenes, the people were attentive. The most opposite expressions of opinion were endured with admirable patience, and no hisses or groans prevented the orator arriving at the end of his discourse.

At Sparta, eloquence was scarcely known, because the government was conducted on different principles by an aristocracy which possessed fixed traditions of policy that rendered debate unnecessary. But the Athenians refused to act till after full discussion had produced conviction in their minds. Eloquence was allowed to be the spring of their government, and the orators were termed leaders of the people, δημαγωγοί, because they induced action and determined every resolution.

Contradictions of existing laws were prevented by special magistrates called νομοφύλακες or guardians of the laws, seven of whom surveyed the assembly from lofty seats, as representatives of Law, which is raised above the people. If any orator attacked a law that was still in force, these officers immediately stopped his speech and bade the assembly disperse. No votes could then be taken. Other precautions there were, as, for instance, the law which punished every orator who gave bad advice to the people, and that other law which prohibited further speech from any orator who had thrice proposed resolutions contrary to existing laws.

It was thoroughly recognized as a truth at Athens that

---

[1] See Aristoph., *Wasps*, 711 (689); *Scholiast*.
[2] Aristoph., *Knights*, 1119.

democracy could only maintain itself so long as it continued to respect the laws. The Thesmothetæ considered what changes in existing legislation might be useful, and their proposals were reviewed by the Senate, which could reject them but not convert them into laws. If it approved of the new ideas, the Senate convoked the assembly and imparted the proposal of the Thesmothetæ. But the people could not immediately decide upon anything. The discussion was put off to another day, and five orators were appointed to defend the old law and shew what inconveniences might result from the change. Then the people met anew on the day agreed on, and heard first the counsel for the defence of the old law, and next those in favour of the innovation. Even after the discussion, the people did not yet decide, but contented itself with naming a numerous commission of men who had formerly been judges, who once more listened to the orators, and examined the proposal. The unfavourable decision of this commission was without appeal. But if they approved, the people were re-assembled the third time definitively to vote or to reject the law.

If in spite of all these precautions an injurious proposition was accepted, the author of it, whose name had been attached to the law might be prosecuted and punished, for he was still held responsible, whilst the sovereign people could do no wrong.

Another point that strikes one is the hard work that this democracy required of its votaries. If we consider the daily life of an Athenian we find him continually at state-work. One day it is a meeting of the deme he has to attend, another day it is an assembly of his tribe. There are examinations of accounts to be made, nominations of officers, and arrangements for festivals. Thrice a month the Athenian must be present at the general assembly of the people, for he may not fail in his attendance; and he must be there not merely to vote but also to hear all the speeches of the orators. He feels it a serious matter to consider who shall be his political and military chief, for his individual interests are inseparably united to the state, and an error may have to be atoned for either by money or blood. On the day when the disastrous expedition to Sicily was voted, there was not a citizen but knew some one dear to him would take a part in it, and that all the power of his mind ought to be exerted to strike the balance between the dangers and the advantages of it.

The duty of the citizen was not confined to voting. In his turn he became magistrate either in his deme or in his tribe. As a general rule, one year out of two each citizen had to be heliast ;[1] and that year he spent in the courts of justice, occupied in listening to the pleadings and in applying the law. Again, the same man at least twice in his life must be a Senator, and then he had to sit from morning to night, receiving the depositions of the magistrates, demanding their accounts, answering foreign ambassadors, and looking into all matters that would have to be submitted to the people. Besides which it might fall to his lot to be archon, general, or astynome, if chance or the choice of his fellow citizens so designated him. So it was a heavy charge that had to be borne by every citizen of a democratic state, there being occupation for the greater part of a man's life, and very little time left for personal labours and domestic intercourse. So Aristotle justly said that the man who had need to work for his livelihood could not be a citizen. Such were the exigencies of democracy. Every citizen then, like state-servants now, owed all his time to his country. He gave his blood in war and his time in peace, and instead of neglecting state matters to attend to his own, it was his own that must be neglected for the other. Thus men spent their lives in governing themselves. In fact, democracy could but exist on condition that the citizens toiled incessantly, corruption and decay supervening if their zeal slackened, as in a body where the blood has ceased to circulate.

---

[1] There were 5000 heliasts out of 14,000 citizens, and from 3000 to 4000 of these would be set aside by the δοκιμασία.

CHAPTER XLIX.

RICH AND POOR; DEMOCRACY PERISHES; TYRANTS ARE POPULAR.

WHEN men could no longer fight about principles and rights, because they were at last all equal, then they fought about property. In some states this period of contention rapidly followed the establishment of democracy; in others it did but appear after several generations had succeeded in governing themselves peaceably. But sooner or later every city fell into these deplorable struggles.

Indigence had been unknown in patriarchal times, because the head of the γένος must feed all his dependents, but the day that men saw themselves freed from the bonds of clientship, they were brought face to face with the stern necessities and hardships of existence. Independence brought toil and exposed men to all the chances of life; and now everyone must look after his own welfare, and get rich by energy or remain poor. Inequality of fortune must necessarily exist when society gets beyond the patriarchal or tribal state. And so far from doing away with poverty, democracy caused it to be more keenly felt, because the equality of political rights brought out the inequality of fortunes. Besides which there was neither any authority over both rich and poor to make them live together in peace, nor were they forced into mutual agreement by the prevalence of right economical principles and true conditions of toil. Had they but stood in such need one of the other that the rich man could not get wealth but by employing the poor, whilst the poor man found an honourable maintenance in working for the rich; then the inequality of fortunes would have stimulated the activity and the intelligence of the indigent, and not begotten, as it did, corruption and civil war.

But many cities were absolutely devoid of manufactures and commerce, and therefore could not augment the sum of the public wealth so as to give part to the poor man without robbing the rich. And where there *was* commerce nearly all the advantage of it fell to those who were already rich, money being at an exaggerated price. Also what manufacture there was, was done by slaves, for the rich at Athens and Rome had work-shops of weavers, chisellers, armourers, and others, who were all slaves. Even the liberal professions were almost shut against the citizens. The doctor was often a slave who cured diseases for the profit of his master. So bank-clerks, many architects, ship-builders, and lower officers of state were slaves. Slavery became a scourge to society itself; for the citizen, after finding but little employment or work to be done, became idle, and seeing only slaves at work learnt to scorn toil. And so economical habits, moral dispositions, and prejudices all united to prevent the poor man issuing from this wretched condition and living honestly. In short, wealth and poverty were not constituted in a way to settle down in peace together.

It is true the rich and poor had equal political rights, but the want of daily bread made the poor man often wish that fortunes were equal too. And no long time elapsed before he perceived that the equality he did possess might be made useful towards acquiring the equality which he did not possess, and that, owning a vote he might also arrive at owning wealth.

He began by wishing to live by his right of suffrage, and being paid for attending the assembly or acting as juryman in the court of justice. Where the city could not pay for such services, the poor man had other resources, and by selling his vote, of which he had many chances, he managed to live. At Rome this traffic took place regularly and openly, men selling themselves as witnesses, since there they had no part in administering justice. At Athens, men sold their honesty as judges, or rather jurymen, but less openly.

When these expedients failed, more energetic measures were made use of, and a regular war was organized against wealth, a war at first disguised under legal forms charging the rich with public expenses, with heavy taxes, with the building of ships, and the giving of great feasts. Afterwards, fines were multiplied and property was confiscated for very light faults. Vast numbers were condemned to banishment for no other reason in real truth than that they were rich. Then the banished man's estate went into the treasury, and came out again into the hands of all the poor under the form of the triobolon, or fee for public service.

But even all this did not suffice. The number of the needy still continuing to increase, they next proceeded by means of their votes either to decree a general abolition of debts or else a grand confiscation of goods, whereby all peace was upset. The old principle, by which the right of property reposed on religion, had been entirely forgotten, and wealth was no longer sacred, or the gift of the gods. He who had it not desired to lay hold on what chance seemed to have bestowed on another. A man's need seemed to him the measure of his right, and covetousness ceased to be impiety.

The power of the state in ancient times was almost limitless, individual liberty being all but unknown; and the decision of the state seemed, to the Greeks at least (things were not so bad at Rome), to have made their gross iniquities quite just. We may cite the following instances of robbery of the rich by the state.

At Megara, Plutarch tells us, after a certain insurrection, not only were all debts abolished by public decree, but the creditors were ordered to repay the interest they had received, in addition to the loss of their capital.

Aristotle writes: "At Megara, as in other towns, the popular party having seized the power, began by decreeing a confiscation of goods against certain wealthy families. But once started on this way, there was no stopping; some new victim was required daily; and at last the number of the rich who had been exiled and despoiled was so great that they formed an army."

In 412, the people of Samos put to death two hundred of their adversaries, exiled four hundred more, and divided amongst themselves their lands and houses.

At Syracuse, scarcely were the people rid of the tyrant Dionysius, than at their first meeting they decreed a partition of land.

In short, at this period of Grecian history, every time we hear of a civil war, the rich are on one side and the poor on the other, the latter wishing to seize the wealth of the former, and the others to defend their possessions, or to recover them. "In every civil war," says a Greek historian, "it is a question of transferring property;" and every demagogue acted like Molpagoras of Ceos, who gave up to the mob the possessors of money, massacring some and exiling others, and distributing their goods to the poor. At Messina, as soon as the popular party got the upper hand, they exiled the rich and shared their lands among themselves.

✓ Unfortunately, in ancient times the upper classes never had intelligence enough or cleverness enough to set the poorer people to work, or to help them to get honourably out of their wretchedness and corruption. The nobler spirits who attempted it failed. Consequently their cities were ever fluctuating between two revolutions, one that stripped the rich of their wealth and the other that reinstated them in their fortunes. This continued from the Peloponnesian war to the conquest of Greece by the Romans.

So in every city the rich and the poor were two foes living alongside one another, the one greedily hankering after the wealth of the other, who indignantly regarded his covetousness. They had no concerns with one another, nothing in common; no service or work was done for the rich by the poor; nor could the latter obtain any share of the others' superabundance except by robbery. The rich could but defend himself by extreme care and watchfulness, or by force. And the two watched one another with eyes full of hatred. A double conspiracy was going on in every city; the poor conspired through greed and the rich for fear. And Aristotle says that the rich had pronounced this oath in private: "I swear to be always an enemy of the people and to do them all the harm I can."[1]

Which of the two factions committed the most crimes it would be hard to say. Hatred effaced in the heart of both all feelings of humanity.[2] At Miletus there was war between the rich and poor. At first the poor had the best of it, and

---

[1] Aristotle, *Pol.*, viii., 7, 19 (v. 7f. Plutarch, *Lysander*, 19.
[2] Heraclides of Pontus, in Athenæus, xii., 26.

obliged the rich to flee. Afterwards, being sorry that they had not been able to kill their enemies, they took their children, and laying them on a threshing-floor, had them crushed beneath the feet of oxen. Then the rich, regaining possession of the town, took possession of the children of the other party, and having smeared them with pitch, burnt them alive."

Although Athens has been accused of excess in her struggles against the aristocracy, she deserves praise for being the only Greek city which did not witness these fearful atrocities wrought on each other by rich and poor. The advantage of labour had been recognized at Athens from the beginning, and there toil was honourable. By the laws of Solon, every man who had not a work to do was deprived of political rights; and similarly, Pericles would let no slave put a hand to any of the great monuments that he was raising, but reserved all the work for free men. Also, the land of Attica was divided amongst a very great number of small proprietors, so that at the end of the fifth century before Christ, by a census then taken, there were ten thousand. The result was that Athens, by having an economical régime somewhat superior to the other cities, was less disturbed, and did not see such excessive violence in the struggle between rich and poor.

True democracy perished in these frightful contentions; since this sort of government requires the strictest rules and the most careful behaviour. Only factions now held power, and even the magistrate had become a partizan. No command seemed to have a sacred character or to be legitimately exercised, nor was any obedience rendered otherwise than of necessity by men who promised themselves retaliation by and bye. Plato truly said that those cities were but assemblies of men whereof one party was all masters and the other all slaves. When the rich were in power, the government was called aristocratic; and democratic, when the poor were supreme; but the real truth was true democracy had perished, having been corrupted by material interests. Democracy with the rich at the helm was a violent oligarchy; and with the poor in power it had turned to tyranny. From the fifth to the second century before our æra, one can perceive in all the cities of Greece, Rome still excepted, that republican forms of government are in danger and odious to one party.

R

And it is always easy to see who are they that would destroy them, and who are they that would preserve them. The rich, being more enlightened and more conservative, remain faithful to republicanism, whilst the poor, valuing political rights less, are quite ready to be led by a tyrant. The experience of many civil wars, after each of which the rich did not fail to regain their power, convinced the poor that the struggle would always have to be recommenced, if they did not institute a monarchy in their own interest, which should for ever repress the opposite faction and ensure them the fruits of their victory. Thus they made themselves tyrants ; and now parties changed their names : there was no more aristocrat or democrat, but the one fought for liberty, the other for tyranny. But it was still rich and poor that were fighting under these two appellations. Liberty meant a government where the rich would be uppermost and could defend their wealth ; and tyranny meant the contrary.

It is a general truth, to which there is hardly an exception, that the tyrants of Greece and Italy were all of the popular party, and opposed to the aristocrats. Aristotle says " the tyrant's only mission is to protect the populace against the rich. The tyrant begins by being a demagogue, and is essentially the foe of the aristocracy." "And," again he says, "This is the way to become a tyrant : win over the mob, by declaring yourself a foe to the rich, as did Pisistratus at Athens, Theagenes at Megara, Dionysius at Syracuse."

The tyrants were obliged to be harsh, from their position. We hear that at Megara, when Theagenes found the flocks of the rich in the country, he slew them all. At Cumæ, Aristodemus abolished debts, and took away the lands of the rich to bestow them upon the poor. So also did Nicocles at Sicyon, and Aristomachus at Argos. All these tyrants are represented to us as most cruel ; most likely they were not so by nature, but the pressing necessities of their position obliged them always to give land or money to the poor. Nor could they maintain their power any longer than they satisfied the covetousness of the mob or pandered to its passions.

Nothing in these days can give us an adequate idea of the ancient tyrant. For he was a man who lived in the midst of his subjects, without ministers or go-between, and he smote them directly. He was not in the elevated position of the head of a great state; on the contrary, he felt all the passions of a private man, was not insensible to the profit of a confiscation, was accessible to anger and the desire of vengeance; he feared; he knew that he had enemies close at hand, and that public opinion would approve of his assassination. It may be guessed what sort of government such a man would carry on. With one or two honourable exceptions, all the tyrants who were raised to power in Greece during the fourth and third centuries could only reign by flattering the worst feelings of the mob, and violently suppressing whatever excelled in the way of birth, wealth, or merit. Their power was unlimited; and nothing was clearer to Greek minds in those days than the facility with which a republican form of government, which pays no great respect for individual rights, can be turned into despotism. Such vast authority had been given by the ancients to the state, that, from the day when the tyrant laid hands on this excessive power, men had no longer any security against him, and he was legally the master of their life and fortune.

CHAPTER L.

THE REVOLUTIONS OF SPARTA.

WE must not suppose that Sparta existed ten centuries without seeing any revolutions. So far is this from being the case, that Thucydides says it was more troubled with dissension than any other Grecian city. No doubt the history of these internal disputes is very little known to us; but that is because the Spartan government made it a rule to surround itself with the profoundest mystery. The greater part of the struggles which agitated her have been hidden and consigned to oblivion, but we know at least enough to be able to say that if the history of Sparta differs sensibly from other towns, she did not less go through the same series of revolutions.

The Dorians were already formed into a popular body when they invaded Peloponnese. What made them leave their country,—whether the cause was foreign aggression or interior revolution, we know not. What seems certain is, that at this period of their national life the system of the $\gamma \acute{e} \nu o s$ had already disappeared. We find amongst them no patriarchal rule, no religious nobility, no hereditary clientship, only equal warriors under a king. A first social revolution had taken place either in Doris or on the way to Sparta. For in the ninth century before Christ the Dorian society was much more advanced than the Ionian, though the Ionians afterwards outstripped the others.

Nevertheless, some relics of the patriarchal system still clung to the Dorians in Sparta. Such were the rights of primogeniture and the inalienability of a man's patrimony. And these institutions had power very soon to re-establish an aristocracy.

Every tradition proves that when Lycurgus appeared, two classes of Spartans were at variance. Royalty naturally took the part of the inferior orders; but Lycurgus, who was not king, made himself leader of the aristocracy, and with one stroke of policy took away the power from royalty and subdued the people. Perhaps of all the cities that have been on earth, aristocracy ruled most harshly at Sparta; there also there was least equality. As for a fair division of land, there was none worth mentioning, for if ever there was a partition it was not maintained. In the time of Aristotle, some possessed immense domains, whilst others had scarcely anything at all; and the whole of Laconia was in the hands of about a thousand owners.

Not to speak of the Helots and Laconians, we find in Spartan society a hierarchy of classes placed one over the other. First of all were the Neodamodæ, or former slaves who had been enfranchised; next the Epeonactes, who had been admitted to fill up the gaps caused by war in the Spartan ranks. A little higher in position were the Mothakes, who, like to domestic clients, lived with their masters, followed in their train, partook of their feasts, their work, and fought at their side. Then came the class of bastards, descended from true Spartans, but kept apart by religion and law; next a class called the inferiors, $\dot{v}\pi o\mu\epsilon iove\varsigma$, who were most likely the portionless younger sons of the great families. Finally, above all these was the true aristocratic class, called the Equals, or Ὅμοιοι. In fact, they were but equal amongst themselves and very superior to all others. What was their exact number we cannot say; all that is known is that it was small. An enemy counted them one day in the market-place, and found but sixty amidst a crowd of four thousand. Still none but they had a share in the government of the city, and to be outside of this body, according to Xenophon, was to be outside of the body politic. Demosthenes says that "the man who entered the class of the Equals by that very fact became one of the masters of the government." "They are called Equals," he says, "because equality ought to reign between the members of an oligarchy."

It seems that this body was recruited by election, but the right of election belonged to the body itself, and not to the people at large. To be admitted a member was called, in the official language of Sparta, the reward of virtue. We know not how much was required of birth, merit, or age, to constitute this virtue. It is clear that birth alone sufficed not, because there was an election; it is more probable that riches went for much in a city where the love of money existed to a very high degree, and where every thing was allowed to the wealthy."

Certainly, wealthy men alone had the rights of citizens, and alone composed the assembly. By themselves they made up what at Sparta was called the people. From them were elected the Senators, who by the constitution had great authority, since Demosthenes says that the day a man entered the Senate he became a despot for the common herd. This Senate, of which the kings were but ordinary members, governed the state according to the habitual method of aristocratic bodies; out of their own number they chose annual magistrates called ephors, who, as acting for the Senate, had absolute authority. Thus Sparta had a republican form of government and all the outward forms even of democracy, king-priests, annual magistrates, a deliberating Senate, and an assembly of the people. But then this people was but the assemblage of two or three hundred men.

Such was the government of Sparta after Lycurgus, and especially after ephors were appointed. An aristocracy composed of certain wealthy men held down beneath a yoke of iron the Helots, the Laconians, and even the greater part of the Spartans; and for five centuries, by dint of energy, astuteness, and unscrupulous disregard of morality, though exciting cruel hatred, and having to suppress a great number of insurrections, it maintained its sway.

Of the plots and conspiracies of Helots and of Spartans, we have scarcely anything to record, the government having been too clever not to stifle even the recollection. Nevertheless, history could not forget some of them. Thus it is known that the colonists who founded Tarentum were Spartans who had attempted to overthrow the government; and a slip of the poet Tyrtæus let Greece into the secret that, during the Messenian wars, one party had conspired to obtain a partition of land.

What saved Sparta was the extreme division she knew how to place between inferior classes. The Helots agreed not with the Laconians; and the Mothakes despised the Neodamodes. Thus no coalition between these different classes was possible; and the aristocracy, thanks to its military education and the close union that subsisted between its members, was always able to make head against a single and unsupported class.

But the kings attempted what no one order could bring about. Each king who aspired to rise above the state of inferiority in which the aristocracy held him down, looked for support amongst the inferior orders. During the Persian war, Pausanias formed the project of at once raising royalty and the lower classes, by overthrowing the oligarchy. The Spartans put him to death on a charge of having dealings with the Persians, but his true crime was his intention of freeing the Helots.[1] It may be gathered from history that numerous kings were exiled by the ephors; and if we could not guess the cause of their condemnation, Aristotle tells us that the kings of Sparta, in order to make head against the ephors and the Senate, turned demagogues.[2]

In 397, the conspiracy of Cinadon nearly overthrew the oligarchical form of government. He did not belong to the order of the Equals, and gained adherents to his plot by taking into the forum any man whom he wished to initiate, and bidding him count the citizens. These only amounted to about sixty-six, including kings, ephors, and senators. Then Cinadon would say, "Those are our enemies; the rest of the people in the forum, about four thousand, are our allies." And he added, "When thou seest a Spartan in the country, see in him a foe and a master; all the other men are our allies." This time Helots, Laconians, Neodamodes, ὑπομείονες, were all associated, and accomplices of Cinadon; "for," says the historian, "all hated their masters so much that not one would not have liked, according to his own confession, even to eat them raw." But the Spartan government was well served, and the ephors said the entrails had revealed the plot. The conspirators were secretly put to death, before they had time to act, and the oligarchy was once more saved.

---

[1] Aristotle, *Polit.*, viii (v., i.) Thuc., i., 132.
[2] Aristotle, *Polit.*, ii., 6, 14.

With such a form of government, the inequality that already subsisted went on increasing, and though money flowed into Sparta after the Peloponnesian war and the Asiatic expeditions, yet the manner of its distribution was as unfair as existing institutions, and only enriched those who were already wealthy. At the same time, the number of small land-owners decreased, until the thousand that had existed in Aristotle's time were reduced to one hundred a century later. The soil was entirely in certain hands at a time when there were neither manufactures nor commerce to give the poor something to do, and when the rich had their vast domains tilled by slave-labour. In Plutarch's lives of Agis and Cleomenes, we see that at Sparta an unbounded covetousness was the universal passion. The few, who could indulge in luxury, strove to augment still more their fortunes, whilst beyond them was nothing but a needy crowd, destitute of political rights, full of envy and hatred, condemned to wish for revolution.

The pent-up waters burst at length; and democracy brought with it social as well as political changes. But it was a king and none of the people who commenced the revolution, for the true Spartans at this time were but seven hundred, counting all the classes, and long oppression had debased their character. Agis increased the difficulty of his enterprise by attempting to do it legally. He brought forward before the Senate, that is, before the rich themselves, two projects of laws for abolition of debts and partition of lands. We need not be surprised that these laws were accepted, for doubtless Agis had taken measures to ensure this. But when the laws had once been voted, the difficulty was to put them in execution. The opposition of the ephors forced Agis out of his legality, for he deposed them by his own authority and named others, arming his partizans at the same time and establishing a reign of terror. Then he put in execution the laws that abolished debts, and burnt all the papers relating to these debts in the forum. But he had not time to divide the lands. Whether he hesitated from fear, or whether the oligarchy spread abroad injurious accusations, we cannot say; but it is certain the people separated themselves from him and allowed him to fall. When the ephors had killed him, the aristocratic government was re-established.

However, the projects of Agis were taken up again with more address and less scrupulousness by Cleomenes. He began with massacring the ephors and suppressing their office, which was hateful both to the kings and to the popular party. He then proscribed the rich, decreed a partition of lands, and made citizens of four thousand Laconians. It is worth while remarking that neither Agis nor Cleomenes would allow that it was a revolution they were effecting, but affirmed they were only re-installing the old constitution of Lycurgus. But this is far from being the truth; for Cleomenes was absolute master of the state, with no authority to balance his own. In fact, he reigned like the tyrants of the other Greek cities, his people appearing to be satisfied with the lands they had got, and to trouble themselves very little about politics.

But, unfortunately, Cleomenes tried to spread his democratic system throughout the Peloponnese, just when Aratus was striving to establish a rule of free and sober aristocracy. An insurrection of the lower classes in favour of Cleomenes (for they thought they should get lands as the Spartans had done) obliged Aratus to have recourse to the aid of Antigonus Doson, king of Macedon, the declared foe of tyrants and democracies. Antigonus invaded the Peloponnese, and with the aid of the Achæans defeated Cleomenes at Sellasia. The Spartan democracy was once more suppressed, and the old form of government restored by the Macedonians, B.C. 222.

Still the oligarchy could not keep the upper hand, and troublous times succeeded. One year three ephors, who were favourable to the people, killed their two colleagues; and the next year, when five ephors of the oligarchical party were elected, the people took up arms and killed them all. Then the oligarchy refused to have any more kings, but the people were as obstinate in their favour; and they named one who was not of blood-royal, a thing hitherto unknown at Sparta. The king, whose name was Lycurgus, was twice dethroned, once by the people because he refused to divide the lands, and a second time by the aristocracy, because they thought he then wanted to do it. What his end was is not recorded, but after him we find a tyrant named Machanidas, sure proof that the popular party had got the upper hand.

Philopœmen, who at the head of the Achæan league everywhere made war against democratic tyrants, conquered and slew Machanidas. Whereupon the Spartan democracy immediately took to themselves another tyrant, Nabis, who made citizens of all free men, raised the Laconians to the rank of the Spartans, and emancipated the Helots.

This new democratic Sparta was not without a certain greatness; for Nabis not only introduced into Laconia a degree of order which it had not seen for long, but he also subdued Messenia, part of Arcadia, and Elis, and seized Argos, and then, quitting entirely the traditions of the Spartan aristocracy, formed a fleet, ruling the isles about the Peloponnese and extending his influence as far as Crete. His principle being to establish democracy everywhere, as soon as he was master of Argos he confiscated the possessions of the wealthy, abolished debts, and divided the lands. The intense hatred of the Achæan league for this tyrant, as it may be seen in Polybius's history, was the cause of their inducing Flamininus to make war upon him in the name of Rome; but the identification of the cause of the tyrant with that of the democracy is shewn by the fact that when Nabis wanted to make peace after one defeat from Flamininus, the people refused, and had to be defeated a second time before they would cease from contending. Even then the Romans allowed him to reign on at Sparta, because it either suited them to have a power to balance that of the Achæan league, or that things had now gone too far for the old aristocratic rule to be restored. Nabis was afterwards assassinated by an Æolian, but neither did his death bring back the oligarchy. The changes he had effected in the social state of his country were maintained after him, and Rome itself would not restore Sparta to her old condition.[1]

---

[1] Polyb., ii., xiii., xvi. Livy, xxxii.

CHAPTER LI.

NEW BELIEFS; PHILOSOPHY ALTERS THE RULES OF POLITICS.

THE ruin of the political system of ancient Italy and Greece is to be attributed to two chief causes; 1st, the change in popular belief; and 2ndly, the Roman conquest. And these two different facts were brought about together during the six centuries which precede our æra.

The primitive religion, whose symbols were the domestic fire and the ancestral tomb, and which had not only constituted the ancient family, but also in a great measure the city, had lost much of its influence with the course of time. New beliefs had been formed by the human mind, which had attained both superior notions of what the soul is, and also a loftier idea of the divinity. For although old superstitions were not easily uprooted from the hearts of the vulgar, yet reflecting men even in the fifth century B.C. had freed themselves from old errors, and no longer believed that dead men remained in their graves feeding on offerings. Some expected annihilation after death; some had imagined a second existence, where departed souls are punished for their crimes, or received the reward of their good deeds in the Elysian fields; and no one now deified any dead man but those whom gratitude or flattery placed above humanity.

The divinity which at first had been attributed to departed souls of men, and afterwards to the grander powers of nature, was being gradually transferred by thinking minds to One who is above and beyond nature. The Heroes and the Lares therefore lost respect; and the sacred fire, likewise, if it still received offerings and adorations, only did so from habit and not of faith.

Similarly, the sacred fires in the prytanea of the cities fell into discredit, because men had forgotten their meaning; and now it was only from respect to old custom that they were still kept up, that sacred hymns were sung before them, and public repasts still eaten there. Superstition prevented men ceasing to do what their ancestors had always done, but the ceremonies were all as vain as unintelligible.

Even the divinities derived from nature, whose images men had placed beside the sacred hearth, gradually altered their character. Already their influence had been extended from the family to the city, as the circle of society grew wider; and now men began to perceive that all those different beings whom they called by the names of Jupiter, Pallas, and Juno might after all be but one. In fact the intellect, being embarassed by the number of its deities, felt the need of reducing them by generalization; and thus the world was given to them as their domain instead of a family or a town. Next, poets went about from house to house teaching men no longer the old city hymns, but new songs in which was no mention of the gods, the Lares, nor yet of the town-deities, but legends of the great gods of earth and sky; and these superior works of art and imagination soon caused the old chants to be forgotten. At the same time, some great sanctuaries, like those of Delphi and Delos, attracted men from all quarters to the prejudice of their local worships; and the mysteries, with the doctrines implied in them, brought scorn on the comparatively meaningless religion of the city.

Thus an intellectual revolution was slowly and obscurely wrought out, and the more surely that there was no opposition; since the priests were satisfied so long as the sacrifices were regularly performed, clinging to outward rites whilst faith was perishing.

Then Philosophy appeared, upsetting all the old rules of politics; for it is impossible to alter the principles of men without also eventually deranging the fundamental principles of government. Pythagoras, for instance, having acquired some notion of a Supreme Being, despised the local worships; and from that went on to reject the ancient way of governing mankind, and to attempt to found a new sort of society.

Anaxagoras, in like manner, because he had a conception of an intelligent God who reigns over all men and all things, could offer no more worship to the gods of the prytaneum, nor fulfil his duties as a citizen. As he avoided the public assembly and refused to be a magistrate, it was felt that his doctrines were dangerous to society as then constituted, and the Athenians condemned him to death.

The Sophists, who came next, exercised a more powerful influence, because they imagined they had received a mission to combat old errors, and went about from town to town preaching a justice that differed from the old in being less exclusive, more humane, and more rational. They seem to have had no definite doctrine on things in general, only they saw the inadequacy of existing rules for the conduct of life. As they boldly attacked old prejudices and customs, and disturbed, as Plato says, what had been hitherto held unalterable, they stirred up a storm of opposition and hatred. Despising ancestral ways and unchangeable tradition, they placed the rule of politics as well as of religion in the conscience, and taught the Greeks to persuade men's minds, and to appeal to free will instead of commanding in the name of superstition. Logic and rhetoric were made motive powers in place of those which former generations had been wont to employ, and now to dead tradition they opposed intellect and oratory.

So thought was aroused, and men wanted a reason for their faith and for their institutions. Other principles dawned upon their minds, in a way to put to shame the so-called justice of their old social laws. Plato puts the following beautiful words in the mouth of a Sophist: "I look upon all you who are present as relations to one another, since nature, in default of law has made you fellow-citizens. But law, that tyrannizes over man, often does violence to nature." It is clear that the opposition between nature and tradition, thus insisted on, cuts at the root of ancient policy; and indeed, though the Athenians banished Protagoras and burnt his writings, yet they could not undo the immense effect that had been produced. The authority of the national gods and of all old institutions perished, and the habit of free examination was established both in private houses and in the forum.

Socrates, also, though he reproved the Sophists' abuse of their right to doubt, yet like them rejected the empire of tradition, and appealed to conscience for a rule of conduct. His superiority over them consisted in his religious determination to find in conscience the obligation to be just and to do good. But he cared not for law and custom in comparison with truth and justice. In times before him duty had been looked upon as what was ordered by the ancient gods; but he separated morality from religion, and asserted that the principle of duty is in the soul of man. In all this, whether he would or no, he was fighting against the city worship. In vain he was present at all sacrifices and all feasts, for his words and his beliefs belied his conduct. He founded a new religion opposed to that of the city, and he was justly accused of no more adoring the gods whom the state adored. He was put to death for having attacked ancestral customs and belief, or, as they said, for having corrupted the present generation. One can only understand the unpopularity of Socrates and the anger he excited, by remembering the religious habits of the city of Athens and its numerous and powerful priests. Still the revolution, which the Sophists begun, and which Socrates more cautiously carried on, was not to be stopped by the death of one old man, and every day Greek society more and more freed itself from obsolete institutions and beliefs.

After him other philosophers freely discussed the rules and principles of human association, and treatises on politics were written by Plato, Crito, Antisthenes, Speusiphus, Aristotle, Theophrastus, and others. Very many examined the great problems of state organization, of authority, and obedience, of rights and obligations; and intellect generally made great strides.

Plato seems at first sight to have remained behind his times in political thought. His model state does but consist of 5000 citizens, and it is ruled upon ancient principles; moreover, the end which his legislation proposes is not so much the perfection of man as the safety and greatness of the association. He stifles the family to make more room for the city. The state alone can own land. The state alone is free; alone can exercise its will; alone can choose a religion and belief; and whoever thinks not as itself must perish. Nevertheless, in the midst of all this, new ideas begin to peep through. Plato proclaims, as well as Socrates, that the rule of morality and politics is in ourselves, that tradition is worthless, that reason must be considered at all times, and that laws are only just when in accordance with human nature.

In Aristotle these ideas are still more precisely stated. He says, "Law is reason," and teaches that we must seek not what agrees with the customs of our fathers, but what is good in itself, adding that as time progresses we must modify our institutions. Respect for ancestors he sets aside in the following words: "Whether our first parents were born out of the earth or survived some deluge, it is most likely they resembled what is now-a-days most common and ignorant amongst men. It would be quite absurd to hold to the opinions of such persons." Like all the other philosophers, Aristotle failed to perceive the religious origin of Greek society. The sacred fire and the local worships he ignores. "The state," he thought, is but an association of equal beings seeking in common an easy and happy existence." But that is because philosophy rejected the old principles of society and sought a new foundation whereon to repose the idea of country and the laws of cities.

But the Cynical school went further, denying the very idea of country. Diogenes boasted of having no city of his own anywhere, and Crates that contempt of others was his country. They added this truth, which was new at that time, that man is the citizen of the universe and that his country is not the narrow circuit of a town. Municipal patriotism seemed to them a prejudice, and they would not reckon the love of one's country amongst the number of sentiments.

So through scorn or disgust, the philosophers held more and more aloof from public affairs. Plato had so far interested himself in the state that he would have reformed it, but Aristotle was more indifferent and did but look on, making of the state an object of scientific study. The Epicureans followed the precepts of their founder, who said, "Meddle not with public affairs, unless obliged by superior force." But the Cynics would not even be citizens.

The Stoics, however, reverted to politics, and Zeno,

Cleanthus, and Chrysippus wrote numerous treatises on government. But their principles were very far removed from those of the old-fashioned cities. Witness, for instance, the false Plutarch (Fortune of Alexander, I.), who speaks as follows of their doctrines: "Zeno wished to shew us in his treatise on government that we are not inhabitants of such a deme or such a city, separated one from another by peculiar privileges and exclusive laws, but that we ought to behold fellow-citizens in all men, as if we all belonged to the same deme and to the same city." This shews us the progress of ideas since Socrates' time; for Socrates held himself bound to adore as much as he could the city-gods; and Plato had conceived of no other government than that of a city, but Zeno goes beyond the narrow limits which ancient religion had assigned to the associations of men, and having conceived the idea of a God of the Universe, so he can imagine a state into which all mankind might enter.[1]

Moreover, we observe the entrance of a new principle into the doctrines of the Stoics, since, whilst they enlarge so much the bounds of society they will no longer allow that the citizen should be the slave of the state. Though they encouraged their disciples to mix in public affairs, they yet clearly marked off one part of a man which should remain independent; and that part was the conscience; for that is what they mean when they say that a man must look within himself, and there find duty, virtue, and reward. Self-amelioration was to be man's great object and the individual conscience unforced. Here was a great principle, hitherto disregarded by antiquity, but yet destined to become a most valued principle in politics. So other duties begin to be recognized than these toward the state, and other virtues than the civic. A man's country is no longer the sole object of his life, the end of all his toil and all his ambition, his standard of the true and honourable. Zeno teaches that man, as man (and not merely as a citizen), has a dignity of his own, that he has duties of his own, and may please the Deity of the Universe. If these virtues may be characterized as somewhat selfish, and if they allowed national indepen-

---

[1] The idea of the universal city is expressed by Seneca, *Ad Marc.*, 4; *De Tranquill.*, 14; by Plutarch, *On Exile*; by Marc. Aurel., who says, "As Antoninus, I have Rome for my country; as man, the world."

dence to perish, yet at all events by means of them the individual grew and waxed stronger. The personal virtues, though they had to struggle both against general corruption and a despotic government, yet by degrees took root in humanity and made a shew in the world, till at last, they could not be ignored by governments, and the rules of politics had to be modified in their favour.

A desire sprang up for larger forms of society than the ancient city ; and men even aspired to unity during the two centuries which preceded our æra. It is true that the fruits produced by these revolutions of opinion ripen very slowly. But, as we shall see in studying the Rôman Conquest, events marched along with ideas, upsetting the old municipal system and preparing new forms of government.

CHAPTER LII.

THE ROMAN CONQUEST.

IT seems very surprising at first that amongst the thousand cities of Greece and Italy, one of them should have been found able to subdue all the others. Nevertheless, this great fact is to be explained by the ordinary causes which determine the course of human affairs. And the wisdom of Rome consisted in simply profiting by the favourable circumstances that fell in her way.

Two periods may be distinguished in the work of the Roman Conquest; one coinciding with the time when the old municipal spirit still prevailed, and when Rome had most obstacles to overcome; and the other belonging to the days when that municipal feeling was weakened, and when, consequently, the conquest met with less difficulty and proceeded rapidly.

§ 1. *On the origin and the population of Rome.*

The peculiar character and exceptional career of Rome receive much explanation from a knowledge of the original composition of its people. For the Roman was a very mixed race. Its main element was Latin, and came from Alba. But these Albans themselves, according to traditions which we are not authorized in rejecting, were composed of two associate and yet separate populations. The first of these were true Latins of aboriginal race; but the others were strangers, said to have come from Troy with Æneas the priest founder of Alba. This colony seems to have been few

---

[1] The Trojan origin of Rome was believed in, before Rome had regular communication with the East. In a prediction which is to be referred to the Second Punic War, the soothsayer applies to the Romans the term Trojugena. Livy, xxv., 12.

in numbers, but was of much account from the institutions and worship it brought with it.

These Albans, who were thus a mixture of two races, founded Rome in a spot where there was already another town of Greek origin, Pallanteum. This Greek population continued to subsist in the new town, and the rites of the Greek worship were still retained there.[1] There was also on the spot where afterwards was the Capitol, a town said to have been founded by Hercules, and whose families preserved themselves distinct from the rest of the Roman population during the whole period of the republic.

Thus at Rome all races met and mingled,—Latins, Trojans, Greeks, and by-and-bye we shall hear of Sabines and Etruscans. On the Palatine Hill is the Latin city which had been the town of Evander, whilst the Capitoline, which had been the dwelling-place of Hercules' companions, becomes the abode of the Sabines and of Tatius. The Quirinal received its name from the Sabine Quirites or the Sabine god Quirinus. The Cœlian from the first seems to have been inhabited by Etruscans.

Of the three names of primitive tribes, the ancients always supposed that one was Latin, the second Sabine, and the third Etruscan. For in truth Rome was not one town, but a confederation of several, and each of these attached to some other confederation. It was a centre of re-union for Latins, Etruscans, Sabellians, and Greeks.

The first king of Rome was a Latin, the second a Sabine, the fifth the son of a Greek, and the sixth an Etruscan.

Its language was composed of the most diverse elements, the Latin being dominant; but Sabellian roots were numerous, and there were more Greek words than in any other dialect of central Italy. As for its very name, no one could be certain as to what language it belonged; for some said it was a Trojan word, some a Greek; there are reasons for believing it Latin, but some ancients thought it Etruscan.

So, also, the names of the Roman families prove a great diversity of origin. There were still fifty families in Augustus' time, which could trace back the line of their ancestors to

---

[1] Livy, i., 5. Virgil, viii. Ovid, *Fasti*, i., 519. Plutarch, *Quest. Rom.*, 56. Strabo., v., p. 230.

the companions of Æneas.[1] Others declared themselves sprung from the Arcadians of Evander, having carried on their shoes from time immemorial a little silver crescent, as their distinguishing badge.[2] The families of the Potitii and Pinarii were descended from those who were called the companions of Hercules, and their hereditary worship of this god seemed to prove their lineage. The Tullii, Quinctii, Servilii, had come from Alba after the conquest of this town. Many other families joined on to their name another, which called to mind their foreign origin. Thus we have Sulpicius Camerinus, Cominius Auruncas, Sicinius Sabinus, Claudius Regillensis, Aquillius Tuscus. The Nautian family was Trojan; the Aurelian was Sabine; the Cæcilian came from Præneste, and the Octavian from Velitræ.

The consequence was that Rome had family ties with every people she knew, and could call herself Latin with the Latins, Sabine with the Sabines, Etruscan with the Etruscans, and Greek with the Greeks.

Her national worship, also, was a collection of many other distinct worships, of which one or other attached her to each of these peoples. She had the Greek worships of Evander and Hercules, and boasted of possessing the Trojan Palladium. Her Penates were in the Latin town of Lavinium, and from the very beginning she adopted the worship of the Sabine god Consus. Another Sabine god, Quirinus, fixed himself so firmly there that he was associated with the founder Romulus. Rome also had Etruscan gods, with their feasts, their augurs, and priestly insignia.

When religion was very exclusive, and when no man could be present at the religious feasts of a people who did not belong to this nation by birth, the Roman had the incomparable advantage of appearing at the Feriæ Latinæ, at the Sabine and Etruscan feasts, and at the Olympian games.[3] And religion was a powerful bond of union. Cities which had a common worship called themselves akin. They looked upon one another as allies, and felt bound to afford mutual help. Indeed, religion was the only acknowledged tie in primitive times. Therefore, Rome cherished with the greatest

---

[1] Dionysius, i., 85.   [2] Plutarch, *Quæst. Rom.*, 76.
[3] Pausanias, v., 23, 24. Cf. Livy, xxix., 12; xxxvii., 37.

care whatever could attest this much-prized relationship with other peoples. She had her traditions about Romulus for the Latins, her story about Tarpeia and Tatius for the Sabines; to the Greeks she could recite her old hymns about Evander's mother, hymns which she continued to sing long after their meaning had been lost. Not less anxiously did she keep up the recollection of Æneas, for if through Evander she could claim relationship with the Peloponnesians, through Æneas she was related to more than thirty cities scattered in Italy, Sicily, Greece, Thrace, and Asia Minor, all of which had Æneas for their founder, or were colonies from towns founded by him, and therefore had a common worship with Rome. In the wars waged in Sicily against Carthage, as well as in Greece against Philip, one may perceive the advantage Rome derived from this ancient relationship.

§ 2. *First aggrandisements of Rome* (730 *to* 350 B.C.)

It is said that the first act of the new city was to carry off some Sabine women, but the story seems very improbable when we reflect on the sacred light in which marriage was looked upon amongst the ancients. Unless two cities had a common origin, marriage between their members was forbidden by the municipal religions. So the first Romans could intermarry with the Albans, who had sent them out as colonists, but not with their neighbours the Sabines. In order to gain this right of intermarriage, Romulus knew he must establish a common religion, and therefore adopted the worship of the god Consus, and celebrated his festival. The tradition adds that during this festival the Romans carried off the Sabine women; but if this were true, the marriages could not have been celebrated duly, since the first and most important act was the delivery of the girl by her father, *traditio in manum*; and thus the Romans would have missed their aim. But the presence of the Sabines and their families at this religious ceremony so united the two peoples that intermarriage could no longer be refused. There was, therefore, no need for any violence, the right of *connubium* being a natural consequence of the feast. Thus also says the historian Dionysius of Halicarnassus, who consulted the texts and the sacred hymns; and Plutarch and Cicero confirm his statement, that the Sabine women were married according to the most solemn rites. And it is worth while noticing that the first effort of the Romans tended to remove a barrier raised by municipal religion between themselves and a neighbouring people. No similar story has come down to us respecting Etruria ; but it appears certain that Rome had the same relations with Etruria, as with Latium and the Sabines. She was clever enough to unite with herself either by worship or by blood all that surrounded her ; and what proves she appreciated the advantage of having *connubium* with other cities, is the fact that she would not allow her subject cities to have this right amongst themselves.

Next follows the long series of Roman wars. The first was against the Sabines under Tatius, and ended with a religious and political alliance between those two small peoples. Afterwards Rome made war against her mother-city, Alba ; for it was necessary to her greatness to do away with the religious supremacy naturally exercised by a metropolis. So long as Alba stood, Rome must be a dependent city and her destiny was for ever arrested.

When Alba had been destroyed, Rome was no longer content with her emancipation from the condition of a colony ; she wanted to raise herself to a metropolitan position, and to inherit the religious supremacy which Alba had hitherto exercised over her thirty colonies in the Latium. Long wars were waged until she gained the right of presiding at the *feriæ Latinæ*. No other means of acquiring the superiority she wanted was then thought of.

In the city of Rome was built a temple to Diana, whither the Latins were forced to come and sacrifice, and even Sabines as well.[1] Thus two peoples were habituated to partake with her, and under her presidency, in prayers, and festival, and the flesh of victims. She joined them under her religious supremacy.

Again, Rome was the only city of those times clever enough to increase her population by war. For she brought within her walls the population of conquered towns, and gradually turned the vanquished into Romans. At the same time she sent colonists into the conquered countries, and, so

---

[1] Livy, l., 45. Dion. Halic., iv., 48, 49.

to speak, sowed herself everywhere; for these colonists, whilst they formed cities which may be called politically distinct, yet maintained a religious community with their mother-city, which was enough to subordinate their policy to hers, to make them obey, and help her in war.

Another remarkable feature in Roman policy was her way of attracting to herself all the worships of the neighbouring cities, and taking as much pains to conquer a god as a town. Thus she possessed herself of a Juno from Veii, of a Jupiter from Præneste, a Minerva from Falerii, a Juno from Lanuvium, a Venus of the Samnites, and many others that we know not.[1] "For," says one of the ancients,[2] "it was the custom of Rome to bring home the worships of all the conquered towns, which she sometimes distributed amongst her *gentes*, and sometimes placed as portions of the national religion."

Montesquieu praises what he calls the refined policy of the Romans in not having imposed their gods on the conquered peoples. But this conduct would have been quite opposed to all ancient notions. Rome took the gods of the conquered and did not give them hers, wishing to possess more worships and more tutelary deities than any other city. The bonds of a common origin, the conquest of the connubium, of the presidence at the feriæ Latinæ, of other foreign gods, and the right which she claimed to sacrifice at Olympia and at Delphi, were all made use of at a later period for purposes of domination. No other city made religion thus useful for aggrandisement. The rest of the cities were but isolated by their worship; but Rome had the skill or the good-fortune to use religion as a means of winning and mastering all others.

§ 3. *How Rome acquired empire* (350 *to* 140 B.C.)

Whilst Rome was making use of religion to increase her power, the social and political changes which we have already detailed began to take place. Then the alteration of religious belief and the progress of democracy coincided with the great strides of Roman conquest. These two events acted

---

[1] Livy, v., 21, 22; vi., 29. Ovid, *Fasti*, iii., 837, 843. Plutarch, *Parall. of Gr. and Rom. Hist.*, 75.
[2] Cincius, quoted by Arnobius; *Adv. Gentes*, iii., 38.

and re-acted upon one another. The conquests of Rome would not have been so easy had not the old municipal spirit been extinguished everywhere; whilst we may say that the municipal system would have lasted on some time longer if the Roman conquest had not given it its death-blow.

The strong old feeling of patriotism, which partook so largely of religion, which looked to the sacred fires, the household and the city-gods, had perished, and men loved their country now from different motives. A man now expected his country to give him good laws, wise institutions, equal rights, and security against conquest. In the funeral oration which Thucydides puts in Pericles' mouth, the reasons which made Athens beloved are said to be "the gift of liberty and the opening of the path to honour; the maintenance of public order, the assured authority of the magistrate, the protection of the feeble, and the presentation to all of spectacles and feasts which educate the soul." "For this reason," he continues, "our warriors died bravely rather than let this country be taken from them; for this reason the survivors are still ready to suffer on her behalf." So that a man is still held to have duties towards his country; but these duties are derived from another principle than in old times. If a man is prodigal of his blood it is not for the hearth of his sires, or the god of the city, but to defend the advantageous institutions which he appreciates in the city.

And this new sort of patriotism had not the same effects exactly as the old. It fluctuated with the government, and perished with the goodness of the laws and institutions which it wanted. Bad laws and bad systems of ruling, or even what a man thought bad, alienated his affections. So each man's opinion became more sacred in his eyes than his country, and the triumph of his faction dearer than the safety or glory of his city. If a man's native city could not supply him with institutions that he loved, perhaps some other could. Emigration and exile seemed less formidable; and to lose sight of the prytaneum and be deprived of holy water was less awful now than in times of yore.

It was but a step further to take up arms against a man's own country; and many citizens would not scruple to ally themselves with a hostile town in order to ensure a party-triumph at home. Thus, of two Argives, one would desire an aristocratic government, and lean to Sparta; the other, being of the democratic side, would prefer Athens. Neither stickled much for the independence of Argos, or would mind being the subject of a foreign city, provided that city would uphold his faction at Argos. The duration of the Peloponnesian war was clearly prolonged by the prevalence of this state of mind. At Platææ, the rich were on the side of Thebes and Lacedæmon, but the democrats clung to Athens. At Corcyra, the popular faction was for Athens, and the aristocracy for Sparta. Athens had allies in all the cities of Peloponnese, and Sparta in all the Ionian towns. Thucydides and Xenophon agree in saying there was not a single city where the people were not favourable to Athens and the aristocracy to Sparta. In fact, the war seems to represent a general effort made by all the Greeks to establish everywhere the same constitution, under the leadership of one town; only whilst one side wished for aristocracy under the protection of Sparta, the others sought democracy with the support of Athens. It was the same in Philip's time: everywhere the aristocratic party invoked the Macedonian domination. Parts were changed when Philopœmen flourished, though feelings were unaltered, and it was the popular party now which courted Macedonian rule, whilst everybody who sided with the aristocracy joined the Achæan league. Thus the city was no longer the object of men's hope and aspirations. Few Greeks were not ready to sacrifice municipal independence for the sake of a constitution which they preferred.

As for the honest and scrupulous, the perpetual dissensions which they witnessed disgusted them with the municipal rule. A state of society where men had to fight every day, where rich and poor were ever struggling, where popular violence alternated with aristocratic vengeance, could not possibly retain their love; and they desired to escape from a system, which, if it once had produced true grandeur, now only begot suffering and hatred. Many men began to wish there were some sort of sovereign power to maintain order and force these turbulent little societies to keep the peace. Thus Phocion, who was a good citizen, advised his countrymen to accept the authority of Philip, promising the enjoyment of safety and concord at this price.

---

[1] Thuc., iii., 47. Xenoph., *Hellenic*, vi., 3.

Things were not different in Italy from what they were in Greece. The cities of Latium, of the Sabines, and of Etruria, were troubled with the same revolutions and the same struggles, and there too the love of the city was disappearing. As in Greece, every body would join a foreign people to further the prevalence of his own opinions and of his own interests at home.

And these dispositions made Rome's fortune. Everywhere she had supported the aristocracy, and everywhere, also, the aristocracies were her allies. Let us mention some instances. The Claudian gens quitted the land of the Sabines because Roman institutions pleased it better than those of its own country. At the same time, many Latin families emigrated to Rome because they did not like the democratic rule in Latium, and because Rome had just set up patrician institutions.[1] At Ardea, the aristocracy and the plebeians being at variance, the former gave up the city to the Romans,[2] whilst their adversaries were appealing to the Volscians. Etruria was full of dissensions. Veii had overturned its aristocratic government, and the Romans attacked it; wherefore the other Etruscan towns where the sacerdotal aristocracy still ruled refused to help the Veientines. The legend adds that in this war the Romans carried off a Veientine sooth-sayer, and made him declare what would win them the victory. May not the meaning of this be that the Etruscan priest-nobles opened the city to the Romans?

Afterwards, when Capua revolted against Rome, it is noticeable that the knights, or aristocrats, took no part in the insurrection.[3] In 313, the cities of Ausona, Sora, Minturnæ, and Vescia were given up to Rome by the aristocratic parties in them. And when we find an Etruscan coalition against Rome, the meaning is that a popular government had been established there, and if one town, Arretium,[5] refused to enter the coalition, that was because Arretium was still aristocratic. When Annibal was in Italy all the cities were in a state of agitation, but it was no question of independence that disturbed their repose; but in every one the

---

[1] Dion. Halic., vi., 2.
[2] Livy, iv., 9, 10.
[3] Livy, viii., 11.
[4] Livy, ix., 24, 25.
[5] Livy, x., 1.

aristocracy was for Rome, and the populace for the Carthaginians.[1]

Perhaps the way in which Rome was governed may account for this preference that the aristocracy entertained for her. If the series of revolutions which we have explained influenced Rome as well as all the other cities, yet at all events it did so more slowly. In 509, when the Latin cities were already having their tyrants, a patrician reaction had succeeded in Rome. Afterwards the democracy rose in opposition, but with much deliberation and self-restraint. The Roman government was longer aristocratic than any other, and long continued to be the hopes of the aristocratic party.

It is true that democracy eventually prevailed at Rome, but even then the proceedings and tricks of government, if we may use the expression, remained aristocratic. In the comitia centuriata votes were taken on the principle of wealth. Nor was it altogether different in the comitia tributa as a matter of fact, though, theoretically, riches had no weight. The reason was that the poorer class belong altogether to the four city tribes, and had but four votes to set against the thirty-one of the land-owners. Besides, in general nothing was quieter than these assemblies, where no one spoke but the president or the person whom he called upon, where oratory was scarce heard, and where discussion hardly existed; where men voted yes or no, and spent a great deal of time in counting votes. Besides, the Senate was not renewed, as in Greece, every year, but sat for life, recruiting its members itself, and was indeed an aristocratic body.

Moreover at Rome, men's manners were even more aristocratic than their institutions.

The Senators had places reserved for them at the theatres. Service in the cavalry was permitted only to the rich, and high rank in the army was mostly held by members of great families. Scipio was but sixteen when he commanded a squadron.

The wealthy kept their power longer at Rome than in any other city: which may be accounted for in two ways. First, the great conquests enriched the class that was already wealthy; for theirs were the conquered lands, they seized

---

[1] Livy, xxiii., 13, 14, 39; xxiv., 2, 3.

on the commerce of the conquered cities, adding to it great gains from taxes and the administration of provinces. Hence certain families in the course of time became enormously opulent, and severally constituted a mighty power against the people. Secondly, poor men at Rome seemed to have an innate respect for the wealthy; and, long after the true condition of client had disappeared, revived the name under the form of homage rendered to large fortunes, a custom having arisen of the proletarii waiting on wealthy persons every morning to salute them.

The struggle of the rich and poor was not unknown at Rome, but it only commenced at the date of the Gracchi, when the conquest of the empire had been nearly achieved. And then the struggle was not so violent at Rome as elsewhere. The lower orders were not very covetous, at least they but feebly supported the Gracchi, scarcely believing these reformers were working for them, and abandoning them at the decisive moment. The agrarian laws were but demands of the State-lands, and never proposed to take away from the wealthy their own property. Partly by inveterate respect, partly by their habit of inaction, the poorer class liked to live on beneath the shadow of their wealthy neighbours. Again, this class had the wisdom to admit into its number the most considerable families of the towns which Rome had conquered or made allies. All the wealthy men of Italy one after another were received amongst the rich of Rome, so that it was a body that grew in importance and became master of the state. As it cost much to buy a magistracy, no one else filled office; and no one else could be a Senator, because a large fortune was a necessary qualification. Thus we observe the practical paradox, that in spite of laws which were democratic, a body of nobles was formed, and the omnipotent people allowed these men to raise themselves above them, without making any real opposition.

Therefore, in the third and second centuries before our æra, Rome was the most aristocratically governed city of Greece or Italy. But we must observe that there was a difference within and without. At home, the Senate was obliged to let the people have their own way, whilst in foreign politics, it remained absolute master. It was the Senate which received ambassadors, made alliances, assigned provinces and legions, ratified the acts of generals, and determined the conditions to be exacted from the conquered; all which things were settled elsewhere by the popular assembly. Therefore, foreigners in their concerns with Rome had never anything to do with the people. The Senate was all they heard about, and the idea was kept up in their minds that the people had no power. And in this sense a Greek expressed himself to Flaminius, saying, "In your country riches rule; and everything else is subject."

In Greece therefore, about 199 B.C., when Rome made her appearance in Greece the aristocratic party were ready to give themselves up to her, not thinking it so much a question of national independence, as a measure to be taken against the opposite faction. In every city one man was for Philip, or Antiochus, or Perseus, and another for Rome. It is easily gathered from Polybius and Livy that, if Argos opened her gates, in 198, to the Macedonians, the reason was that the people had got the upper hand;—that next year it was the faction of the wealthy who gave up the town of Opus to the Romans;—that in Acarnania the aristocracy had made an alliance with Rome, but that the treaty was broken next year because the people had got the best of it;—that Thebes was allied with Philip as long as the popular party was the stronger, but goes back to Rome as soon as the aristocracy are masters;—that the mob of Athens, Demetrius, and Phocæa hated Rome;—that Nabis the democratic tyrant fights against Rome;—that the Achæan league, so long as it is governed by the aristocracy, is favourable;—and that men like Philopœmen and Polybius long for national independence, but prefer the Roman rule to that of the democracy;—that even in the Achæan league there comes a time when the popular party rises in turn; and that henceforth the league is hostile to Rome;—that Diæos and Critolaus are chiefs of the popular faction and generals of the league against Romans;—and that they fight bravely at Scarphæa and Leucopetra, but perhaps less for the independence of Greece than for the triumph of democracy.

Such facts account for the triumph of Rome. Not merely was the municipal spirit gradually disappearing, and party-feeling now much stronger than patriotism, but the barriers which had hitherto separated town from town and made each a little world to itself, were gradually falling away. Two groups of men only were now to be found throughout Greece and Italy, on one side the aristocratic class, and on the other the popular party, of which the former invited the domination of Rome, whilst the other rejected it. And as the aristocracy was the stronger, Rome won the empire of the world.

§ 4. *Rome everywhere destroys the municipal system.*

The institutions of the primitive city had been weakened and exhausted by a series of revolutions, and the effect of the Roman sway was to complete their destruction.

We must not imagine that the different people conquered by the Romans resembled at all the annexations of powerful kingdoms in these days. Conquest then did not increase the Roman state *(civitas Romana)*, which continued to comprise only those families who were present at the census. Nor was the Roman territory *(ager Romanus)* of any wider extent; for that remained within the unalterable boundaries traced by the kings, and re-traced by the Ambarvales every year. Only one thing was increased by every conquest, and that was the dominion of Rome *(imperium Romanum)*. So long as the republic lasted it never entered into the head of any body that the Romans and the other peoples could form one nation. Rome might individually receive some vanquished families, place them within her walls, and eventually transform them into Romans; but she could not assimilate a whole foreign population to her own, and a whole foreign territory to hers. This was not the peculiar policy of Rome, but was the result of a principle common to all antiquity, a principle which perhaps she would have departed from more willingly than any other city, but from which she could not entirely free herself. When, then, any people was subdued, it did not join the Roman state as provinces are now united to a capital. Rome knew but two sorts of union between her people and herself, and those were subjection and alliance.

After this, it might seem that municipal institutions should still have remained standing in the conquered towns, and the Roman world become an assemblage of distinct towns with a mistress-city at their head. But it was not so. The Roman conquest effected a complete change in the interior of every town.

There were, in the first place, the *dedititii*, or subjects who had utterly surrendered to the Roman people their "persons, their walls, lands, water, houses, gods." So that they had not merely given up their city government, but also all that was thereto attached in those days, viz., their religion and their private rights. The buildings of their town might be intact, but their civil association had perished, and though they continued to live together, it was without laws, institutions, magistrates. The arbitrary authority of a præfect sent by Rome maintained order amongst them.[1]

Secondly, there were allies, *fœderati* or *socii*, who were less ill-treated. It had been stipulated that each of these should keep their city government, and their municipal organization. Hence they all had their own constitution, their own magistrates, senate, prytaneum, laws, and judges. The city was reckoned to be independent, and had to do with Rome only as one ally with another. Yet in the terms of the treaty drawn up at the time of the conquest, Rome would insert such a formula as the following : " *Majestatem populi Romani comiter conservato* :" " Let the allied state kindly observe the majesty of the Roman people :"[2] words whose vagueness was to the advantage of the stronger. These cities were called free, but received their orders from Rome, obeyed proconsuls, paid taxes to the publicans, sent in their accounts through their magistrates to the governor of the province, and appealed to him also from their judges.[3] Now such was the nature of the ancient city, that it must have complete independence or must cease to be. Between the maintenance of city institutions and the authority of a stranger there was a contradiction, that might not appear so glaring perhaps to modern eyes, but which could not help striking every man of that period. Municipal freedom and the rule of Rome were irreconcilable ; the first was but a shew, to blind the eyes of men who submitted in reality to the latter. Each of these cities yearly sent a deputation to Rome, and its most intimate affairs were minutely regulated in the Senate. It still

---

[1] Livy, i., 38 ; vii., 31 ; ix., 20 ; xxvi., 16 ; xxviii., 34. Cicero, *De Leg. Agr.*, i., 5 ; ii., 32. Festus, V°. *Præfectura*.
[2] Cicero, *Pro Balbo*, 16.
[3] Livy, xlv., 18. Cicero, *Ad. Attic.*, vi., 1 ; vi., 2. Appian., *Civil Wars*, i., 102. Tacit., xv., 45.

retained its magistrates, archons, and generals freely elected at home, but all the archon could do was to write his name on the public register to mark the year, whilst the general whose predecessors had led armies, was now a way-warden, and inspector of markets.[1]

The difference between Rome's allies and subjects was that the former retained the appearance of municipal institutions, whilst the latter did not. But in neither case was there left anything approaching the original idea of the Urbs Antiqua. This only remained within the walls of Rome.

Moreover, when Rome destroyed the ancient city system, she put nothing in its place. Her own institutions were not imparted to the peoples from whom she had taken their own, nor yet any others. Never was any constitution given to the people of her empire, nor any rules set up by which they might be governed. Even the authority which she exercised over them was as irregular as it could be. They made no part of her state, and therefore they were not under her regular legal action. Rome's subjects were foreigners to her; and in respect to them she had that irregular and unlimited power which primitive municipal law gave the citizen against a stranger or a foe. It was on this principle that Roman administration was long regulated; and its course of proceeding was as follows.

A Roman citizen was sent into a country, which was made his *provincia*, or peculiar business and personal affair. The city stripped herself for a time of her *imperium* and conferred it upon him, who was therefore absolute master. For it was he who settled the amount of the tax, who exercised military power and rendered justice. No constitution settled his relations to his subjects or allies. From his judgment-seat he ruled as he pleased, and neither could the laws of the provincials touch him, because he was a Roman; nor the law of the Romans, because he was judging provincials. It was needful for the governor himself to make whatever laws there were to be. Hence the *imperium* with which he was invested included legislative power. Wherefore the governors, as they had the right, so had they the habit of publishing a set of laws, called their Edict, when they entered upon a

---

[1] Philostratus, *Life of the Sophists*, i., 23. Bœckh., *Corp. Inscr.*, passim.

province, and of course were morally bound to abide by these laws. But as the governors were changed every year, so were the codes of laws, for the reason that Law had no other source than the will of the person who was in power there for the moment. And this principle was applied with such rigour, that when an outgoing governor had pronounced a judgment, if his successor arrived before execution, the process must recommence from the beginning.

The governor, in fact, was the living law; and as for invoking justice at Rome against his violence or crime, the provincials could only do so when they had found a Roman citizen to be their patron. For of themselves they had no right to invoke the city law or to speak before its tribunals. They were strangers, in juridical language *peregrini*; and all that the law said about the *hostis* applied to them.

It is evident from the writings of the Roman lawyers that the inhabitants of the empire were considered as having neither their own laws any more, nor as having yet acquired a right to the Roman laws. According to Roman jurisprudence, a provincial was properly neither husband nor father, since the law recognized in him neither conjugal nor paternal authority. Neither could he be an owner of land, correctly speaking, for two reasons: first, he himself was not a Roman citizen; and, secondly, complete ownership could only exist within the limits of the ager Romanus. It was a principle, then, of Roman law, that provincial soil could never be private property, and that men could only have the temporary enjoyment of it. And what was said of the provincial soil in the second century of our æra, had been equally true of Italian soil till Italy obtained Roman citizenship.

It is true that practically these hardships were much softened to the subject peoples. For instance, paternal authority had its place in men's manners if it had none in the law. If a man had not ownership of land, he had occupation (possessio), and might till, sell, or will it away. They never said that the land was his, but that it was like his, *pro suo*. It was not his property, *dominium*, but it was amongst his goods, *in bonis*: and so a number of artifices and fictions were imagined for the good of the subjects. Doubtless though municipal tradition forbade the making of laws for the vanquished, yet Roman sense could not let society fall to

T

pieces. Those who were without the pale of the law yet lived as if they were within. But beyond this toleration of the victors, all the institutions of the vanquished were allowed to fall into disuse, till, at length for generations the Roman Empire presented this spectacle, a single city erect, with its institutions and laws intact, whilst the remaining part, that is to say, a hundred million souls, had no longer any sort of laws, or at least none that were recognized by the mistress city. The world was not altogether a chaos, but in default of laws and principles, force, arbitrary will, and convention alone sustained society.

Such was the effect of the Roman conquest on the peoples who were successively its victims. Of civil association every valuable part perished; first religion, then government, then private law; whilst municipal institutions, already shaken, were now uprooted and overthrown. But no regular society or system of government immediately replaced what was disappearing. A sort of pause seems to have occurred between the dissolution of the municipal system and the rise of another sort of society. Nations did not immediately succeed to cities, because the Roman Empire in no wise resembled a nation. It was a confused multitude, with true order only existing in one central spot, the humblest obedience elsewhere only purchasing a factitious and transitionary calm. Subjects only won organization when they had wrested from Rome the rights which she wished to retain for herself. They were obliged to force an entrance, so to speak, into the city and to change her also, that one body might be made of them and Rome. And we shall see that this was not a light or easy task.

§ 5. *Successive entrance of the subject peoples into the city.*

It may be conceived how ardently the conquered people longed to win the place of Roman citizens, so as to have rights at last and count for something. Latins, Italians, Greeks, then Spaniards and Gauls, struggled hard to gain an entrance into the city, and succeeded in pretty much the same order as that in which they had entered the Empire. This is the last act of the social transformation which we are studying: and to understand it thoroughly we must go back to the fourth century before our æra.

Latium had then submitted to Rome, half of its forty little populations having been exterminated, some more stripped of their land, and the rest being called allies. The latter having found out, by 347, the detrimental nature of this alliance, and observing with grief that they were yearly forced to spend both blood and money to the sole advantage of Rome, formed a coalition against her; and their leader, Annius, thus expressed their claims before the Roman Senate: "Let us have equality; let us have the same laws; and form one state with you, *una civitas*, with the name of Romans for all alike." To the Romans this seemed monstrous, for indeed it was contrary to the old religion and to the old city-law; and the consul Manlius accordingly exclaimed that if such a proposition were accepted, he himself would come girt with his sword to slay the first Latin who should sit in the Senate; and then turned to the altar and said, "Thou hast heard, O Jupiter, the impious words of this man; couldest thou endure it, that a stranger should come and sit in thy sacred temple as a senator?" For the old religious sentiment of repulsion towards strangers was not extinct. And indeed this wish of Annius, thus expressed in 347, and afterwards conceived by all the peoples of the empire, was not completely realized until five centuries and a half had rolled away.

In the war that followed the demands of Annius, the Latins were beaten and compelled to make surrender of their cities, their worships, their laws, and their lands. But a consul said in the Senate that if Rome would not be surrounded by a desert, she must shew some mercy to the Latins. What was done is not too clear in Livy's account; but, if we may believe him, the empty name of Roman citizen was accorded, without right of voting or of intermarriage; and we perceive that these so-called new citizens were not counted in the census. Moreover, the unsatisfactory nature of the arrangement is shewn by the speedy revolt of several cities of the Latins.

If we go on a hundred years, again we receive direct light from the historian, but still a change has evidently come over Roman policy. Now the cities have their own municipal government, laws, and magistracies, and are not called Roman citizens, but a narrow door is opened to real citizenship. Every Latin man who had held office in his native town became a Roman citizen at the expiration of his term.[1] This time the right to citizenship was complete and unreserved: votes, census, magistracies, marriage, private law, were all included. Rome agreed to share with the stranger her government and laws; only her favours were bestowed on individuals and not upon whole towns. So she won whatever was richest and best amongst the families of Latium. To those who became possessed of the envied privilege, the advantages were a voice in the important elections of Rome, and a power of becoming even consul; or without aiming so high, marriage was possible into a Roman family; a man might establish himself at Rome and be an owner of land; or he might enter into commerce in that most central place of business; or he might enter a company of publicani and share the great gains derived from farming the taxes and speculating on the *ager publicus*. Besides which there was most ample protection in all parts of the empire; the municipal magistrates were powerless over the Roman citizen; and it was something also to be able to disregard the whims of the Roman officers. Thus the Roman citizen had honour, wealth, and safety; and it was natural for the Latins to try every means of becoming such. It was discovered once that 12,000 of them had obtained the distinction by fraudulent means. But in general Rome wisely winked at the measures by which her population was augmented and her losses in war repaired. Of course, however, the Latin cities lost as much as Rome gained by this transfer of their wealthiest members. The taxes were made heavier by the exemption of these new Roman citizens, and it was harder every year to furnish the required contingent of soldiers. And the more men obtained the envied right, the more deplorable was the condition of those left. An outcry was raised against the bestowal of citizenship as a privilege; and the Italian cities now joined the Latin. After a subjection of two centuries they found themselves in the same circumstances as their predecessors, and their position was aggravated by the agitation of agrarian laws at Rome. The principle of these laws that no subject of Rome nor ally could own land, without a

---

[1] Appian., ii., 26.

formal grant from the city, and that the greater part of the land in Italy was the property of the republic. And there was always a party demanding that these lands, which were mostly occupied by Italians, should be resumed by the state and distributed to the poor of Rome. The Italians then were threatened with general ruin, and keenly felt the need of having civil rights, which only accompanied Roman citizenship.

The war which ensued was called the Social War, and was fought to decide whether or not Rome's allies should become Roman citizens. Though victorious, Rome was obliged to yield all that had been demanded, and the Italians now received the right of citizenship. They could vote in the forum, and were governed by Roman laws in private life; also they could now become owners of land; and henceforth the Italian soil for purposes of property was equal to the Roman. Then was established the jus Italicum, which was the right not of any Italian person, because now the Italian was equal to the Roman, but of the Italian soil, which was made capable of being owned as though it had been *ager Romanus*. Henceforth Italy formed but one state.

In considering the unification of the provinces with Rome, we must draw a distinction between the Western provinces and Greece. As before the conquest Gaul and Spain had not known the true municipal system, Rome proceeded to create it amongst them, either not knowing how else to govern them, or supposing it necessary for them to pass through the same experience as the Italian populations had done. Hence the emperors, whilst suppressing all political life at Rome, cherished every form of political liberty in the provinces. So cities were formed in Gaul, each with its Senate, its aristocracy, and its elective magistrates; nay, each had its tutelary god and its local worships, after the fashion of ancient Greece and Italy. And this municipal system prepared men for arriving at Roman citizenship. The steps of the scale to be mounted before arriving at Roman citizenship were as follows. First the allies had laws and governments of their own, and no legal bond of union with the citizens of Rome. Secondly, the colonies had the civil rights of Romans, but not political rights. Thirdly, came the cities of Italian privileges, that is, those cities to whom Rome had granted complete ownership of their land, just as if those lands had been in Italy. Fourthly, were the cities of Latin right, whose inhabitants, according to the old custom established in Latium, might become citizens after having filled a municipal office. These distinctions were so profound that neither marriage nor any legal relation was possible between persons of two different categories. But the emperors took care that in course of time each city should be able to raise itself step by step from the condition of subject or ally, to the jus Italicum, and from the jus Italicum to the jus Latinum. When a city had arrived at this, its chief families became Roman one after the other.

Greece also entered by little and little into the Roman State. At first every city, having manifested a great desire to preserve its autonomy, was allowed to remain under the forms of the old municipal system. But when a few generations had passed away opinions had altered, and ambition as well as interest made every Greek burn to be a Roman citizen. Indeed, the Greeks never seem to have felt for Rome that hatred with which foreign masters are generally regarded. Rather, they felt for Rome a sort of veneration, and offered her worship in temples which they raised as to a god, the city divinity being replaced by the goddess Rome, or the god Cæsar. And these new divinities were honoured with the most-carefully-prepared festivals, whilst the first magistrates had no higher function than to celebrate with great pomp the Augustan games. Thus men became accustomed to lift their eyes above their city; seeing in Rome the chief city of all, the country and prytaneum of every people. Thus a man's native town seemed small in his own eyes, and its interests ceased to occupy his thoughts. He cared not for the honours of the provincial city, but aspired to be a Roman. And if under the emperors political rights were not conferred by the title of Roman citizen, yet still more solid advantages were bestowed, for it carried with it the rights of ownership, of inheritance, and of marriage, with paternal authority and all the jus privatum. The laws of every man's own town were merely tolerated, and had neither sure foundation nor any certainty, The Roman despised them, and the Greek himself had but little regard for them. Whosoever would have fixed law, law allowed of all and truly sacred, must find it at Rome.

We do not find a formal demand for this right of citizenship set forth either by Greece in its entirety or by any Greek city: only men toiled severally and individually to acquire it, and found Rome willing enough to yield in this way. Some obtained it by the favour of the emperor, and others bought it. It was given to those who had three children, or who had served in some divisions of the army. Sometimes the construction of a merchant-ship of a certain size, or the conveyance of corn to Rome, constituted a sufficient claim. One very ready method was for a man to sell himself as a slave to a Roman: then he might instantly be set free according to the proper forms, and he became a citizen.[1] It resulted from the principle already laid down, viz., that a man could not belong to two cities at the same time, that the person on whom Roman citizenship had been conferred, no longer belonged either civilly or politically to his native city.[2] Although he might continue to reside there, he was really a stranger to it, owing obedience neither to its laws nor its magistrates, nor liable to its pecuniary charges. After some generations every Greek city contained a considerable number of these persons, and those generally the wealthiest. So the municipal system perished slowly and as if by a natural death. The hour arrived when the city-lists had no names left upon them, when the local laws applied to scarce a soul, and when the municipal judges were without justiceable persons.

Finally, when eight or ten generations had sighed and longed for Roman citizenship, and when every one who was worth anything had obtained it, then was published an imperial decree granting it to all men without distinction.

Caracalla, who was destitute of all exalted views, is credited with this step. But the historians of the period thought so little of it, that we only gather the fact from a short mention of it by Dio Cassius,[3] and two vague passages

---

[1] Suet., *Nero*, 24. Petron., 57. Ulpian., iii. Gaius, i., 16, 17.

[2] He became also a stranger to his family, unless they were citizens as well as himself, so that he could not inherit property from them. See Cicero, *Balb.*, 28; *Archias*, 5; *Cæcina*, 36.

[3] It is known that Caracalla styled himself Antoninus in public acts. (To this day the lane that leads to his baths is called Via Antonina.) Consequently, the following passages apply to him:—" Antoninus Pius

in law-books. Nevertheless, this decree suppressed for ever all distinction between the dominant people and the subject peoples, and even the still older distinction between one city and another. This seems important enough, but in truth the changes had practically been effected long before, and Caracalla's motive was to get the tax of a tenth on enfranchisements and successions from a larger number of contributors.

The title of citizen henceforth began to fall into disuse, or if it was still employed it was used to mark the condition of a free man as opposed to that of slave.[1] Henceforth all that belonged to the Roman Empire, from Spain to the Euphrates, truly formed but one people and one state. The distinction between cities had disappeared, and that between nations made but a feeble show. All the inhabitants of this immense empire were Romans alike. The Gaul and the Spaniard assumed the title of Roman as eagerly as the Thracian and the Syrian. There was now but one name, one government, one Law.

It is not our task to consider what followed this system, or whether it deserved to be displaced by what followed immediately. We halt where antiquity ceases.

---

jus Romanæ civitatis omnibus subjectis donavit." Justinian, *Novell.*, 78, ch. 5. "In orbe Romano qui sunt, ex constitutione imperatoris Antonini, cives Romani effecti sunt."

[1] It seemed natural that emancipated slaves should not pass all at once to the enjoyment of Roman citizenship. So in Ulpian and the Code we find, still, mention of peregrini, Latins, and citizens. For these were intermediate steps between the two conditions. In like manner, traces long remain of the distinction between land which had the jus Italicum, and provincial property: Code, vii., 25; vii., 31; *Digest.*, Bk. L., tit. i. Tyre, even after Caracalla, had the jus Italicum. The fact was that the Emperor's peculiar treasury derived a benefit from provincial lands, which were therefore retained as such.

CHAPTER LIII.

CHRISTIANITY ALTERS THE CONDITIONS OF GOVERNMENT.

THE social transformation whose commencement we placed six or seven centuries before our æra, was not finished till the arrival and triumph of Christianity. We must remember that according to the old religion each god exclusively protected a family or a city. It has been shewn that from this religion sprung the ancient laws of property and inheritance, which regarded not so much the principles of natural equity as the needs of ancestral worship. Government, whether patriarchal or civic, flowed from the same source. In those times the State had the nature of a religious community, the law was a sacred form of words, and the king or magistrate was a pontiff or a priest; patriotism was piety, and exile excommunication; individual liberty was not; and every stranger was a foe; men were enslaved to the state in their body, in their goods, and in their souls; the boundary of the city was the limit which shut in a man's notions of justice and love; and it was impossible to lay the foundations of any great association. Such were the chief characteristics of Greek and Italian society for a period, which we may put down as having lasted for fifteen centuries.

But things slowly altered, as we have seen, and changes were effected, first, in belief, then in law and government. Law and politics during the five centuries which preceded Christianity were being gradually weaned from religion, and the old principles of human asssociation were gradually upset by the struggles of oppressed classes, by the defeat of the sacerdotal caste, by the progress of thought, and the labours of philosophers. Then, when men could believe no longer in the old family and city religions, they struggled unweariedly to free themselves from its thraldom; and in law and statecraft at last they got free from its bonds. Only this sort of divorce of politics from religion arose from the disappearance of old beliefs; nor did law or governments become independent except at the expense of faith. Religion only relaxed her hold upon mankind when extreme debility had befallen her. Whence the question arises (since religion is restored to vigour once more under the shape of Christianity), shall we not behold the old confusion of priesthood and statecraft, of faith and law again complete. It will be seen by-and-bye that this was not the case. When religion was restored in Christianity, it assumed a loftier and purer expression. God was now conceived of as apart from humanity in his essence, and mankind scorned the former deities which it had formed to itself out of the powers of nature or the souls of dead men. God now appeared to man as a being unique, incomprehensible, all-pervading, the only mover of the Universe, and alone able to satisfy man's need to adore. Whereas in other ages the religions of Greece and Italy had been but collections of rites practised without meaning, or a series of formulas that had become obsolete, now were put forth a chain of consistent doctrines concerning a worthy object of faith. Prayers, therefore, were no longer mere incantations, nor was it man's main religious duty to offer food to his god. In short, religion became spiritual instead of external, and the wearisome fear of having offended some irritable power was replaced by a trustful love of the Great Father of all.

Moreover, this new religion belonged to no caste and to no family. For Christ had said, "Go, and make disciples of all people." And this principle was so new and unheard-of, that it is easy to see some apostles at first refused to spread their doctrines beyond their own nation. The God of the Jews, according to their idea, could not be the god of foreigners; and it seemed to them alike opposed to interest and duty to diffuse the name and worship of the peculiar protector of their race.

It is true that during the centuries which immediately preceded the advent of our Lord, all thinking persons began to revolt against the exclusiveness of cotemporary religions. The Jews sought proselytes and Greeks bestowed citizenship.

Moreover, often since Anaxagoras had philosophy taught that the God of the Universe receives the prayers and worship of all nations, though it was not in the power of philosophy to arouse any lively faith. There was also in Greece one form of religion, namely, that taught at Eleusis, which regarded not the distinctions of cities; though even into that initiation was necessary, and not always directly obtained. There were besides forms of worship, like those of Serapis and Cybele, which for generations had been passing from people to people, but these did not take hold of men's whole power of feeling, and were incorporated too readily into the mass of the old mythology. For the first time in the west Christianity made man bow before one God, the Ruler of the Universe, who had no peculiar people, and cared not for families, races, or countries.

For this God there were no more strangers. Neither was His temple profaned by their presence, nor His sacrifice spoilt by the sight of them. Every believer might kneel at the shrine, and, as religion was no more a patrimony, the priesthood was no longer hereditary. The worship was not kept hidden as something secret, but ceremonies, prayers, and doctrines were gladly explained, and truth, instead of waiting to be sought, went in search of believers; for the spirit of propagandism took the place of exclusiveness.

Great consequences resulted from this, both as to the government of states and the relations of peoples between one another. For the latter, mutual hatred was no longer commanded by religion. Rather they were commanded to love as children of the same Father. The barriers between races and nations were removed, and the meaning of the *pomœrium* forgotten. "Christ," said the Apostle, "has broken down the wall of partition;" "There are many members, but one body;" "There is neither Greek nor barbarian, Jew nor Gentile, bond nor free."

As for government of States, Christianity altered it entirely by simply letting it alone. For in old times Religion was the State and the State was Religion. Every people adored its own god, and the god in turn governed his own people, and one code sufficed for men's relations to God and to one another. In those times religion, being mistress of the state, appointed its chiefs by lot or by taking the auspices; whilst the state in turn, mixing itself up with the domain of conscience, punished every infraction of the city's rules of worship. But now with the words, "My kingdom is not of this world," Christ separated religion from government. And we have the first distinction ever drawn between God's affairs and the State's in that other saying, "Render unto Cæsar the things that be Cæsar's, and unto God the things that be God's." When this was said, Cæsar was still Pontifex Maximus, the chief-priest of the Roman religion. Public worship was his province, and he was the guardian and interpreter of belief. Wishing to re-assume the traits of ancient royalty, Cæsar was little likely to forget the divine character which antiquity attached to her king-pontiffs and priestly founders. But Christ broke through this bond of union which Paganism and Empire wished to tie again. He proclaims that a line is now to be drawn between religion and state, and that to obey Cæsar is no longer the same thing as to obey God.

Though Christianity was able to overthrow local worship in all places, and extinguish the sacred fires of all cities, yet it refused to take the position of the religion which it rejected. On the contrary, it declared that religion and state-craft had nothing in common; but that what all antiquity had joined together must now be put asunder. For three centuries the new religion lived apart from all state interference, being perfectly able to dispense with its protection, and even to hold its own against governments. The history of those three centuries have established a great gulf between politics and religion; and the recollection of that glorious period has never yet nor ever will be wiped out, but will always be regarded by the wisest servants both of Church and State as exemplifying an important principle.

Already this principle has produced the greatest results. On the one hand, politics have been freed from the strict rules which ancient religion marked out for them. It has been found that men may be governed without conforming every act to the requirements of some belief, such as consulting oracles and taking auspices. And the march of political economy has been made freer and bolder, now that it is shackled by nothing but the laws of morality. On the other hand, conscience also gained; for if in some matters the authority of the state has been rendered more absolute, in others its power was limited. The better half of every man was emancipated. Christianity teaches that man only belongs to society by one side, being bound to it corporeally and in his material interests, so that he may yield obedience to a tyrant, or give his life for his country, but that no claim can be made upon him for his soul, which is free and pledged to God alone.

Stoic philosophy had already marked this separation, restoring man to himself and having founded inward liberty. But that which was the mere attempt of a brave sect was fixed by Christianity as the universal and unalterable rule of posterity; and the consolation of a few became the common good of mankind.

And if it be only remembered what we said above concerning the excessive power of the state in ancient times, and the degree of authority assumed by the city in virtue of its sacred character, then it will be seen that this new principle announced by Christianity was the source from which we have derived all individual liberty. For when the soul and the conscience were once emancipated, the greatest difficulty had been overcome. Liberty became possible in society.

And not only were political principles altered, but at the same time were transformed the sentiments and manners of mankind. Christianity has made a distinction between private and public virtues which were hitherto confounded. The latter have been abased and the former raised in general estimation. It is no longer the supreme idea of duty to give one's time, and strength, and life to one's country. At present there are notions which take precedence of one's native land, namely, duty to self, to family, to God.

Law has altered in like manner. Having been subject to religion, from which also it derived its rules (for the laws of the Hindoos, Persians, Jews, Greeks, Italians, and Gauls, were written in their sacred books), Christianity now for the first time confessed that law was not her work or business. She has claimed to occupy itself with men's duties and not with their material interests. With property, succession to estates, and contracts, she has no proper concern. Law, therefore, being thus left independent, could take its rules from man's innate idea of justice, and could alter them at will, and follow the progress of morality without obstacle, accommodating itself to every need of successive generations.

Roman Law could only get nearer to natural equity by artifice and in round-about ways. Its regeneration was attempted by jurisconsults and prætors, but could only be achieved when complete freedom was granted by a new religion. As Christianity gained ground, new rules were established without subterfuge and without hesitation. When the household gods had been overthrown and the sacred fire extinguished, then the primitive constitution of the family disappeared for ever, and all its regulations with it. The father lost the absolute authority which his priesthood had given him, and only retained that which nature bestows for the good of the infant. The wife rose to a moral equality with the husband. Also the nature of property was changed, being now derived from *labour* and not from religion, whilst its acquisition was rendered more easy and the old formalities were abolished.

Thus the disappearance of the old domestic religion was entirely altered in constitution; and in like manner the loss of the *State's* official religion changed for ever the rules of human government.

At this line of separation between ancient and modern history we stop. What we have tried to set forth has been the history of a belief. Along with the establishment of this belief human society was constituted. But when the belief was modified, society was subjected to a series of revolutions. When eventually it disappeared, society was radically altered. Such is the history of ancient times.

THE END.

G. B. Smith, Printer, Chipping Norton.

www.ingramcontent.com/pod-product-compliance
Lightning Source LLC
Chambersburg PA
CBHW032042230426
43672CB00009B/1441